LINGUA FRACTA

Toward a Rhetoric of New Media

NEW DIMENSIONS IN COMPUTERS AND COMPOSITION

Gail E. Hawisher and *Cynthia L. Selfe*, editors

LINGUA FRACTA

Toward a Rhetoric of New Media

Collin Gifford Brooke
Syracuse University

HAMPTON PRESS, INC.
CRESSKILL, NEW JERSEY

Printed in the United States of America

Library of Congress Cataloging-in-Publication Data

Brooke, Collin Gifford.
    Lingua fracta : toward a rhetoric of new media / Collin Gifford Brooke
        p. cm. -- (New dimensions in computers and composition)
    Includes bibliographic references and index.
    ISBN 978-1-57273-892-8 (hardbound) -- ISBN 978-1-57273-893-5 (paperbound)
1. Rhetoric. 2. Rhetoric--Study and teaching. 3. Hypertext systems. I. Title.
    P301.B66 2009
    808--dc22

                                2009021921

Hampton Press, Inc.
23 Broadway
Cresskill, NJ 07626

For
Allen & Aideen
Charlie & Bert
and
Karen

CONTENTS

LIST OF FIGURES

IN (NEW) MEDIA RES,
A PREFACE

The beginning. That's always the hard part. Once you get into
the flow of things, you're always haunted by the way that things
could have turned out.

Paul Miller (2004)

Where to begin?

This project began several years ago, during what Robert Coover has
referred to as the "golden age" of hypertext. This book shares a title
(although not a subtitle) with the dissertation that I wrote during that hey-
day, at a time when critics were just beginning to lash back at the over-
whelmingly celebratory discussions of hypertext. Although there remain to
this day some important points of resonance between hypertext and poststructuralism, my own response to the equivocation of the two terms/cate-
gories was to choose a much different starting point—the canons of classical rhetoric. In my dissertation, the canons served a heuristic function,
focusing my critical attention on specific elements or claims made on
behalf of this new form of writing.

Some years later, hypertext no longer enjoys the novelty it once did. As
many critics have pointed out, the first wave of hypertext theory was too
closely bound to literary contexts, too concerned with making idealistic,
sweeping claims that were either impossible to achieve or impractical to
apply. Hypertext was at the same time too grand and too narrow an idea
to serve as a productive category. Because hypertext has been subsumed
into the more loosely defined and more modest category of new media, so
too has my own thinking about what I call discursive technologies changed.
Conceptually, this project leans more toward contemporary theorizing

xi

about new media than it does hypertext theory of the mid-1990s. The range of possibilities enabled by discursive technologies has continued to grow beyond what hypertext theory once envisioned, enough so that it is probably more accurate to speak of posthypertextuality as Michael Joyce does. Hypertextuality is already diffused into any number of new media that are considered to be distinctly separate—blogs and wikis, for example, are hypertexts, albeit in different ways than that first wave of thinkers conceived them.

Along with a title, this book shares with my dissertation an abiding interest in the canons of classical rhetoric. Kathleen Welch (1999) observes in *Electric Rhetoric* that the canons "have recurred in different forms and with different emphases in varying historical eras" (p. 144), and my project attempts to take this claim to heart. Disciplinarily, *Lingua Fracta* is located in between technology and rhetoric, using the canons to come to grips with new media at the same time that it acknowledges the changes that the canons must undergo in the context of new media. We shape our technologies even as they shape us, a fact that influences the approach that this book takes to its subject matter. Ultimately, this book attempts to stage an encounter between rhetoric and technology; each functions as a lens through which we might consider the other, and neither is left untransformed by the encounter.

To work with terms such as *rhetoric* and *technology* is to beg the question, however. In the context of this project, both terms map out for me a middle space. In *Rhetoric of Motives*, Kenneth Burke (1969a) describes three sets of terms: positive, dialectical, and ultimate. Positive terms represent for Burke a physicalist vocabulary; that is, they name visible, tangible things accessible to us for the most part through our senses. At the other end of the spectrum, ultimate terms are those ideas that totalize, creating an order that places competing voices in a hierarchy or developmental sequence. Dialectical terms are those where there are competing voices without recourse to a single unitary principle that orders them. Burke speaks of the "rhetorical advantages of an ultimate vocabulary as contrasted with a vocabulary left on the level of parliamentary conflict" (p. 197), but it is that latter vocabulary that invites discussion. In other words, dialectical terms provide a site for rhetorical practice to take place. For too long, we have treated the canons as if they belonged to one end of the spectrum or the other. As organizing principles behind a composing process, and having lasted as long as they have, we might argue that some see the canons as an ultimate vocabulary. It also could be argued that we tend to treat them as positive terms. Although invention and style have both been studied and debated in some detail over the past 40 years, few would suggest that arrangement, memory, or delivery constitute vital sites of disagreement for our field.

One way of describing this project, then, would be to say that it attempts to restore the dialectical character of the rhetorical canons, seeing them as terms that "belong, not in the order of motion and perception, but rather in the order of action and idea" (Burke, 1969a, p. 184). As actions, as practices, the canons always occur within a particular technological context; obviously, this book considers them in the context of *new media*. I do not spend much time in this book worrying over definitions of new media, however. Lev Manovich (2003) offers several definitions in his foreword to *The New Media Reader*, none of which necessarily settle, once and for all, the question of what new media actually is, and I do not propose to add to the discussion with this project. The danger with extended discussions of definition is that they ultimately distract from what are (for me) more important questions, the practices that these technologies enable and assist. For my purposes, new media are notable for the importance they place on interfaces. As I explain in chapter 1, the interface is not an object in the same way that more traditional media are. In other words, I resist treating various new media as positive terms.[1] At the same time, interfaces are typically customizable; although they restrict the range of available practices on the part of a user, even that restricted range is much broader than those available in older media forms. By definition, certain uses of an interface are no better nor worse than others—they are simply individual performances made possible by the interface. The interface functions as a dialectical space, in Burke's terms, and a rhetorical space *par excellence*. The interface, then, is where rhetoric and technology meet to serve as the focus of this project.

Among other things, new media invites us to rethink (or reinvent) the canons of classical rhetoric, understanding them as practices that might, in turn, be used to understand the proliferation of interfaces that surround us. In chapter 2, I draw on the idea of ecologies to articulate this relationship, an articulation that attempts to capture the mutually transformative encounter I am describing here. We encounter interfaces as part of our individual media ecologies, and those interfaces each serve as ecologies of rhetorical practice, where the canons shift, overlap, intermingle, and combine, sometimes as a direct result of our choices and sometimes despite them. At the same time, new media occupy an increasingly relevant focus within the disciplinary ecology of rhetoric, challenging traditional binaries and boundaries, some of which we have retained since rhetoric's inception. My hope is that the following project will simultaneously demonstrate the value of rhetoric for the study of new media, as well as the reverse.

LINGUA FRACTA?

From the central moltenness, where all the elements are fused into one togetherness, there are thrown forth, in separate crusts, such distinctions as those between freedom and necessity, activity and passiveness, cooperation and competition, cause and effect, mechanism and teleology.
—Kenneth Burke (1969b)

The title of this book attempts to capture some of the "middling" that occurs within, by means of what Gregory Ulmer calls a *puncept*, a play on words that provokes us to think through a set of terms in more detail. In this case, the pun is based on the idea of a *lingua franca*, which was the term given to the mercantile language that emerged in various countries surrounding the Mediterranean in the Middle Ages. Traders in coastal cities, faced with the need to communicate with customers from diverse ports and countries, developed a pidgin language containing elements of Italian, French, German, Greek, and Arabic. More recently, of course, *lingua franca* served as the name of a periodical that covered trends, significant publications, and the occasional scandal in the academy, before its demise in late 2001. In both cases, the phrase connotes connections, the crossing of boundaries whether linguistic or disciplinary, for the purpose of shared interests.

Technology has served as a *lingua franca* in recent years, both within and outside of the academy. From McLuhan's vision of a "global village" to more recent advances in social and networking software (a designation that includes dating sites, weblogs, and various forms and models of online networking), computers and the Internet more generally have helped millions of people forge connections to one another. Advances in digital telecommunications has helped to make the world a much smaller place for those who are privileged enough to have access. Within the academy, technology is transdisciplinary, cutting across the traditional boundaries of disciplines to serve as a cornerstone of Bill Readings' managerial "university of excellence," as a crucial site for innovative pedagogies, and as a increasingly pressing demand in an already overburdened postsecondary educational system. Whether construed as a positive or a negative force in each of these instances, technology is a shared interest, however.

The second layer of my titular puncept incorporates the Latin verb *fractare*, to break, from which we receive the English word *fracture*. At the same time that technology connects us to one another in various ways, it also encourages different axes of separation. Within our own country, access to technology is no less uneven than access to other material goods, and that is to say nothing of the colossal gaps in access that separate our country from much of the rest of the world. Online networking might enable us to forge new connections without concern for geography, but those connections may come at the cost of our more immediate, local connections. We may appreciate our "up-to-the-minute coverage" of events around the world, but these events are still mediated for us, albeit in a fashion that often tropes on immediacy. Listserv discussions may transcend temporal and geographic boundaries, but the cost is often misunderstanding, and sometimes, outright flame wars. In other words, as often as technology may provide us with connections, to each other and to the world around us, it is just as capable of distancing us.

Adding *fracta* to my title, then, is one way of acknowledging this double edge, one way of following Burke's insight that identification implies division, that we congregate with certain people only by segregating ourselves from others. But there is a third layer to this hybrid term as well because fracta also implies fractal. In the 1960s, French mathematician Benoit Mandelbrot discovered what he called *fractal geometry*, figures that are characterized by an ambiguity of scale. Composed of smaller versions of themselves, fractals retain their shape to a greater degree than Euclidean figures, regardless of the distance from which they are perceived. The shapes of fractals persist across different scales of magnification, and this self-similarity opens up questions for technology that I hope this project engages to a degree. In chapter 2, I describe this specifically as an issue of scalability, and it is an issue that goes unexplored too frequently. At its most basic, we frequently assume that our individual (or even community) experiences with various technologies can be extrapolated to all users, or that the values of those experiences are the same at every level of interaction. In the composition classroom, many scholars identify a tension between helping students improve as writers and preparing them for a marketplace that will exploit them, and this is a tension of scale.[2] In other words, *lingua fracta* as fractal calls our attention to the fact that our understandings of technology frequently depend on the scale at which we choose to consider them.

Lingua fracta also connotes the in-between-ness that I attempted to describe in the last section. Euclidean geometry locates dimensions as integers: a point is one dimensional, polygons two dimensional, and our perceptual space is three dimensional. Fractal geometry, in contrast, describes figures whose dimensions are fractional and permanently so. In this way, they reverse our traditional understanding of dimensions, treating stable, integer dimensionality as a deviation from naturally occurring figures that possess these fractional dimensions. Similarly, technologies rarely can be described purely as a matter of identification or division, connection or alienation, liberation or oppression, celebration or depression, and so on. For almost any value claim about technology, there are corresponding examples of the opposite value—examples that are no less relevant. The space marked out by fractals, however, does not represent for me a compromise or a golden mean between opposite extremes, but rather a space from which those extremes occasionally emerge.

In *Grammar of Motives*, Burke (1969b) discusses the value of the "representative anecdote," and, in a particular sense, the puncept behind the title of this project serves this function. The associative process by which I arrived at the title, thinking through first one and then another extreme, only to arrive eventually at a place that in fact precedes those extremes, is something more akin to a mood of thought than an actual anecdote. Personally speaking, the phrase *lingua fracta* is the one part of this project that has remained constant over the past several years; as such, it is less representative of the ideas in this book than it is of my own attitude or approach to this material. The ideas gathered together in this project represent a particular performance of the kinds of speculation, research, reflection, and rhetorics in which I engage. A fractal set is never finished because there is always another scale of magnification from which to view it, and my attempt to articulate a rhetoric of new media shares this quality.

ABOUT THIS BOOK

This project is laid out in a fairly simple manner. The first two chapters provide the framework elaborated on in the subsequent five chapters, and I close the book with a short afterword. Chapter 1 argues that any rhetoric of new media should begin with an understanding that our unit of analysis must shift from textual objects to medial interfaces. We have inherited a critical attitude from our long association with English departments that focuses on individual texts, on the one hand, and large theoretical structures, on the other. This book argues that the excluded middle of such an attitude is, in fact, rhetoric and specifically, interfaces as rhetorical practices that may span multiple texts without achieving the level of abstraction of literary theory. In the absence of research that attends to this middle space, many in rhetoric and composition have turned to the concept of remediation; the latter portion of the chapter distinguishes the project that follows from Bolter and Grusin's terminology.

Chapter 2 begins from the question of what a rhetoric that attends to interfaces might look like and draws on two sets of vocabulary from classical rhetoric, the trivium and the canons of classical rhetoric, to answer it. If the interface is our unit of analysis, then we need a framework that enables analysis without discounting the overlaps and dynamic relationships among interfaces. I turn to the increasingly popular notion of ecologies to situate my inquiry. I argue that we might reenvision the trivium of grammar, rhetoric, and dialectic/logic, seeing them less as separate disciplines and more as scales of activity that focus our attention in different ways. I suggest that a revised trivium comprise ecologies of code, practice, and culture and, furthermore, that the canons of classical rhetoric provide a robust example of an ecology of practice—one that we might use to both interrogate and produce new media. Within this broad ecology of practice, each of the canons designates a site where various practices are gathered together, juxtaposed, combined, interrogated, discarded, and so on. In short, the concerns named by the canons persist to this day, but our means of articulating and fulfilling them changes as information technologies change. Because the canons have been adapted to process pedagogy in our textbooks and writing classrooms (cf. Welch), they have been truncated and sapped of much of their explanatory and productive power. Viewing them in light of new media can both restore the canons' relevancy and supply us with an effective framework for understanding new developments in discursive technology.

In chapters 3 through 7, I examine each of the canons in turn, renaming them to distinguish their manifestations in new media from our more traditional understandings. These new terms are intended less as absolute assertions, however, than they are meant as heuristic in nature, as means of demonstrating the various practices made possible by contemporary technology. These chapters do not seek to invalidate prior work in and on the canons, but rather to help us resist the tendency to restrict the canons to their traditional meanings. Chapter 3 ("Proairesis") borrows a term from Roland Barthes to discuss the ways that new media shift invention from the generation of new material toward a resistance to closure. It surveys both recent treatments of invention in rhetoric and composition and a related focus on authorship in technology studies scholarship, concluding that much of this work tends toward the closure of the textual object. Chapter

4 ("Pattern") begins from early scholarship on hypertext, which often emphasized the obsolescence of arrangement, and turns to a similar emphasis in more recent discussions of the database as a cultural form. I argue that arrangement can be productively thought of in terms of patterns rather than sequences, and that the navigation of databases requires us to work with such patterns as the hierarchal lists of search results, the network maps generated by data mining, and even the tagclouds that appear on weblogs.

Chapter 5 ("Perspective") revisits Richard Lanham's classic distinction between *looking at* and *looking through*, suggesting that with new media a third term is needed, *looking from*, that captures the positionality of users. This argument concludes an exploration of recent work in visual rhetoric and literacies, which often relegates the canon of style to the ecology of code. Chapter 6 ("Persistence") questions the separation of memory into personal acts of memorization, on the one hand, and public memorial acts, on the other, which I read as the bifurcation of this canon into ecologies of code and culture, with little room allowed for memory *practice*. In the ecologies of code and culture, memory becomes an issue of presence or absence. I argue that N. Katherine Hayles' semiotics of virtuality, which adds the terms *pattern* and *randomness* to presence and absence, might help conceive of memory practices that are constructive rather than purely reflective. Finally, chapter 7 ("Performance") examines two recent attempts at reclaiming the canon of delivery: *delivery as medium* and *delivery as circulation*. Although each of these formulations has strengths, I argue that they run the risk of returning to a transitive understanding of the canon, one that asserts discourse as an object to be transmitted. Rethinking delivery as performance captures the productive elements of the canon lost when the canons were rethought according to their relevance for print technologies.

A FINAL NOTE

There is a paradoxical mix of ambition and modesty at the heart of this project. It is modest in the sense that we have taken for granted the effect that technological contexts have on the practice of rhetoric. It is no secret that, with the onset of print, the canons of memory and delivery were largely abandoned as unnecessary. In this sense, suggesting that the canons shift in emphasis with changes in discursive technology borders on the obvious. At the same time, however, suggesting new terms for the canons—although it is not my intent here to supplant the Greek, Latin, or English terms for them—is a wildly ambitious, and perhaps presumptuous, endeavor. Yet it is precisely the weight of millennia that I seek to avoid here through my redescriptions of the canons. We are far too quick to assume that we understand the canons because we are comfortable with that vocabulary. So although I readily admit the presumption of this project, I do not think it too much to suggest that we revive discussions of the canons at a time when their context is changing in important ways.

That we are faced with an unprecedented proliferation of discursive technologies provides us with an ideal exigence for engaging in such a project. Time and again, we have come up against the fact that our disciplinary structures, designed and revised in print contexts, are insufficient to the task of understanding what is happening around us. This does not require us to abandon the knowledge we have already achieved in the study of writing, but it should compel us to revisit even our most cherished assumptions about discourse and its production and reception. Too often our discussions of technology center around "making room" in our courses for it, at a time when the idea of writing is being transformed all around us. Rebuilding our discipline not just to cope but to contribute to such change seems to me the least of our obligations as writing teachers and researchers.

NOTES

1. For example, consider electronic discussion lists. Positively speaking, a discussion list is little more than a list of e-mail addresses, where sending a message to the list address forwards the message to all of the addresses subscribed. But this no more describes a discussion list than a guest list for a party describes the conversations that take place there.
2. This is perhaps our contemporary, disciplinary version of Burke's (1969a) famous example of the shepherd, who "acts for the good of the sheep" at one level, even as "he may be 'identified' with a project that is raising the sheep for market" (p. 27).

ACKNOWLEDGMENTS

The book before you is the culmination of a long and layered history, spanning my time at three different institutions. It began as my dissertation at the University of Texas at Arlington, and while the current volume shares little with that document beyond a title and an abiding interest in the classical canons of rhetoric, it's difficult for me not to think of this project as an inevitable outgrowth of my work as a graduate student ten years ago. In that time, however, my thoughts on rhetoric and technology have been honed, challenged, supported, and complicated by friends and colleagues at UTA, Old Dominion, and Syracuse, and there is no question in my mind that they have helped me to push my thought further than I ever could have on my own. Under normal circumstances, I would take this opportunity to thank as many of them as possible; I am grateful for their support and mentorship over the years, certainly, but I believe that they will understand if I fail to mention them here by name.

While this book was in press, my father, Charles Winston Brooke, passed away after a protracted battle with cancer. Even now, some months later, it is difficult for me to write those words, or to grasp fully the facts behind them. We are faced in our lives with losses and joys at every turn—I am not so self-centered as to imagine that my own experiences in this regard are unique—but with my father's passing, I have struggled to regain what was at one time my unquestioned faith in the sufficiency of language. I have struggled to articulate the conflicted mess of emotion and experience that has been my near-constant companion for the past year. It has not been something have I have felt especially comfortable either talking or writing about, and even now, I have my doubts. But this is what I remember:

- Saturday morning errands to the library, the hardware store, the firm
- Dad's Club softball, YMCA soccer, and playing kickball at dusk in the summers
- Our annual trips to Missouri to buy fireworks for the 4th of July
- Youth group canoe trips to the Boundary Waters
- My father trying to learn to play the flute. Trying.
- The first Quad-City Symphony Riverfront Pops concert
- Going to Wrigley Field in the summers
- Borrowing my father's clothes for debate tournaments
- Being able to attend any college that accepted me
- Exploring cemeteries in Indiana tracking down our family history
- Struggling to understand graduate school my first go-round
- Living in and renovating the saltbox on 13th Street
- Deciding to give graduate school another try
- Landing my first tenure-track position
- Driving the UHaul from Virginia to New York
- Watching my father be sworn in as Mayor of Davenport
- Going to Busch Stadium last summer

In one sense, I never had the chance to thank my father for any of these things. But as I spent time with him last summer, even though we never talked about it, I like to think that I showed my gratitude each day. I think it frustrated him to be treated as someone who was dying, when in fact each day was another day of life. And we spent those days doing crosswords, watching baseball, eating out, reading, catching movies, and talking local politics. For the past few years, every time I left Iowa to return home, I did so not knowing if I'd see him again, but when I was there, I was *there*, in the moment, nothing more, nothing less.

Through all the good times and the bad, my father was *there* for me, and that's something I don't know that I fully appreciated until it was my turn to be there for him. Here's a final memory. In May of 1997, I received my first job offer from Old Dominion, which was contingent upon completing my dissertation. I had to choose between turning down the offer and spending another year in Texas or spending the entire summer doing nothing but writing. Without a second thought, my father loaned me the money so that I could finish my dissertation and accept that offer. Of all the layers that comprise the history of this book, one of the deepest is the support I received over the years from my father. He may not be around to read it, but he's here in these pages. The name on the front is mine, but the book itself is ours.

Hope you enjoy it, Dad.

—cgb

1

INTERFACE

In 1999, the electronic journal *Kairos* published "Hypertext Is Dead (Isn't It?)," (Fig. 1.1) an electronic essay containing the positions and ideas of some of the leading figures in the specialty of computers and writing and focusing specifically (as the title indicates) on the vitality of hypertext. But this essay did not begin as such. Instead, it began as an e-mail conversation associated with the online portion of the 1999 Computers and Writing Conference. Portions of that conversation were collected, coded, and connected to produce the form that appears in *Kairos*. Readers can follow the conversation sequentially or access individual contributors' posts, or some combination of the two. The first page of the essay provides an overview that identifies the context for the conversation and options for accessing the text. Otherwise the editor (who is unnamed in the essay) has designed the nodes "to represent the discussion and dialogue as close to the original form as possible."

"Hypertext Is Dead" is a distinctive example of scholarship in the field of rhetoric and composition, partly for the multiple layers of mediation it passed through to arrive in its published form. Accounting for that form requires us to acknowledge three such layers. First, there is the "town hall" conversational format, which is a distinctive feature of several Computers and Writing Conferences. Town hall discussions typically involve several

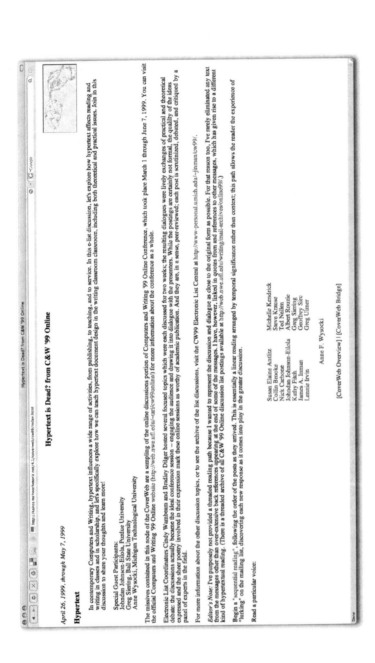

Figure 1.1. A screenshot of the *Kairos* essay

discussion leaders, a common topic, and the attempt to generate wide-ranging discussion among a large group of face-to-face participants. The online component of Computers and Writing provides a second layer; C&WO is a venue both for conference attendees and those who are unable to attend, and it frequently extends beyond the temporal boundaries of the onsite conference as well as the geographical. The editor of "Hypertext Is Dead" acknowledges as much, going so far as to explain the success of the discussion as "the ideal conference session," praising its lively exchanges and audience engagement. On a conference listserv, then, "Hypertext Is Dead" began as an emulation of a town hall conversation. The anonymous editor also provides the rationale for its translation into a third and final form, the *Kairos* article, writing that "the quality of the ideas expressed and the sheer poetry involved in their expression mark these online sessions as worthy of academic publication."

One thing that makes "Hypertext Is Dead" distinctive is the fact that all three of these layers are made explicit on the front page of the essay: Its emulation of the "ideal conference session" supplies the motive behind its preservation, its remediation of an e-mail conversation provides part of the text's organization, and the rationale justifies its status as a publication. The text is distributed across these layers, which distinguishes it from more traditional, scholarly writing processes. It is hardly unusual, for example, to turn a conference paper into an article for publication or a dissertation chapter into an oral presentation for a campus visit, but in those more common cases, each "text" is expected to stand on its own—to satisfy the generic, formal, and conceptual expectations associated with the situation. In challenging such expectations, however modestly, "Hypertext Is Dead" announces itself as a "new media text" according to Anne Wysocki's (2004) definition:

> I think we should call "new media texts" those that have been made by composers who are aware of the range of materialities of texts and who then highlight the materiality: such composers design texts that help readers/consumers/viewers stay alert to how any text—like its composers and readers—doesn't function independently of how it is made and in what contexts. Such composers design texts that make as overtly as possible the value they embody. (p. 15)

"Hypertext Is Dead" is not a particularly radical or mysterious example of the kinds of texts Wysocki describes. Indeed, the editor's description takes pains to make it recognizable to an audience accustomed to more tradition-al texts. Yet despite such effort and despite the modesty of the challenge to traditional academic discourse that the article represents, texts like "Hypertext Is Dead" remain largely invisible to rhetoric and composition.

One mode of this invisibility is institutional. In recent years, a great deal of effort has gone into revising tenure and promotion guidelines for those of us who define our work in terms of technology,[1] but such guidelines are slow to change, and "Hypertext Is Dead" offers an interesting test case. It is mercenary perhaps to reduce institutional recognition to lines on one's *curriculum vitae*, but such a reduction is not especially unusual. Who, then, should receive credit for "Hypertext Is Dead," which is, after all, a publication in one of our most visible electronic journals? There are 15 "authors" whose permission was secured prior to publication, but it is unlikely that any of them—and I say this as one of the discussion participants—thought to list the article as a publication. It is hard to imagine a tenure committee treating a handful of e-mails as equivalent to a peer-reviewed journal article. The organizers of the discussion are even less likely, except insofar as they participated in the conversation; taking credit for a conversation they initiated seems even less defensible. Perhaps a case can be made for attributing this essay to the editor who collected it for *Kairos*, but that person remained anonymous. Intentionally or not, the editor of "Hypertext Is Dead" only serves to reinforce the attitudes toward what constitutes recognizable scholarship. Institutionally, an essay like this one is all but invisible. Despite multiple layers of effort, some fairly renowned contributors, and the editor's attempt to place the article within an institutional economy, "Hypertext is Dead" is not really the kind of work that is recognized by our institutions.[2]

But its invisibility extends beyond the pragmatic lens of the "line on the vita." In her description and definition of new media, Wysocki (2004) also articulates a need for work that bridges the gap between "two broad categories [of scholarship on new media]: there is writing about how to analyze or design isolated individual texts and there is writing about the broad contexts and functioning of media structures in general" (p. 6). This is not simply a niche that Wysocki is asking us to fill, however. Accounting for "Hypertext Is Dead" and other new media texts requires us to inhabit the gap about which she writes. This essay is neither isolated nor individual, intertwined as it is with the efforts of many contributors and several layers of media. Nor is it really recognizable as a text, except in the etymological sense of the word as *weaving*. The hypertext binds together a variety of positions, tones, voices, authors, and contexts, but it does not do so in the interests of a single thesis or focus. Although unpacking this chapter may tell us something about one particular context or media structure, it would be difficult to generalize from that process to "media structures in general." On first glance, neither of the categories Wysocki describes seems especially suitable for understanding "Hypertext is Dead," and, in fact, they haven't been. These categories are in fact critical strategies, ones that (as I discuss later in this chapter) represent two extremes of a spectrum and that continue to prevent us from understanding new media *qua* new media as long as we adhere to them.

This is one of the central premises of this book. Like Wysocki (2004), I believe that, as teachers and students of writing, scholars in composition and rhetoric are indeed uniquely positioned to contribute to discussions and debates about new media. Such contributions, however, depend on our ability to rethink some of our own cherished and unexamined assumptions about writing; new media will transform our understandings of rhetoric as thoroughly as our training and expertise in rhetoric can effect a similar impact in discussions of new media. But this presumes that we recognize the various contributions that information technologies make to rhetorical situations. Rhetoric and composition has emerged, over the past century, within the disciplinary context of the study of literature, and that context has predisposed us to print literacies and textualities. That predisposition is strong enough that we tend to neglect the technological specificity of various rhetorics, and this, in turn, has kept us from bridging the gap that Wysocki observes. This gap, between the local particularity of the individual text and the global generality of media structures, is a space that we already occupy as writers and writing scholars; bringing what we know to bear on new media is the next logical step in the growth of our discipline.

There is more at stake behind this premise than simply recognizing a particular article or ensuring that someone receives credit for it. "Hypertext is Dead" and other "essays" like it are symptomatic of broader changes in the range of informational, communicative, and expressive potentials embodied in new media. Our tendency has been to treat discursive technologies as if they were simply another specialty among many in our discipline, the province of a handful of experts, one of whom could be hired into a department thereby satisfying that particular "area." This attitude, another of our legacies inherited from English departments, has left us underprepared for the shift from page to screen; technology is transdisciplinary, cutting across the full range of activities we engage in as professionals, rather than subdisciplinary. The longer we wait to realize this, the harder we will have to struggle for respect and relevance as experts in writing.

My tone here is perhaps more apocalyptic than it needs to be because it is not simply a matter of breaking from print literacies or arguing that such literacies are obsolete. At the same time, we cannot simply neglect the technological changes happening around us. New media writers may draw on more traditional strategies to make their work recognizable to us, but just as frequently, older media become sites of innovation, drawing on the rhetoric of new media. In the early days of compact disc players, for example, some artists specifically designed new releases to take advantage of the unique features of CD players, like the shuffle button.[3] Similarly, with the emergence of the Web, it has become more common to find books that attempt to simulate links, books as disparate as Celia Pearce's (1997) *The Interactive Book* and historian Jacques Barzun's (2000) *From Dawn to Decadence*. The presence of websites for our print journals has slowly begun to change the way we think about them. The point here is not that rhetoric and composition risks obsolescence any time soon if it continues to bracket off technology as a specialty—if anything, institutional change is even slower than disciplinary change—but rather that the conversations about technology, conversations to which we can and should contribute, are taking place around us right now. They are taking place in interdisciplinary programs, at conferences jointly sponsored by academia and industry, on listservs, and in blogspace, and it is high time that we seek them out.

Of course, calls to action such as this one are rife in our field, and not only with respect to technology. It is relatively easy to level critiques or calls for action at a discipline, but it is more difficult to lay down a coherent path for that action to take. Since Cynthia Selfe's CCCC Chair's Address in 1998,[4] computers and writing scholars have urged the larger discipline to pay critical attention to technology; a corollary of my premise above is that a focus on technology requires critical attention to rhetoric as well, and this book represents my own attempt to fuse rhetoric and technology both critically and productively. The remainder of this chapter, as well as the second, lays some groundwork for this fusion. In this chapter, I argue that new media challenges us to reconceive our basic unit of analysis; the mutability of new media means that we should be shifting our focus from textual objects to medial interfaces. Chapter 2 introduces the idea of ecology as a framing strategy that can help us enact this shift, and it argues that the classical canons of rhetoric can be rethought in ecological terms, as an *ecology of practice*, that can provide us with a great deal of insight regarding new media. Chapters 3 through 7 put this claim to the test, articulating each of the canons as rhetorical principles for both reading and writing new media, principles that avoid both the particularity and the universality of the categories that Wysocki observes.

In other words, if bringing new media and writing studies together is one of the central premises of this book, perhaps its overarching claim is that the rhetorical canons, revised for technological specificity, supply us with a powerful means of doing so. They allow us to inhabit Wysocki's gap, to find some middle space between the analysis of texts in isolation and the proclamation of theoretical absolutes. The canons are by no means the only way to accomplish this goal, but they have the advantages of familiarity for rhetoric and composition scholars and flexibility as a framework that has persisted across a number of shifts in medium in the centuries since their inception. As helpful as the canons can be for understanding new media, however, it is equally important to acknowledge the degree to which new media can help us rethink the canons. Staging this mutually transformative encounter is the primary aim of this book.

NEW NEW CRITICISM

> The object of criticism is not "the world" but a discourse, the discourse of someone else: criticism is discourse upon a discourse; it is a second language, or a metalanguage (as the logicians would say), which operates on a first language (or language object).
>
> Roland Barthes, *Critical Essays* (1972)

Bringing new media and writing together, as I hope to demonstrate throughout this book, is not simply a matter of taking what we know as writing scholars and applying it to a new set of texts or language objects as Barthes terms them. Such an approach decontextualizes both the knowledge and the objects to which it is applied. As I argue later in this section, this strategy appears frequently in early hypertext criticism as part of the rush to locate poststructuralist principles in the workings of those texts. For the moment, however, I want to consider the two broad categories of scholarship that Wysocki identifies: "writing about . . . isolated individual texts and . . . writing about the broad contexts and functioning of media structures in general"—in more detail, both as a means of articulating what I mean when I advocate a shift from text to interface and as an example of the kind of fundamental rethinking that I believe we must bring to our core disciplinary assumptions if we are going to bring new media and writing together.

Earlier I described these categories as *critical strategies*, a designation that requires some explanation. *Critical* is an overdetermined word, both in rhetoric and composition and in the humanities more generally. If we consider the range of perspectives, ideologies, and inflections implied by its appearance in phrases like critical literacy, critical thinking, and critical theory, *critical* begins to look a lot like *excellence* as Bill Readings critiques the term in *The University in Ruins*. In other words, just as *excellence* has come to function as an empty signifier in the institutional discourses of the academy, it is hard to imagine *critical* as much more than a generic statement of value. But the term's contemporary overdetermination has emerged from a more specific tradition, one signified in the title of Barthes' (1972) *Critical Essays*. For Barthes, and for generations of scholars in humanities disciplines, *critical* refers specifically to criticism and designates a particular set of aims and practices common to the scholarship of several disciplines.

Although a full-scale history of criticism is beyond the scope of this chapter, it is important to acknowledge that this history, or at least that part of it that takes place in English studies, has had an impact on rhetoric and composition, both in terms of what counts as scholarly work and in terms of how we go about such work. Robert Scholes and others have written at length about the privilege attached to the *reception* (rather than *production*) of texts in English departments, and there is copious evidence to suggest that this emphasis prefigures the status of rhetoric and composition in such departments. More recently, Patricia Harkin has called attention to our discipline's reticence in considering issues of reading, and reader-response theory more specifically, as if to do so would be to "sleep with the enemy" of literary study. Maxine Hairston's landmark "Winds of Change" is perhaps the most famous expression of this suspicion, but the years that have passed since her CCCC Chair's Address have done little to ease it, as Richard Fulkerson's recent attempt at rehabilitating Hairston's position, and his recasting of it as "content envy" on the part of our discipline, suggests. Regardless of whether rhetoric and composition manages to achieve some sort of institutional autonomy or separation from English studies more broadly (e.g., in the case of free-standing writing programs), intellectual autonomy seems almost certain to take longer to achieve.

Wysocki's diagnosis of these broad categories of new media scholarship underscores the magnitude of such an achievement. The first category that she identifies, with its focus on "isolated individual texts," should be familiar to us as one of the guiding principles behind New Criticism in literary studies. In the first half of the 20th century, New Criticism navigated between the competing traditions of historical-cum-philological scholarship, on the one hand, and an impressionistic, subjective eulogizing, on the other hand, neither of which, it was felt, focused on the texts. Terry Eagleton characterizes the New Critical "urge to convert the poem into a self-sufficient object" by contrasting it with the Romantic tendency to "bow low in reverent silence before the unfathomable mystery of the text":

> . . . the New Critics deliberately cultivated the toughest, most hard-headed techniques of critical dissection. The same impulse which stirred them to insist on the "objective" status of the work also led them to promote a strictly "objective" way of analyzing it. A typical New Critical account of a poem offers a stringent investigation of its various "tensions," "paradoxes" and "ambivalences," showing how these are resolved and integrated by its solid structure. (pp. 48-49)

The emphasis that Eagleton places on the "objectivity" of this method is no accident because New Criticism grounded itself in the literary text as language *object*, separated from its author, its readers, as well as any social, historical, or political context. New Criticism may no longer serve as anything more than an episode in the history of English studies, but its influence has lasted much longer. As the traditions that made New Criticism "new" faded from relevance, New Criticism became less of a movement, diffusing instead into standard operating procedure for most literary critics. New Criticism simply became criticism or "close reading," a species of analysis that survives to the present day[5] in the form of rhetorical analyses, for instance, that urge students to locate instances of ethos, logos, and pathos in particular texts.

New Criticism began to lose steam as a movement, however, with the influence of Continental philosophy, imported by departments of English and Comparative Literature as "literary theory," and this turn in English studies parallels the second of Wysocki's categories, discussions of the "broad contexts and functioning of media structures in general." New Criticism began with a call to return to the texts, but as Eagleton's characterization makes clear, their method of close reading privileges particular forms and functions when it comes to literary value: paradoxes, ambivalences, and so on. Hence, New Critics focused on individual, isolated texts as the objects of their close reading, but they did so with a particular set of values in mind, so as to be able to distinguish the "great" works of literature from those that were less so. These New Critical values, then, end up functioning as both a context for and a description of the "functioning" of "[literary] structures in general." If anything, the arrival of Theory-with-a-capital-T in English studies cements this particular strategy because literary theory had little effect on the actual practice of criticism. Instead, literary theory challenges the set of values institutionalized by New Criticism, introducing any number of alternative contexts and structures among which literature plays various roles—conservative, subversive, normalizing, obfuscating, and so on. So-called *theory* corresponds to that second category that Wysocki identifies if we read the "functioning of media structures in general" as broadly as possible, and countenance the substitution of various theoretically contested terms—gender, class, race, sexual preference, language, literature, art, politics, culture—for "media."

In other words, these two categories end up functioning as a single category, opposite poles (particular and universal) of a single, *critical* approach to texts. The close reading of an object (and as the shift toward cultural studies has demonstrated, that object need not be textual or linguistic) depends on some prior theoretical commitment on the part of the reader. At the same time, the value of a particular theoretical perspective, the test of its claim regarding the functioning of structures in general, is going to depend on its applicability to individual texts and upon, as Susan Miller (2002) puts it (somewhat parodically), "the projection of individual perspicacity that is practiced as hermeneutic interpretation" (p. 43). It is no more possible to consider individual texts without some type of theoretical principles for one's judgments than it is to advance claims about generalized structures or contexts in the absence of concrete application. Although it was no doubt tempting at one time to dismiss New Criticism as naively atheoretical, no less tempting than it may be now to accuse literary theory of abstract impracticality, these two mo(ve)ments in the history of English studies are really two sides of the same coin.

Nevertheless, there is nothing intrinsically wrong with the scholarly practice of criticism, with its twin poles of close reading and theoretical judgment, nor should the growth of new media criticism necessarily be a cause for concern. We should be concerned, however, as Wysocki is, with the limitations that criticism entails, with its emphasis on evaluating work that *has been* done, rather than focusing on invention—on what *might still* be done with new media. Criticism is, at heart, a method of reading and, as such, is perfectly worthwhile, but criticism should no more exhaust our understandings of and our approaches to new media than literary study exhausted the study and practice of writing. In part, we must bear in mind, as the epigraph from Barthes reminds us, that criticism requires an object in a specific sense. Professional, "objective" criticism, of the sort that the New Critics advocated, requires an object that is stable, isolated (in principle, at least), and consistent. Ten different readers may offer 10 different interpretations of a given literary text, but the practice of criticism presumes that they are not reading 10 different material objects or else the criticism would become meaningless. It would be difficult, if not impossible, to argue convincingly that one critic's reading of text X is more accurate than another's reading of text Y.

To put it another way, criticism depends on the shared experience of a text, something that the standardization of print publication allows us to take for granted. In the case of new media, however, the absence of shared experience can become part of the infrastructure of a text, as is the case with frequently updated weblogs or particularly contentious pages on a wiki[6] (Fig. 1.2). If we turn back to early hypertext theory, the mutability and variability of the text was celebrated as a virtue. Yet few of those who praised this aspect of hypertext took the time to think through its implications. One exception comes from Steven Johnson's (1997) *Interface Culture*, where he discusses his initial enthusiasm over Michael Joyce's (1990) *Afternoon, A Story,* one of the canonical examples of hypertext literature.

> After I finished with *Afternoon,* I rang up a few friends who had also meandered through it, looking for feedback. In each phone call, we talked excitedly for a minute or two about the medium and its possibilities, but the second we turned to the content of the story, the conversation grew stilted and uneven. We were talking, it turned out, about very different stories. Each reading had produced an individual, private experience. (pp. 126-127)

Johnson's experience is emblematic of the problems that any attempt at a criticism of new media faces; although he does not put it in so many words, Johnson and his friends were confronted with the *social* dimension of criticism and, in particular, the ability of new media to frustrate that dimension. Criticism of "the content of the story" relies on an implied social contract among critics, enforced by the publishing industry and intellectual property laws, that fixes textual objects, thereby making them available for readers in different locations and at different times.

In a recent issue of the *Journal of Digital Information* (*JoDI*), devoted specifically to the question of hypertext criticism, Richard Higgason (2003) extends Johnson's observations, imagining a scholar who has given a conference presentation on a particular hypertext, only to be asked by a member of the audience how a "rape scene" fits into her analysis ("A Scholar's Nightmare"). What happens when the scholar has not read the scene in question? The simple answer to this question is to say that a rigorous scholar should leave no node or lexia unread. Although such a reading would be exhausting, in both senses of the word, this answer would seem to work

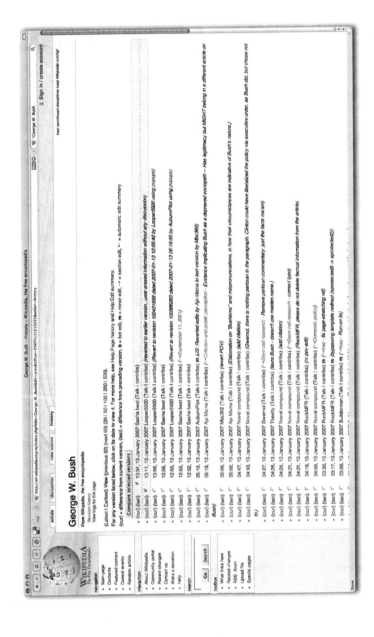

Figure 1.2. The history page from the Wikipedia entry on George W. Bush

against the spirit of hypertext as it has been characterized by its advocates and impossible with hypertextual media like weblogs and wikis that extend diachronically. If, as Jay Bolter (1991) writes, there are no hypertexts, but only readings, then an exhaustive mapping (physical, narratological, or cognitive) of a given text wouldn't really be a "reading" at all, but rather the generation of a sort of ur-text that can not possibly exist for any reader.

In fact, this is the strategy adopted in much of hypertext criticism. In the second edition of *Hypertext*, George Landow (1997) reviews several pieces of hypertext literature, including Joyce's *Afternoon*, Shelley Jackson's *Patchwork Girl*, and Carolyn Guyer's *Quibbling*, a section that attempts to accomplish both of Wysocki's "broad categories" of scholarship, reading individual texts in terms of broad claims regarding literary-theoretical structures. What is striking about much of this section of Landow's text, for all that he engages in criticism of each work, is the degree to which such criticism pulls back from the text. The section on Joyce, for instance, rumi-nates on the theories of Gerard Genette, Claude Lévi-Strauss, and J. Hillis Miller far more than it does on Joyce's work. Landow's description of Guyer's *Quibbling* owes far more to French feminist thought and Guyer's own account of the resonance she feels with ideas from Gilles Deleuze and Félix Guattari than it does to any specific reading of her hypertext. This strategy makes sense in the face of the "nightmare" offered by Higgason. If hypertexts vary from one reader's experience to another, then as Johnson's account demonstrates, the "shared experience" rests at the scale of medium or system, rather than individual readings. But deploying this strategy entails a certain degree of decontextualization or abstraction; it is no accident that the theoretical concepts that Landow employs throughout his book are poststructuralist abstractions, such as Deleuze and Guattari's "smooth space," Barthes' "writerly texts," Bakhtin's "multivocality," Derrida's "decentering," and many others.

Yet there are a couple of problems with this approach. In Landow's (1997) account of Guyer, a section called "*Quibbling*, A Feminist Rhizome Narrative," there is no real explanation of how Deleuze and Guattari's idea of the rhizome is embodied by *Quibbling*. The connection between Guyer's work and Deleuze and Guattari's *A Thousand Plateaus* comes from Guyer's own account of having encountered their work subsequent to composing, and, at least in the remarks referenced in Landow's text, she does not make mention of rhizomes. This is not to deny the potential affinity between Deleuze and Guattari's notion of "smooth space" and Guyer's experience in composing *Quibbling*. Yet from a critical perspective, there is little evidence for this connection beyond Guyer's claim, as author, that it exists. If the evidence for theoretical criticism is the kind of close reading discussed earlier, it may not be possible to marshal evidence beyond authorial statements (both Joyce and Jackson, it should be noted, include theoretical material in their hypertexts, making the framework for their reception part of the texts). In other words, if new media provide us with objects that are not stable enough for the kinds of shared, close reading to which we are accustomed in print culture, then locating theoretical values behind the texts will largely be a matter of assertion, rather than demonstration. New media "objects" lend themselves neither to close reading nor really to demonstrating the broader values represented by the theoretical concepts that Landow deploys.

A second problem with this approach is more pragmatic, and it is one that opens onto the broader themes of my own project. Landow's book is relatively unique among volumes of new media criticism in that, in addition to critical accounts, he attempts a corresponding description of what he describes as "rhetoric and stylistics."[7] However, we would be hard put to find much consistency between the principles he advocates in response to the question "How Should We Write Hypertext?" (the subtitle of this section) and those he celebrates in his readings of various examples throughout his work. Continuing with the example of Guyer, and in stark contrast to the rhizome, Landow's (1997) account of the "rhetoric" of linking is largely rule-based. Arguing that "the very existence of links conditions the reader to expect purposeful, important relationships between linked materials" (p. 125), Landow identifies four "rhetorics" that govern linking—orientation, navigation, departure, and arrival—all of which imply the purposeful relationships that he asserts as intrinsic to links. But these "rhetorics" bear little resemblance to Deleuze and Guattari's (1987) *rhizome*, the idea that Landow alludes to in the subtitle for his discussion of Guyer. Unlike the link driven by utility and scarcity, the rhizome, for Deleuze and Guattari, is much less orderly:

> Principles of connection and heterogeneity: any point of a rhizome can be connected to anything other, and must be. This is very different from the tree or root, which plots a point, fixes an order. . . . The coordinates are determined not by theoretical analyses implying universals but by a pragmatics composing multiplicities or aggregates of intensities. (pp. 7, 15)

In fact, it is not too far off to suggest that Deleuze and Guattari argue, in the first chapter of *A Thousand Plateaus*, precisely against the kind of well-ordered, purposeful linking that Landow offers as a "rhetoric of hypertext."

Yet neither vision of links is incorrect or wrong. Ultimately, it is not a matter of choosing between purposeful or profligate linking in an effort to determine which is the "correct" model for hypertext. From a rhetorical perspective, it is possible to imagine contexts where each model of linking, and many more besides, would be appropriate, contexts where particular writers' goals range from precise and careful orientation, on the one hand, to defamiliarization, on the other hand. The pragmatic concern that Landow's book raises (as do other examples of new media criticism) is one that the field of rhetoric and composition in some ways has emerged to address. The assumption that we learn to write by reading exemplary texts by professional (or "great") writers is one that carries little credibility in the field. Yet if we turn to critical accounts of new media in order to fashion a rhetoric, we are falling prey to this assumption all over again. This is not to suggest that there is no value in a text like Landow's; it is simply to note that *Hypertext* (and other critical projects like it) will never provide us with the kind of rhetoric we seek. A rhetoric of new media lies in the middle space identified by Wysocki, the space between analyses of individual texts on the one hand, and the theoretical values allegedly demonstrated by those texts, on the other hand. A rhetoric of new media, rather than examining the *choices that have already been made* by writers, should prepare us as writers to *make our own choices*. Such a rhetoric cannot be achieved through the reactive lens of critical/theoretical reading.

REMEDIATION

One way to cope with the provocation of novel art is to rest firm and maintain solid standards. . . . A second way is more yielding. The critic interested in a novel manifestation holds his criteria and taste in reserve. Since they were formed upon yesterday's art, he does not assume that they are ready-made for today. . . .

Leo Steinberg, *Other Criteria* (1972)

In chapter 2, this book offers a framework for such a rhetoric of new media, one that the subsequent chapters spell out in more detail. Before moving to that portion of the argument, however, it is worth our time to consider another strategy for approaching new media, one that has received a fair amount of exposure in rhetoric and composition in recent years, Jay Bolter's and Richard Grusin's (1999) idea of remediation. Although remediation is a claim about "media structures in general" (and would thus seem to fall in the second of Wysocki's categories), scholars who are taking it up tend to apply it at a smaller scale, investigating the relationships among specific media. This would suggest that remediation has some potential for bridging the gap between the criticism of individual texts and the assertion of theoretical generalities. However, a review of the scholarship that applies this concept, either explicitly or implicitly, suggests that this potential is limited at best. Following a brief introduction to remediation, this section examines two studies that take the remediation approach to new media, concluding that we have asked remediation to bear too much conceptual weight in our research.

Bolter and Grusin (1999) introduce the concept of remediation in their book of the same name, in part to provide a corrective to technology theorizing in the 1990s that posited various new media as breaking radically with more "traditional" media. The classic example of this kind of hyperbole is Robert Coover's (1992) suggestion in the *New York Times Book Review* that hypertext would result in the end of books. Bolter and Grusin also break from scholarship that posits progress or a teleology in the development of technology. They argue that older media can remediate new ones, and their book demonstrates this idea by including "hyperlinks" among its pages. The majority of *Remediation*, once extreme claims to technological difference and repetition are disavowed, is devoted to demonstrating a more nuanced approach to articulating relationships among media. Building on Marshall McLuhan's (1994) insights in *Understanding Media,* specifically the idea that "the content of any medium is another medium," Bolter and Grusin "call the representation of one medium in another *remediation,* and [...] argue that remediation is a defining characteristic of the new digital media" (p. 45). Remediation is comprised of what Bolter and Grusin describe as "our culture's contradictory imperatives for immediacy and hypermediacy," the desire "both to multiply its media and to erase all traces of mediation" (p. 5). Both imperatives are rooted in a desire, they explain, to "get past the limits of representation and to achieve the real" (p. 53). Immediacy does this by erasing all traces of mediation, hypermediacy by multiplying mediation to the point where "the excess of media becomes an authentic experience" (p. 53) in and of itself.[8] Like McLuhan before them, Bolter and Grusin introduce this idea at the outset of their book and then spend the majority of their pages illustrating its principles.

In this illustration of remediation, Bolter and Grusin (1999) provide a compelling account of the various ways that so-called "new" media emerge from specific social, economic, and technological contexts. In each case, however, remediation is a consequence of their analysis; remediation is the thesis that each chapter demonstrates and/or illustrates. Although remediation has been taken up in rhetoric and composition in a parallel fashion,[9] as a means of articulating the conclusions of a particular study, it is more frequently the premise on which subsequent work is based. For example, Kevin Brooks, Cindy Nichols, and Sybil Priebe (2004), in an essay entitled "Remediation, Genre, and Motivation: Key Concepts for Teaching with Weblogs," offer a rationale for this strategy, one based in Charles Bazerman's (1997) work on genre.[10] Bazerman writes, "When we travel to new communicative domains, we construct our perception of them beginning with the forms we know" (p. 19), and Brooks et al. combine this insight with remediation as a means of setting up a multiyear, multicourse study on weblogs and student motivation. Remediation provides Brooks et al. with at least a partial answer to the question of the rhetoric of weblogs by referring that question to the "print genres that weblogging, as we were presenting it to students, remediate[s]." Although the conclusions of the essay rely more heavily on student surveys than they do on the essay's conceptual premise, it is interesting to see what happens over the course of the essay as a result of their assumption.

They begin by identifying three print genres, all of which are familiar from writing courses—personal journals, academic notebooks, and note cards—and all of which, they argue, are remediated by weblogs. Ultimately, they conclude that "familiarity with a genre does not necessarily correspond to motivation," reaching this conclusion, in part, on the fact that the most "recognizable" genre, that of the note card, received the lowest marks in terms of student motivation when it was remediated into "filter blogging." Although their other conclusions (students prefer personal writing, community feedback helps to motivate "notebook blogging," technology is often motivating in and of itself) seem fairly predictable, the observations about "filter blogging" raised by Brooks et al. merit a closer look. Drawing on Bazerman and David Russell, they conclude that "the filter or note card weblog" may constitute a genre that appears obvious on the surface, but has "subterranean histories that complicate readers' and writers' expectations and practices." At several points, they reference the "complexity of this task."

What makes this unusual, however, is the high number of students who acknowledge their familiarity with note cards. Although there is no necessary connection between familiarity and motivation, certainly there should be a fairly direct relationship between familiarity with a given task and its relative complexity. That there was none in this case suggests a problem with the premise that filter blogging remediates the note card, but this possibility goes unquestioned in the essay. Instead, Brooks et al. (2004) enumerate the various factors they see contributing to the complexity of filter blogging (the need for strong motivation and interest, domain knowledge, the ability to locate and evaluate sites, etc.), many of which are common across all three "types" of blogging that they study (e.g., how to write effectively for their audience). Their description of filter blogging as a complex activity is an accurate one, particularly if their list of features is considered in light of the many popular filter weblogs, such as Metafilter, Slashdot, boing boing, Crooked Timber, and others. But it also raises the question of how useful it is to begin from the perspective of remediation, for the "subterranean histor[y]" of filter blogging hardly corresponds to the note cards with which nearly 70 % of their students were already familiar.

It is worth asking whether my argument goes too far here in attributing what I see as a breakdown in the conclusion of Brooks et al. (2004) to the broader application of remediation, rather than locating it more specifically in their selection of the note card as the antecedent for filter blogging, particularly when I am willing to grant that the other two genres seemed to work just fine within this framework. This objection is a valid one, undoubtedly. But it is also worth considering how remediation functions in its role as this essay's premise and clarifying that my objection here is not with remediation *per se*, but with a particular usage of it. If remediation places conceptual emphasis on "similarities and differences" among technologies as opposed to "similarities or differences," it serves as a useful framework for seeing technologies as intimately connected and culturally emergent. However, Bolter and Grusin's work provides no particular recipe, nor could it, for the relationships between two particular media. In this instance, Brooks et al. end up using the term in a way that flattens the *ratios* among genres, for wont of a better term. To put it more concretely, I would argue that the remediation entailed by moving either journals or notebooks (which in writing courses are already written to the audience of the instructor) online is relatively minimal, whereas the remediation of the note card (which bears little, if any, resemblance to filter blogging) is considerable. This is consistent with the variations found in Bolter and Grusin's illustrations of the concept: Remediation designates less a positive cultural function than it does a framework for examining a range of such functions, each dependent on its own set of factors.

All of which is to suggest that one of the equations treated as a given in Brooks et al. (2004), the notion that filter blogging remediates the note card, is a claim worthy of examination in more detail than the authors are able to provide. The danger of assuming this equation is demonstrated in their essay. When it proves inadequate to the task of explaining the practice, the authors defer their explanation to contextual factors. In the context of their essay, this deferral is more problematic with one of their types than with the others, but it is typical, I would argue, of any similar application of remediation. Remediation holds some value as an explanatory framework, certainly, but it cannot supply us with ready answers to the question of a new media rhetoric. Ultimately, it defers that question to older media. The rhetorics of blogging, insofar as we might generalize so early in the development of its practices, do indeed remediate various "older" genres, but at most this is simply another way of asking the question. At worst it invites us to focus our attention on media and practices that may mislead us, as it does in the case of filter blogging for Brooks et al. The consequences of this misstep are minimal in their essay; the nature of filter blogging is set aside for their purposes. In the next example of remediation, however, the stakes are a little higher.

My second example of remediation is an example in practice, if not in name. "The Limitations of Hypertext in the Composition Classroom" is MaryLynn Saul's (1999) contribution to Scott DeWitt and Kip Strasma's (1999) book *Contexts, Intertexts, and Hypertexts*, a collection that studies "the practical application of hypertext theory within the context of writing classrooms." Published in the same year as Bolter and Grusin's (1999) *Remediation*, Saul's chapter doesn't draw on their vocabulary, but the study she describes is a relevant example of remediation. At the time of the study, Saul was teaching four composition classes at two campuses of the Ohio State University; she decided that, in two of the classes, she would substitute a hypertext assignment for the collaborative research essay that her classes normally completed. As the title of her essay implies, Saul does not find that hypertext provides her with a satisfactory alternative to the essay; it remediates the research essay insufficiently for her purposes. Although it is possible to question her conclusions on methodological grounds, it is similarly possible to see her study as a cautionary tale about the application of remediation.

At the start of her essay, as she lays out the context for her case study, Saul (1999) explains her goals for the writing classroom: "My main goal in teaching freshman composition is to teach students three main skills: to write a clear thesis statement, to maintain a consistent focus on this thesis, and to support the thesis with logical arguments" (p. 41). These goals are not unusual for a writing classroom, but Saul seems to ignore the fact that these goals arise out of a particular medium, the academic essay. A few sentences later, she writes, "I hoped that hypertext would add an interest-ing and fun strategy for working on these goals" (p. 41). The only real dif-ference seems to be that students will be doing what they have done all along, except on a computer, and that this might make it more "interesting and fun." There is no evidence that Saul has considered the possibility that hypertext writing might involve a different set of goals or accomplish dif-ferent rhetorical aims than the traditional essay.

Nor is this the only place where Saul's assumptions undercut her ability to find significant results. At one point, she cites Johndan Johnson-Eilola's (1994) claim that collaborative hypertexts allow for the preserva-tion of multiple voices as one possible reason that "no one in the hypertext group expressed problems with disagreements among group members" (p. 46). This is entirely possible, but a more likely explanation is the fact that, in the assignment, Saul "strongly encouraged groups to take a group stand on the research subject" (p. 46), a directive consistent with her goals for the project and the class as a whole. It is notable that one hypertext group chose to resist this directive by including what Saul calls "two contradicto-ry opinion sections," although their project grade may have suffered for it.

There are other places where the students seem to resist the parame-ters of the assignment. One of the ways that Saul (1999) measures the suc-cess of the hypertext projects is by comparing the number of nodes that contain explicit argument with the total number of nodes. She reports being "disappointed that the groups in the hypertext classes did not use more argumentation." One group in particular is described as typical. "Like several other groups, this group viewed its project as laying out the facts and letting the reader reach his or her own conclusion, despite the fact that this is not how I presented the assignment" (p. 56). Whether she is citing explicit student reactions here or her own interpretation of them is not clear, but it is significant that the idea of shifting authorial responsibilities to the reader is a frequent feature of hypertext theory, although this goes unremarked in the text. Saul suggests two possible reasons for what she calls the "ambivalent attitude" of her students—the fact that they were writing about a new topic or that they had to learn to use StorySpace—but she never considers hypertext or that the students may have been express-ing something other than ambivalence about their topics. Faced with an unfamiliar subject, as well as the prospect of having to learn both a new platform for writing and a different type of writing, Saul's students, I would argue, were not ambivalent because they refused to engage the assign-ment. Rather, they fulfilled the assignment too well. Although Saul does not report the project grades, all indications are that they suffered for failing to restrict their writing process to the parameters of the assignment.

This disapproval carries over to the essay's conclusion. After citing a student who enjoyed the hypertext project, Saul (1999) writes, "This perfectly encapsulates what occurred in the hypertext projects: the students focused on learning a computer program and learning about the research topic, while very little thinking occurred about the process of writing" (p. 60). The fact that her students appeared to resist the assignment, even at the risk of their own grades, suggests that, on some level, they may have thought about the writing process in ways that Saul was not prepared to recognize. It is not surprising that her essay closes by stressing the inability of hypertext to accomplish the goals that she has set for her writing courses. Her study rests on the assumption that hypertext has little to do with writing, that it is simply a technology which can be added or subtracted from a writing classroom without any appreciable effect on the goals, aims, purposes, or strategies of the classroom or of the writers themselves. At the end of her chapter, hypertext stands as a failed remediation of a medium that goes unquestioned.

Neither of these examples stands as a refutation of remediation as Bolter and Grusin (1999) lay it out; as a framework for focusing our attention on the similarities and differences among various media, remediation makes a great deal of sense. Transposed to rhetorical ends, however, remediation has its limitations. Its primary limitation is that it requires some degree of stability on the part of the media under consideration. In each of these examples, there is an attempt to bring a new medium to the writing classroom, and the rhetoric of that new medium is based on older media. Saul's (1999) insistence on values (a clear thesis, a single viewpoint) derived from the academic essay prevents her from embracing the possibilities of hypertext, even in light of her students' exploration of what at the time was an unfamiliar medium. By basing their pedagogical adoption of filter blogging on a medium (note cards) that did not share enough similarity with what they were trying to accomplish, Brooks et al. (2004) leave the centrifugal, linking aspect of weblogs largely unaccounted for in their study. In each case, there is an artificial stability imposed on the new media (they are alike in these ways) that prevents or forestalls any exploration of how they might differ from more familiar, traditional media.

If, as Nancy Barta-Smith and Danette DiMarco (2007) write, "we may find that the most revolutionary ideas about writing and new media emerge . . . as evolving combinations rather than definite conclusions about textuality and new media" (p. 175), then remediation will prove a fairly limited (and limiting) path to those revolutionary ideas. Remediation remains a framework for describing combinations that have already occurred and acquired some degree of cultural stability. However, it provides little guidance for working with such combinations from the inside or for producing them. Such guidance can only come from a new media rhetoric, one focused on production rather than explanation.

FROM TEXT TO INTERFACE

A medium just is a "middle," an in-between or go-between, a space or pathway or messenger that connects two things—a sender to a receiver, a writer to a reader, an artist to a beholder, or (in the case of the spiritualist medium) this world to the next….If media are middles, they are ever-elastic middles that expand to include what look at first like their outer boundaries.

W. J. T. Mitchell, *What Do Pictures Want?* (2005)

The majority of this chapter has concerned itself more with what a rhetoric of new media *shouldn't* be rather than what it *should* be. The two strategies under consideration in the chapter—our literary critical inheritance, on the one hand, and the more recent, McLuhanist remediation, on the other hand—do not so much fail as they fall short of accomplishing the goals that this book sets for itself. There are any number of approaches that we might take for understanding new media and reading the kinds of writing they are helping us generate, but such approaches are ultimately reactionary. Pursuing a rhetoric of new media should involve methods that are, as Paul Miller (2004) puts it, "'actionary' rather than 're-actionary'" (p. 13). As actionary, a rhetoric of new media should prepare us for sorting through the strategies, practices, and tactics available to us and even for inventing new ones. It is the difference between studying the finished products of others and preparing to generate our own. Crucial to this effort, I believe, is a re-vision of some of our basic principles when it comes to rhetoric. Chapter 2 focuses on a couple of formations from classical rhetoric (the trivium and the rhetorical canons), but I would like to close this chapter with an argument about our field's unit of analysis and the challenge that new media poses to it.

Ours is a discipline that emerged in response to and persists in its valuation of the printed page. Although it is tempting to engage in the kind of apocalyptic pronouncements that appear far too often in accounts of new media, claims that print technology will vanish in the near future, the fact of the matter is that our discipline will most likely survive and even thrive with a continued focus on print. Cultural change is glacial, and the commonsense understanding of "writing" will remain tied to the printed page for longer than any of us could reliably predict. At the same time, all but the most recalcitrant of us realizes that change is coming, that the place of the page in our culture's media ecology, while perhaps in no immediate danger, has shifted in recent years. Nevertheless, we still tend to imagine that when we visit websites like Amazon, Ebay, or a friend's weblog, we are viewing static pages that exist even when we have left them, as opposed to the dynamically generated content on which many sites now rely. Certainly, the fact that we still call them "pages" encourages us in this. To take another example, we are still inclined to think of an e-mail message sent to a discussion list as a "single message," rather than the hundreds (or sometimes thousands) of e-mail messages that a single "post" produces and distributes to its subscriber list. We may engage in idiosyncratic behaviors from time to time (the notorious private "Reply" writ public on a list or an attempt to bookmark a dynamically generated page), but, by and large, we are capable of managing without challenging our basic assumptions about textuality.

That challenge is coming, however, and it is no longer simply a matter for the "techies" among us. Our disciplinary insistence on the printed page, if it persists unchecked, will slowly bring us out of step with our students, our institutions, and the broader culture of which we are a part. The unspoken assumption that we can simply react to technological change "just in time" or as we need misunderstands the scope of this change. Understanding what it is *really* that we are doing when we "read" the Web, for instance, is merely a symptom of broader shifts in the ways that knowledge is produced, distributed, consumed, circulated, and sampled today. The development of rhetorics that might assist us in confronting (and shaping) these shifting conditions is only a small step toward that change, but it is an essential step.

In rhetoric and composition, that step begins with a single revaluation, the move from text to interface (or from page to screen, as the collection edited by Michael Joyce and Ilana Snyder would have it). This movement, as I argue in the next chapter, necessitates that we begin thinking less in terms of (textual) objects and more in terms of (medial) ecologies. Interface has become a much more familiar term in the past 20 years or so. As Matthew Kirschenbaum (2004) explains, definitions of the term "typically invoke the image of a 'surface' or a 'boundary' where two or more 'systems,' 'devices,' or 'entities' come into 'contact' or 'interact'" (p. 523). Or as Synne Skjulstad and Andrew Morrison (2005) put it,

> Studied in terms of human-computer interaction (HCI), interfaces have been thought of as intermediary to communication. However, interfaces have come to be understood as more than a static, graphical layer lying between system and user. They exist as devices for shaping and spatialising the organization, selection and articulation of what is to be communicated electronically. As a result, interfaces are now an integral and dynamic part of communication design as a whole. (p. 413)

As Kirschenbaum (2004) notes, in addition to the spatial, "most interfaces also embody temporal, haptic, and cognitive elements," and it is this broader sense of interface with which this project works. Rather than viewing the interface as the boundary or contact point between people and machines, I follow W. J. T. Mitchell (1995) in suggesting instead that interfaces are those "ever-elastic middles" that include, incorporate, and indeed constitute their "outside." My definition, then, ventures a little further than Skjulstad and Morrison's (2005), who argue for an increased awareness of the dynamics within interfaces while leaving the interface as a component (albeit an important one) of the communication process.

In some ways, this expanded version of the interface builds on conceptual work that we have already begun. Over the past 30 or 40 years, we have chipped away at the positivist conception of textuality that a turn toward the interface would have us reject. For example, Wayne Booth's (1983) *The Rhetoric of Fiction* examines how literary texts imply and construct their readers, whereas Michel Foucault's (1977) work on the author function argues that, contrary to our commonsense perceptions, an author is no less an effect of the text than any other. Theoretically, we are capable of seeing communication as much more complicated than the conduit implied by sender, text, and receiver, but, in practice, we have been slower to apply these insights. To return to the example from the outset of this chapter, "Hypertext is Dead" is not a "text" that rests comfortably within our categories for disciplinary practice. It is not the kind of text that we ask our students to generate, nor the kind for which we ourselves seek any kind of institutional credit. Published as a "text" in the online journal *Kairos*, "Hypertext is Dead" is more accurately understood as an interface not only among the various participants in the discussion transcribed there, but among several media even as it is published in the form a hypertext.

Kenneth Burke's (1969b) work provides an analogy for the understanding of interface being advanced here. Where Skjulstad and Morrison (2005) speak of "shaping," Burke emphasizes, at the outset of *A Grammar of Motives,* many kinds of "transformation." He writes that,

Distinctions, we might say, arise out of a great central moltenness, where all is merged. They have been thrown from a liquid center to the surface, where they have congealed. Let one of these crusted distinctions return to its source, and in this alchemic center it may be remade, again becoming molten liquid, and may enter into new combinations, whereat it may be thrown forth as a new crust, a different distinction. So that A may become non-A. But not merely by a leap from one state to the other. Rather, we must take A back into the ground of its existence, the logical substance that is its causal ancestor, and on to a point where it is consubstantial with non-A; then we may return, thus emerging with non-A instead. (p. xix)

Or, as Paul Miller (2004) puts it, "At the end of the day, it's all about reprocessing the world around you" (p. 29). Both Burke and Miller speak to the kinds of "alchemic opportunit[ies]" made possible through new media, opportunities that require us to think in terms of interfaces, the central, medial moltenness, rather than the textual objects that we throw forth.

This does not mean, to paraphrase Jacques Derrida, that there is nothing outside the interface or, to paraphrase Clifford Geertz that it is simply interfaces "all the way down." That is, the world is not one large, undifferentiated, relativistic interface. But the boundaries among interfaces, and the degree to which various interfaces encourage us to locate ourselves outside of them, are part of the processes that both Burke and Miller describe. A turn toward the interface as our unit of analysis would be an acknowledgment that it is not necessary that these processes culminate in products (which can then be decoupled from the contexts of their production), but rather that what we think of as products (books, articles, essays) are but special, stabilized instances of an ongoing process conducted at the level of interface. In some ways, this reversal is simply the logical extension of a transformation that we (try to) effect in our students. We encourage them to shift their own perceptions of writing, urging them not to think of their essays as empty, preexisting containers to be filled, but rather as texts emerging from an ongoing process of reading, thinking, and writing. When it comes to certain forms of new media, such as listservs for instance, we are relatively comfortable with the realization that there is no "product" outside of the interaction that takes place there.

But we have been slow to extend this awareness beyond certain pockets of discursive activity and even slower to consider that the rhetorics driving these and other activities is changing as our technologies do. As the ratio between interface and object shifts with the advent of new media, our rhetorics must shift to account for these new realities and new possibilities.

In short, we must begin to move from a text-based rhetoric, exemplified by our attachment to the printed page, to a rhetoric that can account for the dynamics of the interface.

NOTES

1. See, for example, the CCCC "Promotion and Tenure Guidelines for Work with Technology" at http://www.ncte.org/about/over/positions/level/coll/107658.htm.
2. I am not arguing here that we should be seeking official credit for projects like "Hypertext Is Dead," merely making note of the degree to which our ability to understand such projects often depends on an institutional economy that renders certain forms of writing invisible.
3. For example, the band They Might Be Giants released a CD in 1991 (Apollo 18) that contained eighteen 15- to 30-second sound clips that would intersperse with the more traditional-length tracks on the disc when played with the shuffle function on.
4. An expanded version of the Address was later published as *Technology and Literacy in the Twenty-First Century: The Importance of Paying Attention.*
5. In 2003, Vincent Leitch explained, in reference to New Criticism, that "this type of textual explication remains for many critics not only a viable norm, but, even for its processed enemies, a main methods of classroom teaching and professional demonstration" (p. 10).
6. I am thinking here of Wikipedia and how certain pages on that site are changed repeatedly, particularly those pages where so-called objectivity is impossible. Although the site keeps track of changes to its pages, the "page itself" may change on a daily, if not an hourly, basis.
7. Contrast this with, for example, N. Katherine Hayles' (2002) more recent *Writing Machines*, which is more typical in that it concerns itself explicitly and specifically with textual analysis.
8. Bolter and Grusin's discussion of hypermediacy demonstrates what Kenneth Burke (1969a) called the "paradox of purity," the principle that any value published to its extreme results in its opposite.
9. See, for example, Kendrick (2001).
10. The essay is a chapter in the *Into the Blogosphere* collection.

2

ECOLOGY

A rhetoric of new media requires us to rethink our disciplinary habit of attending to textual objects; however, we do not need to invent this rhetoric wholesale. This chapter argues that the resources provided by the long history of rhetoric will prove sufficient in this regard. Specifically, I argue that we can turn to the rhetorical canons to construct a rhetoric that will allow us to both understand and produce interfaces. First, however, we must approach the canons from a different perspective; centuries of viewing the canons through the lens of print technology have limited their usefulness as a conceptual framework. The first section of this chapter identifies a couple of thinkers who have begun the work of reconceiving the canons that my own project attempts to continue. Although they have survived to the present day, the canons have lost much of their explanatory power in our discipline. The second section builds on contemporary rethinking of the canons, suggesting a new conceptual metaphor on which we might draw to assist in this revision.

The third section of this chapter turns to another of our inheritances from rhetorical history, the classical *trivium* of grammar, rhetoric, and logic. Much like the first two sections attempt to rethink the canons, I argue in this section that the *trivium* should be rethought as layered ecologies, that each element of the *trivium* describes not a separate discipline, but a different scale for thought. A revitalized understanding of the canons, I suggest, provides us with an example of the middle, rhetorical scale, what I describe as an *ecology of practice*. As an ecology of practice, the canons supply a framework for approaching new media that focuses on the strategies and practices that occur at the level of interface, an approach exemplified briefly in the conclusion to this chapter.

This chapter draws on recent work in a transdisciplinary field that has come to be known as media ecology. Thus, I spend time in this chapter examining some of this work, with an eye toward identifying both potential parallels and those places where my own work departs from that of media ecology scholars. Ecology has become a crucial framework in recent years, particularly for scholars who examine media that, paradoxically, grow increasingly interconnected and global, on the one hand, and ever more diverse and intricate, on the other hand. The elaborate dance of competition, cooperation, juxtaposition, and remediation that characterizes our contemporary information and communication technologies has rendered obsolete some of our most venerable models for understanding today's rhetorical practices.[1] As a result, our aims as rhetorical scholars must evolve—no single model is likely to prove capable of returning the sorts of stability that are implied (if imperfectly accomplished) by communication triangles or rhetorical situations, and thus we need to begin thinking about goals other than stability. The ecological thinking that has begun to emerge in rhetoric and composition is less a means of redomesticating rhetorical activity than it is an attempt to come to terms with the dynamics of that activity. Ecologies can achieve a certain level of systemic stability or balance and may even appear stable from a long distance, but they are in constant flux. Ecologies are vast, hybrid systems of intertwined elements, systems where small changes can have unforeseen consequences that ripple far beyond their immediate implications. This means that we must begin to rethink notions of rhetorical effectiveness—whether defined in terms of persuasion, identification, or some other activity—because what is "effective" at one scale or location within an ecology may fail utterly in another context.

Ultimately, the notion of ecology supplies this project with a means of rethinking both the place of the canons in our discipline (a social, textual, and intellectual ecology), as well as the nature of the canons. The subsequent chapters in this book reimagine the canons ecologically and technologically, a revision for which this chapter lays the theoretical groundwork, but my exploration of the canons, the ecology of practice outlined here, will not exhaust the full range of implications of adopting an ecological perspective on rhetorical practice. The test of an ecological perspective will come in part from our attempts to draw on it analytically, but, more important, from our ability to take it up as we read, write, design, mix, and produce new media.

THE RHETORICAL CANONS

Despite having persisted for millennia, the five canons of classical rhetoric (invention, arrangement, style, memory, and delivery) are more like a disciplinary heirloom than they are part of our core intellectual inheritance from antiquity. The canons are really a mixed bag, with what Kathleen Welch (1999) has called a "long and twisting history" (p. 81). On the one hand, invention and style remain central concerns for scholars in rhetoric and composition; on the other hand, despite occasional attempts to revive them,[2] memory and delivery stand as nearly vestigial canons, little more than reminders of rhetoric in a different place and time. Arrangement falls somewhere in between, embodying the necessity of discursive forms, but occasionally lapsing into formulae like the notorious five-paragraph theme. The canons have so completely diffused into our collective conceptions of rhetoric that they are almost beneath our notice, and yet most rhetoric and composition scholars would struggle to explain exactly what the canons are.

It is a curious neglect that the canons suffer from, however, because there is probably no better demonstration of the technological specificity of rhetoric than the canons' imperfect translation from ancient Greece and Rome to the present day. We may recall each of the five canons, but we tend to take for granted the idea that memory and delivery faded in importance once rhetoric shifted from an art of oral presentation to scriptural, written, and printed texts. This narrative of the canons' development is fundamentally inaccurate, as I hope to demonstrate here, but that inaccuracy is even more interesting when combined with our field's unwillingness to pursue this narrative to its logical conclusion. If memory and delivery genuinely were "forgotten" canons, then this would serve as evidence of an irreducibly technological dimension to rhetoric, a dimension that to date remains a "mere" specialization in the discipline, rather than a concern that cuts across all of rhetorical scholarship. If rhetoric were, in our collective understanding of it, intrinsically technological,[3] then we might begin to address some of the crucial cultural issues[4] (e.g., access, intellectual property) that have heretofore been identified as "specialist."

With not only the facts of this story wrong, but its implications all but ignored, it is worth considering just why this perception of the canons exists and even thrives. In part, it is because the canons are beneath our notice that this version has gone uncontested. The canons are simply the canons. Unlike the three modes of rhetoric (forensic, deliberative, epideictic) or the three proofs (*ethos, logos, pathos*), taxonomies that also are part of our rhetorical inheritance, the canons lack a certain wholeness, a sense that they exhaust the given possibilities for the phenomenon they describe. Although it goes largely unremarked, that phenomenon is probably the *writing process*, itself an important conceptual framework for contemporary rhetoric and composition scholars. The canons map loosely across the writing process or more accurately the speaking process. It is not difficult to imagine the canons being taught to ancient rhetors as the stages one must undertake to produce an oration. One must come up with ideas, put them in a particular order, figure out how to express them, memorize the text that results, and finally deliver it. Because the latter two steps are not relevant to the composition of written text, it follows that the corresponding canons have become obsolete.

However, because it is a loose parallel at best, and one that is not really rendered explicitly in our scholarship, the canons suffer the further indignity of being used as a model for a particularly artificial and linear version of the speaking/writing process, one that corresponds neither to ancient nor to contemporary production of discourse. We do not speak of the recursive nature of the canons or of how the canons are unique to each individual speaker or writer. Scholars are not writing chapters and articles about the benefits of postcanonical theories. The canons are not expressive, cognitive, or socioepistemic; they are simply "the canons." They represent stages or steps in a diluted process for the production of discourse. Although on occasion one or another of them has served to focus our scholarship (e.g., the revival of invention), this is normally accomplished by removing one canon and ignoring the other four. Whatever vitality they may have held for ancient rhetors and rhetoricians has not accompanied the canons to the present day.

In an effort to reclaim some of that vitality, it is worth taking a closer look at what I described earlier as the narrative of the canons' development, and specifically at the canons of memory and delivery. These canons are examined in more detail in later chapters (chaps. 6 and 7, respectively), but those chapters assume a relevance on the part of memory and delivery that we can establish initially here, an importance that corresponds to Kathleen Welch's (1999) discussion of them in *Electric Rhetoric*. My argument is *not* that it is only with the emergence of new media that memory and delivery assume a revitalized role. Rather, like Welch, I would contend that these vestigial canons are no less important in print-based rhetorics than they were in oral cultures or will be in digital ones. Our practice of reading the canons through the lens of the writing process has left us unaware of their importance, a misreading that should be corrected.

If there is one canon that would seem to be the least useful for a rhetoric grounded in the printed page, it would be memory. Memory was held by Plato to be one of the chief casualties of a turn to the written word. "If men learn [writing]," he wrote, " it will implant forgetfulness in their souls; they will cease to exercise memory because they rely on that which is written, calling things to remembrance no longer from within themselves, by means of external marks" (*Phaedrus*). Ironically enough, some 2,500 years later, Sven Birkerts (1995) makes a similar argument, only this time against the emergence of digital writing. In a section predicting the "flattening of historical perspective," Birkerts writes,

> As the circuit supplants the printed page, and as more and more of our communications involve us in network processes—which of their nature plant us in a perpetual present—our perception of history will inevitably alter. Changes in information storage and access are bound to impinge on our historical memory. The depth of field that is our sense of the past is not only a linguistic construct, but is in some essential way represented by the book and the physical accumulation of books in library spaces. In the contemplation of the single volume, or mass of volumes, we form a picture of time past as a growing deposit of sediment; we capture a sense of its depth and dimensionality. (p. 129)

In other words, we will cease to exercise *history* because we will rely on that which is *stored in databases*, at least according to Birkerts. There is a sense in which Birkerts' argument might be used to refute Plato's. After all, if Plato's predictions about the demise of memory had proved accurate, Birkerts would not be able to offer his. But both of these arguments are highly generalized. Memory is painted as the victim of technological change in each case, without much thought offered as to how it is being represented or how memory is actually practiced.

Although it is perhaps too early to confirm or deny the various predictions that Birkerts makes, Plato's are little more than a historical curiosity for us. It may be true that our contemporary powers of memory are individually weaker than our ancestors', but it is almost certainly the case that our collective memory is stronger by virtue of our ability to store information with the printed word, audio and video recording, and as bits on our computers. However, the question of more or less—or better or worse—memory is besides the point. Claims of whether or not forgetfulness has been "implanted in [our] souls" or whether our culture's sense of history will languish in a digital age do not speak to the role that memory plays (or no longer plays) in the production of discourse.

For a concrete example of what I mean here, I turn to a study that Christina Haas (1996) conducted and reports in *Writing Technology: Studies on the Materiality of Literacy*. In the second section of that book, Haas reports on two studies designed to elicit information about the cognitive effect that word processing has on writers. One result of these studies is her attempt to articulate one of the crucial differences between pen-and-paper composing and word processing:

> Clearly, writers interact constantly, closely, and in complex ways with their own written texts. Through these interactions, they develop some understanding—some representation—of the text they have created or are creating. This chapter argues that one of the things that writers come to during the course of text production is an understanding of the meaning and structure of their own written arguments; I call this understanding or representation of one's own text a *sense of the text*. (p. 117)

Although Haas focuses, both in this description and in the discussions that follow, on the *representation* implied by *text sense*, it is clear throughout that she is discussing memory. In fact, she links them a few pages later, explaining that, "As the text gets longer and more ideas are introduced and developed, it becomes more difficult to hold an adequate *representation in memory* of that text, which is out of sight" (p. 121, italics added).

Haas' (1996) studies indicate both that writers do not plan as much with word processing (because what they write can be changed easily) and that their sense of text is affected by the limited amount of text their screens can display (leading many writers to print out drafts). A writer's sense of text, she writes, involves "a representation of the text as a spatial and physical object" (p. 119). When she asked the participants in her study to perform a "recall task," this conclusion was borne out because the writers were able to remember significantly more of their work composed with pen and paper than they were when composing similar work with a word processor. In short, Haas' conclusions bear out the fact that memory is not a "dead" canon with the turn toward writing. Rather, she demonstrates that writing calls on us to practice that canon in different ways.

We practice delivery differently with written tasks as well, although it too is often taken to be irrelevant or unnecessary in a print environment. Although Plato refers directly to memory in his indictment of writing, we also might observe on his part a concern with delivery. He attributes to writing "a strange quality" much like painting

> . . . for the creatures of painting stand like living beings, but if one asks them a question, they preserve a solemn silence. And so it is with written words; you might think they spoke as if they had intelligence, but if you question them, wishing to know about their sayings, they always say one and the same thing. And every word, when once it is written, is bandied about, alike among those who understand and those who have no interest in it. . . .

Plato contrasts the written word to the "living and breathing word" embodied in his dialogues. Although he would have his readers believe that this contrast is an essential one, it is more accurate to describe it as a difference between oral and written deliveries.

In Plato's estimation, of course, the delivery of a written text is more accurately perceived as a text devoid of the various qualities of oral delivery; indeed, that is how we have tended to view the fifth canon in the discipline. With few exceptions, we have considered it through the decontextualizing lens of the writing classroom, where "turning in papers" is a near-universal and transparent activity. This transparency parallels Plato's account of writing as well: Written words are encountered, at least in this brief account, in a vacuum, divorced from any context, much less the rich one surrounding the event of spoken discourse.

Certainly, Plato could not have foreseen the technological developments of the following millennia, but that is a poor excuse for our own neglect of the contexts in which we produce and consume writing. One example of an attempt to redress this neglect is John Trimbur's (2000) "Composition and the Circulation of Writing." In that article, Trimbur argues that our focus on the student–paper–teacher transaction "isolat[es] an education in writing from the means of production and delivery":

> To anticipate the main line of thought, I argue that neglecting delivery has led writing teachers to equate the activity of composing with writing itself and to miss altogether the complex delivery systems through which writing circulates . . . delivery has been an afterthought at best, assigned mainly to technical and professional communication and associated largely with such matters of document design as page lay-

out, typography, visual display of information, and Web design. (pp.
189–190)

It is not unusual, in fact, to see claims that recent developments in information technology, and the Web in particular, have resuscitated the question of delivery. Although there is merit to these claims, they leave the neglect that Trimbur speaks of unchallenged. Indeed, we may think more
about delivery when we compose for more visually rich media, but that
does not mean that this canon is irrelevant to print.

Among other things, Trimbur (2000) demonstrates the continued relevance of delivery by looking at periodicals like the *Wall Street Journal* and
the *National Enquirer*. He begins with the "different routes" that the two
periodicals take and suggests that, from a classical economic perspective,
there is little difference between the two. From a Marxist perspective, however, one that attends to circulation (a term Trimbur uses interchangeably
in the essay with delivery), there are marked differences between the two:

> To put it another way, the distribution of the *Wall Street Journal* and the
> distribution of the *National Enquirer* no longer figure simply as equiva-
> lent moments in the circulation of commodities, guided by the law of
> supply and demand. Instead, what gets distributed by these quite dif-
> ferent types of reading matter is the productive means to name the
> world, to give it shape and coherent meaning. (p. 209)

As this analysis suggests, Trimbur (2000) is not merely concerned with
delivery as a procedural or practical matter; his interests in this forgotten
canon are decidedly political, ethical, and economic. In this way, he con-
flates what, later in this chapter, I describe as *ecologies of practice* and
ecologies of culture, but this conflation functions as a counterstatement (in
the Burkean sense) to what Trimbur describes earlier in the essay as the
"foreshorten[ing of] the delivery system" in composition studies in general (and the Elbow/Bartholomae debate of the mid-1990s specifically). In its
focus on the student paper as the writing act *par excellence*, our discipline
has "link[ed] production directly to consumption within the intimate space
of the classroom/home" (p. 194), a connection that leads to the neglect that
Trimbur considers.

There are many other equally compelling instances we might draw on
to demonstrate the relevance of both memory and delivery to writing, but
the work of Haas and Trimbur here should be sufficient at the least to suggest that our discipline's narrative about the development of the canons in
general—and of those canons in particular—is a flawed one. It is accurate

to note, as Plato did, that wholesale changes in discursive technologies are going to transform the practices surrounding the discourses we produce, but we have been too content to define those practices narrowly, such that we have treated memory and delivery as if they are no longer relevant. In other words, we appear willing to acknowledge that rhetorical practice changes as our technologies do, and yet we have maintained an oddly binary vision of that change. As Haas (1996) demonstrates, we are no less beholden to memory for the fact that we may no longer memorize speeches. In tying delivery to relevant, material practices of circulation, Trimbur suggests that we ignore that canon to our peril as writing instructors. Taken together, they suggest that the canons are not simply on/off switches. Rather, as Welch (1999) puts it, they "have recurred in different forms and with different emphases in varying historical eras" (p. 144).

REFRAMING THE CANONS AS ECOLOGY

Welch's insight has been slow to enter into the common sense of the discipline, however, and it is worth our time to pause for a moment and consider the reason for this. After all, the canons have not exactly faded into obscurity. Kathleen Blake Yancey, in her Chair's Address to the 2004 CCCC,[5] called for a "new model of composing" grounded partly in the rhetorical canons, and yet this suggestion has had a limited impact on the discipline. One possible reason, of course, is that the juxtaposition of new technology with the canons of classical rhetoric may strike us as anachronistic. Yancey's other expressions (deixis and circulation) resonate in obvious ways with contemporary information and communication technologies, whereas the canons do not. Much like Welch, however, Yancey is quick to point out that this lack of resonance is less a problem with the canons than it is with the way we have come to understand (or misunderstand) them..

This means that we need to take a temporary step back from the canons and examine the disciplinary context within which we have tried to understand them. If our field is to take up the calls of scholars like Welch and Yancey and to locate the canons more centrally in the discipline, we also must understand why they fell into disuse in the first place.

This understanding cannot happen as long as we continue to view them, as explained in the last section, as a somewhat inaccurate map of the writing process. Although there are undoubtedly overlaps between the two, I hope to demonstrate throughout this book that the canons provide a much broader scope, particularly for our inquiry into new media, than can process theory. This expanded scope requires a different approach to the canons than we have taken as a discipline thus far. We have not denied the existence of the canons. Rather, we simply have not had much use for them, and so the fact that they have changed over time has had minor significance at best. This is particularly so when compared with those frameworks drawn from classical rhetoric that tend more toward the theoretical or universal.[6] It is relatively simple, for example, to use Aristotle's *pisteis* as a heuristic for reading contemporary texts and to analyze the interactions among *ethos*, *logos*, and *pathos*. This is a common enough classroom exercise even today. But the canons are a set of practices that result in the texts thusly analyzed, and, as such, they remain largely invisible. Even those, like arrangement and style, that are visible only provide a final snapshot of the practices behind a given text. For a discipline like ours that depends heavily on textual analysis, frameworks that fail to lend themselves to that activity are simply not going to be especially valuable.

This is a point worth making as directly as possible: I would contend that much of our neglect of the canons to date is the result of an impoverished vocabulary on the part of our discipline. That is, the canons have failed to rest comfortably inside either of the mirror-image fetishes of "theory" and "practice"—the binary around which our field persists in defining itself.[7] As a result, we have paid minimal attention to them as the field has grown. Despite the looseness with which theory and practice are defined and deployed, it would be difficult at best to place them squarely within one camp or the other. Each of the canons names a class of practices, it is true, but each of the canons, not to mention when we take them as a coherent set of such classes, ends up being more abstract than what we typically signify by the term *practice*. For example, to argue that we should be teaching invention in our classrooms is to make a much different claim than to argue that we should be teaching freewriting or mindmapping. To argue, as Yancey does, that the canons should be a centerpiece of a new model of composing is a third type of claim.

For all that we seem to be moving up the ladder of abstraction, from practice to canon to canons, it would be difficult to make a convincing case that there is something at the top of the ladder that we might call "canon theory." Following Stephen Knapp and Walter Benn Michaels, Thomas Kent (1997) offers the following thumbnail sketch of what "theory" means disciplinarily:

By "theory" I mean a special project in composition studies: the attempt to govern the writing act by appealing to an account of the writing act in general. Stated a bit differently, the project of theory attempts to construct a generalized account of writing practice that remains uncontaminated by practice itself...theory provides a formalized structure of understanding to which we may appeal in order to justify and validate our advice to students, our place at the academic trough, and our mission as teachers. (p. 149)

Insofar as the canons appeal to an account of the writing act in general, it is only to observe that the five classes of practices are present in any discursive act. Although this observation runs counter to the narrative discussed in the last section, it seems mild compared with the controversies engendered at one time by competing theories of process or by the various accounts of interpretation generated in the wake of New Criticism and structuralism. In other words, in contrast to the hermeneutic or pedagogical implications for much of what counts as theory in our field, the canons represent a much more innocuous, ontological claim. We may neglect one or more of the canons, and some critical mileage may come of recalling our attention to it/them, but in the final analysis, there is no competing account against which the canons are tested in our scholarship and research because the canons are not theoretical per se.

How then might we frame the canons in our field? How can we understand them in a way that both explains their persistence (despite a long history of neglect) and allows them to occupy the central role that Yancey advocates for them? As I explain in the opening pages of this chapter, the term *ecology* provides an answer to these questions. I close this chapter with an illustration of how an ecological vision of the canons might assist us in looking at new media. For the remainder of this section, however, I want to call attention to some of the history of this term as it has been (infrequently) adopted in the discipline and to make brief note of how my adaptation differs from others'.

The practice of drawing on ecology, a term typically associated with the study of the natural environment, as a metaphor for human activity dates at least back to Gregory Bateson's (2000) *Steps to an Ecology of Mind*. Bateson argues for what we might now call distributed cognition, an epistemology that locates mind not simply within individuals, but socially as well. Bateson writes in "Form, Substance, and Difference" that "The individual mind is immanent but not only in the body. It is immanent also in pathways and messages outside the body; and there is a larger Mind of which the individual mind is only a sub-system." It is not difficult to see parallels between

Bateson's theory of mind and a certain stage in the development of process theory in composition. In fact, although she does not cite Bateson, Marilyn Cooper's (1986) *College English* article, "The Ecology of Writing," is the first to elaborate a connection between ecology and writing.

Cooper (1986) addresses the "growing awareness that language and texts are not simply the mean by which individuals discover and communicate information, but are essentially social activities" (p. 366), a perspective that contemporary writing scholars all but take for granted. Cooper's attempt to seize on this awareness takes the form of a suggestion that we view writing ecologically:

> In contrast, an ecology of writing encompasses much more than the individual writer and her immediate context. An ecologist explores how writers interact to form systems: all the characteristics of any individual writer or piece of writing both determine and are determined by the characteristics of all the other writers and writings in the systems. An important characteristic of ecological systems is that they are inherently dynamic; though their structures are contents can be specified at a given moment, in real time they are constantly changing, limited only be parameters that are themselves subject to change over longer spans of time. . . . In place of the static and limited categories of contextual models, the ecological model postulates dynamic interlocking systems which structure the social activity of writing. (p. 368)

I quote Cooper at length here because I share both her estimation of the value of an ecological model of writing and her delineation of its characteristics. Particularly of note is the constant motion of an ecological system. Although the turn to process in our field has acknowledged the importance of change and motion leading up to the production of discourse, too often that motion is arrested in the emphasis on static textual objects that I discuss in chapter 1. As we turn to the production of interfaces, of digital writing, we require a model capable of taking account of not simply the process leading up to a release, but the activity that follows as well.

If Cooper was the first to detail the connection between ecology and writing, perhaps the most thorough elaboration of that insight has come from Margaret Syverson (1999) in her book *The Wealth of Reality: An Ecology of Composition*. Syverson begins her book by making explicit the terms of Cooper's essay; the adoption of an ecological model for writing is a shift in the "unit of analysis." Syverson explains that, although "writers, readers, and texts form just such a complex system of self-organizing, adaptive, and dynamic interactions," they are also "situated in an ecology, a larger system that includes environmental structures . . . as well as other complex systems operating at various levels of scale" (p. 5). Syverson details what she sees as four attributes of ecological systems: distribution, emergence, embodiment, and enaction. *Distribution* refers to the way that processes of all sorts (including cognitive processes) are "both divided and shared among agents and structures in the environment" (p. 7). *Emergence* describes the way that complex systems, made up of simple components, rules, and/or structures, tend toward self-organization and increased complexity. *Embodiment* is characteristic not just of writers and readers, but of texts themselves, inscription technologies, and the environments where our interactions with language take place. Finally, "*Enaction* is the principle that knowledge is the result of an ongoing interpretation that emerges through *activities* and *experiences* situated in specific environments" (p. 13). In many ways, enaction is the *sine qua non* of complex systems; even as it represents an attribute of such systems, it also is the fundamental condition of possibility for them. Syverson cites Lucy Suchman, who asserts that "The *situated* nature of learning, remembering, and understanding is a central fact" (cited on p. 13). According to Syverson, these attributes manifest themselves across five dimensions: physical-material, social, psychological, spatial, and temporal. Although each is introduced separately, Syverson is careful to note that "they are five aspects of every object, process, fact, idea, concept, activity, structure, event, and so on" (p. 22). That is to say, these dimensions can be conceptually distinguished from one another, but they are not distinct in practice. Furthermore, these dimensions, as well as the attributes that manifest in them, "can be observed at every level of scale . . . in composition studies, from a poet's tiny editorial correction on a draft of a poem to a global literary movement—poststructuralism, feminism, hermeneutics" (p. 23).

This book's ecological approach is less elaborate than Syverson's, deploying it in a somewhat different fashion. Before I move on to that explanation, however, it is important to acknowledge the breadth of the term because rhetoric and composition scholars are not the only writers in the humanities drawing on ecology as an explanatory tool. Media ecology, for example, is a term that has figured in the work of Neil Postman (1970) since the early 1970s, when he wrote that, "Media ecology is the study of media as environments." In her book *Writing Machines*, N. Katherine Hayles (2002) elaborates on this notion (although she uses the term *medial ecology*), explaining that "The phrase suggests that the relationships between different media are as diverse and complex as those between different organisms coexisting within the same ecotome, including mimicry, deception, cooperation, competition, parasitism, and hyperparasitism" (p.

5). Andruid Kerne's (2002) discussion of "interface ecology," drawn, in part, on the work of ecologist Francis Evans offers the following explanation: "With regard to life on earth, ecology investigates the web of relations between interdependent organisms and their surroundings. In the Information Age, people, activities, codes, components, and systems form the same kinds of interrelationships" ("Interface" p. 1).

Bonnie Nardi and Vicki O'Day (1999) appropriate ecology as well, defining an "information ecology" as "a system of people, practices, values, and technologies in a particular local environment" (p. 49). Nardi and O'Day test the idea of ecology against other popular metaphors for technology (technology as tool, text, and system), and they praise what I would describe as its scalability. For example, the focus on technology as a tool encourages us to overlook the fact that "we know that technological tools are embedded in a larger context" (p. 30). At the same time, treating technology as a overarching or deterministic system introduces "overwhelming breadth," neglecting the degree to which technology "responds to local environmental changes and local interventions" (p. 50). Ecology, for Nardi and O'Day, provides a flexibility that other approaches to technology would have a difficult time approximating.

This list is by no means exhaustive: Variations on the ecological model have appeared with increasing frequency in the past few years. A more recent addition, Matthew Fuller's (2005) *Media Ecologies: Materialist Energies in Art and Technoculture*, attempts to draw some distinctions among the various models. Fuller is critical of some of the uses to which the term has been put. For example, he sees *information ecology* as a "saccharin term for the 'natural' structuring of the microscopic to macroscopic dimensions of class composition and command in a workforce" (p. 3), perhaps the latest corporate buzzword for organizational efficiency. Similarly, Fuller connects Postman's use of the term to an older, more humanistic study of technology, one concerned with establishing a "state of equilibrium . . . a resilient and harmonic balance to be achieved with some ingenious and beneficent mix of media" (p. 4). In each of these currents, Fuller locates some broader cultural imperative lurking behind the usage of *media ecology*, a tendency toward the prescriptive rather than descriptive. Fuller's own preference is for the decidedly more poststructuralist adoptions of the term because it is picked up by N. Katherine Hayles, Friedrich Kittler, Joseph Tabbi, and particularly Félix Guattari, whom he sees as having taken up Bateson's original work with the idea of ecology.

As Fuller (2005) himself notes, his book spends little time "fidgeting with a possible hermeneutics of the term," as it focuses more on particular, ecological analyses of sites such as the British pirate radio scene in his first chapter and online surveillance in the fourth. He articulates his approach this way: "Taking such work to exist in an expanded, 'ecological' sense demands an effort at making a nonreductive network of interpretation, with the unfortunate possible result of a certain arduousness" (p. 11). The descriptions that ensue in Fuller's book are far from arduous, but the scope of his interpretation ranges beyond my own, which is focused more specifically on the *rhetoric* of new media. Although Fuller's work avoids it, there is a danger of erring on the side of expansiveness, of allowing ecology to stand as a backdrop, as a synonym for "everything that happens." This project attempts to hold to Fuller's insistence on nonreductive accounts at the same time that it articulates a framework not unlike Syverson's. But where Syverson's axes attempt to encompass an ecology of writing, my own is less certain.

At the beginning of *Datacloud: Toward a New Theory of Online Work*, Johndan Johnson-Eilola (2005) defines the phenomenon from which he draws his title as "a shifting and only slightly contingently structured information space" (p. 4). It is this notion of slight structure, a structure contingent on the shifting dynamics of the various interfaces that allow us to negotiate the datacloud, that this project takes as its goal. That cloud of information is shot through with technologies, media, and interfaces. Where Fuller seeks to trace out the various connections at a cultural level, as I argue in the next section, this project works at the scale of *ecologies of practice*, focusing instead on the strategies and tactics that we bring to bear on new media at the same time that our technologies constrain and empower us. The canons serve this project less as an exhaustive set of terms than they do as analytic and productive starting points from which we might begin a sustained engagement with discursive technologies. As a means of locating the canons conceptually, the next section offers a second set of revised terms from classical rhetoric. My hope is that they help place this project somewhere in between the undifferentiated "backdrop" model of ecology and other, more heavily articulated models.

CLASSICAL RHETORIC 2.0

Cooper (1986) cautions in her article that ecological is not "simply the newest way to say 'contextual'" (p. 367), and any attempt to deploy an ecological framework (as opposed to simply offering ecology as a backdrop for one's activities) must bear this in mind. Contextual models, as Cooper remarks in the excerpt offered in the last section, are composed of what she describes as "static and limited categories," which gives any attempt at a framework pause. The appeal of ecology as a conceptual metaphor is its ability to focus our attention on a temporarily finite set of practices, ideas, and interactions without fixing them in place or investing too much critical energy in their stability. In part, this appeal makes ecology the perfect unit of analysis for examining the interface, itself a momentarily situated encounter among users, machines, programmers, cultures, and institutions.

The challenge, however, is to introduce categories that are somehow not static or limited, delineations that preserve the dynamic flexibility of an eco-logical model while providing us with some ability to distinguish one prac-tice from another. Obviously, I believe that the canons provide us with one such set of categories, and in this section of the chapter, I suggest a second, complementary set, the classic trivium of grammar, rhetoric, and logic. In each case, I perform a somewhat anachronistic discursive strategy, drawing upon classical rhetoric to provide us with insight into contemporary infor-mation and communication technologies, but this strategy is a sound one. In their lead chapter for the book *The Ends of Rhetoric*, John Bender and David E. Wellbery (1990) argue for a "turn" in the history of rhetoric that goes largely unacknowledged in our field, the turn from rhetoric to what they call *rhetoricality*. Characteristic of this turn is a process that they iden-tify in the work of Roman Jakobson, one that they call *displacement*:

> What we find in Jakobson's inquiry, then, is a fundamental displace-ment that affects the traditional terminology of rhetoric, a generaliza-tion of certain terms within that terminology and a wholesale aban-donment of other items. . . . Exactly this shift in the theoretical func-tion and significance of concepts is what we are calling the move from rhetoric to rhetoricality. (p. 30)

The "return of rhetorical inquiry," for Bender and Wellbery (1990), is not simply a repetition of rhetoric as it was figured and delimited prior to the Enlightenment. Instead, they argue, "The contemporary return of rhet-oric presupposes, through its very structure as return, an end of rhetoric, a discontinuity within tradition, and an alteration that renders the second version of rhetoric, its modernist-postmodernist redaction, a new form of cultural practice and mode of analysis" (p. 4).

To put it another way, if pre-Enlightenment rhetorics emerged out of specific political, cultural, social, and technological contexts, then Bender and Wellbery's (1990) rhetoricality, a "generalized rhetoric that penetrates to the deepest levels of human experience" (p. 25), is perhaps truer to both our contemporary context and to classical rhetoric than would be a literal reading and implementation of the ideas of Plato, Aristotle, and/or Cicero. This argument is not in favor of willful misreading, however. Instead, it is a suggestion that we conceive of classical rhetoric less as a set of static absolutes and more as a collection of situated responses to the kind of generalized cultural imperatives that Bender and Wellbery discuss. This does not require us to abandon classical rhetoric. On the contrary, as Susan Jarratt (2002) remarks in one of the few substantial treatments of Bender and Wellbery's article, "Changing practices in the future are underwritten by changed visions of the past" (p. 66). Rhetoricality encourages us to see the inheritance of classical rhetoric as one possibility alongside others.

I raise the issue of rhetoricality at this point because it provides one alternative for avoiding the dangers against which Cooper warns. I take it as an advantage to work here with classical terminology at the same time as I suggest that we consider them in light of contemporary technology. This is one place where our discipline's casual understanding of the canons is beneficial: That individual canons have changed over time is not a controversial claim, and so the canons' historical mutability provides a corrective to the risk of taking them as static categories. Chapters 3 through 7 of this book suggest fresh ways of thinking about the canons, going so far as to rename them for the context of new media, but these revisions or transformations are not intended to replace the canons' classical formation. Rather, they are offered as new layers or dimensions, speculative amendments to terminology that has a long, albeit checkered, history. Translated into Bender and Wellbery's parlance, my presentation of the canons in this book might be described as an example of the kind of work made possible by the idea of rhetoricality.

What does it mean, then, to view the canons as an ecological model? This book offers three answers to this question, two of which I develop briefly in the remainder of this section of the chapter and which lay the groundwork for the third, longer answer: the next five chapters, each of which examines one of the canons in light of new media. Viewing the canons ecologically, it seems to me, requires that we attend to two related questions: First, how does this perspective affect our understanding of the canons themselves, that is, how does it address the neglect discussed in the first section of this chapter? The second question takes a step back and asks how an ecological model of the canons then fits into the broader field of rhetoric and composition. How does a revised model of the canons fit (or complicate) what we might describe as our disciplinary ecology?

The canons have functioned neither as theory nor practice and, thus, as I suggested in the last section of this chapter, they have not fit too comfortably into the field of rhetoric and composition. When we have paid particular attention to one or more canons, it has often been to render it more static. Consider, for example, the various strategies advanced under the umbrella of invention, like freewriting, outlining, mapping, tagmemics, and so on. Although part of viewing invention ecologically must include this repertoire of pedagogical strategies, the emphasis on conscious, visible activity is necessarily a reduction of the canon. An ecological model of invention would treat it at the level of generalized activity. I find it useful to think of the canons as relations rather than categories, and I mean by this something similar to what Kenneth Burke (1969b) does with the ratios among the terms of his pentad. For instance, the canon of invention frames the relationship between given and new information, arranging the relationship between discourse and space, memory the relationship between discourse and time, and so on. These relations are the site of focus for a particular canon, but they are not exclusive or intrinsic to any single one, as I discuss in the final section of this chapter.

The ecology of invention is, of course, composed of far more than a series of directed activities, and two examples from my own experience may clarify what I mean by this. I attend a couple of conferences per year, and each time, starting about halfway through the conference and extending to as long as a week following my return trip home, I am a particularly productive writer. I suspect that many people share this experience. In part, we are trained in the humanities to respond to texts, and usually this is done at the speed of reading. At a professional conference, however, where we are taking in many texts over a short period of time, it makes sense that we would generate potentially productive connections and associations more rapidly. The second example I would offer is my experience with keeping a weblog. When I began blogging, I noticed a shift in my perceptions of the world around me. Much like the t-shirt that promises/threatens "I'm blogging this," a much larger portion of my daily life became available to me as subjects for writing. Over time, the subtle obligation of the weblog has sometimes encouraged me to write when otherwise I would not. In each case, my own particular invention ecology has shifted; although there are professional duties lurking in the background of each activity, those duties do not directly "cause" my writing.

What I am describing as my invention ecology is a personal sensitivity to the conditions under which invention takes place in my own writing. It is not unlike what Karen Burke LeFevre (1987) describes as the "ecology of invention—the way ideas arise and are nurtured or hindered by social context and cultures" (p. 126), although my examples here are less oriented to the shared, visible ecology that LeFevre proposes we study. The impulse behind our projects is a similar one, however. Although we may translate the obligations and imperatives of invention into our own experience—in fact, we cannot help but do this—we are nonetheless drawing on a shared ecology of invention of the sort that LeFevre gestures toward.

That ecology encompasses more than the individual or social development of ideas, however, and requires us to range beyond traditional notions of invention as a stage in the production of discourse. For example, we might consider the feature at Amazon.com that offers book recommendations based on the purchase patterns of other customers: "People who bought this book also bought . . ." (Fig. 2.1). Although their motives for providing this information are primarily economic, this site feature is both social in that it aggregates individual purchases and inventional in that it explicitly marks the relation between the *given* of an individual purchase and the *new* of other volumes tracked by their databases. It also is notable because this feature on Amazon is an instance of invention that is built into the interface, without the (necessarily) conscious participation of the consumers providing the data. As I argue in the next chapter, new media are a site of invention in ways that traditional discursive objects are not.

For the moment, however, it is enough to observe that an ecological approach to the canons treats each as an almost virtual repertoire of practices. The canon of invention does indeed include the various, conscious pedagogical strategies that have circulated in our field, but as any practicing writer understands, invention is not a practice that can be reduced to a handful of activities. Each of us draws our own set of practices from that larger repertoire, which includes other writers, particular sites and materials, texts, the various cultures we negotiate, and so forth. If we recall Johnson-Eilola's (2005) definition of datacloud, "a shifting and only slightly structured information space" (p. 4), the canons provide us with one means of structuring that space, of differentiating our activity within it.

There is a second axis along which I want to differentiate the information space suggested here, an axis that provides another, tentative answer to the questions raised at the beginning of this section. If each of the canons is an ecology of various practices, sites, and activities, what then might we make of the canons as a system? One potential drawback of the ecological approach is the danger that it will become too expansive, becoming simply a backdrop or synonymous with "everything that happens." On the contrary, I would suggest that the canons represent an *ecology of practice*, one scale at which we might examine new media (or media in general) and which is embedded in an even more generalized ecology. I have found it particularly useful to differentiate three scales in particular within this broader ecology and to use the classical notion of the trivium

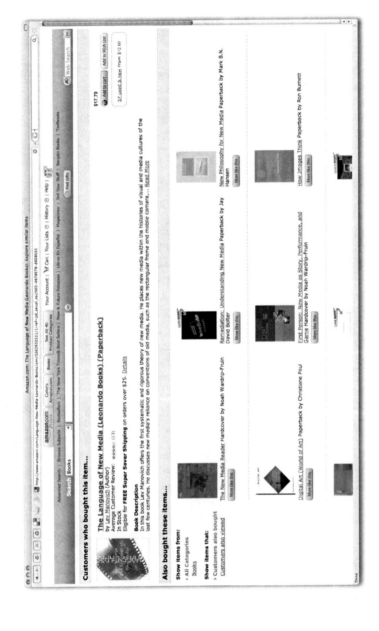

Figure 3.1. A screenshot of Amazon's automated recommendations

(grammar, rhetoric, and dialectic/logic) to do so. I want to close this section of the chapter by laying out a more contemporary version of the trivium, which I label ecologies of *code, practice,* and *culture.* I also discuss some of the precursors I have drawn on for this model, and I consider a couple of its more relevant implications for this project.

For nearly 2,000 years in Europe, from ancient Greece up until the Middle Ages, the trivium designated the course of study leading to a bachelor of arts degree (with the quadrivium of music, arithmetic, geometry, and astronomy the curriculum for a master of arts). The trivium occupies the same kind of limbo reserved in our field for the canons. On the one hand, the study of rhetoric is grounded in this tradition; on the other hand it does not hold much relevance for curricula today.[8] Perhaps the most enduring legacy of the trivium is comprised of the disciplinary distinctions among linguistics, speech, rhetoric, philosophy, and literature. But as these disciplinary distinctions have been instantiated into departmental and institutional forms, any organizing or structuring force that the trivium might have at one time possessed has by now faded. Yet the three categories of the trivium are qualities of discourse, not of disciplines or departments.

I want to suggest that, particularly in the case of new media, there is some value to be found in the trivium, specifically if we think of each of the three as different scales or units of analysis. Some of the worst arguments about new media (and about technology in general) suffer primarily from an unwillingness to consider the possibility that what is true at one scale of activity may not translate up or down to another. To put it more positively, the trivium is valuable because it may help us understand that *the most important changes wrought with and by new media are changes in our ecologies of practice.* This is not to deny that technologies make changes at other scales, but it is to suggest that the transition from one scale to the next is not necessarily seamless, an assumption I have labeled elsewhere the "fallacy of scale." One canonical example of this comes from Kenneth Burke's (1969a) *Rhetoric of Motives,* where he discusses the shepherd who treats sheep well as a means of increasing their value for market. The shepherd's practice of caring for sheep may be no different from that of a child who keeps a lamb as a pet, but the cultural logics behind these practices are certainly different.

If one of the advantages of the trivium is its ability to distinguish conceptually among different scales, one of its disadvantages is the unevenness of the three categories themselves, and this is part of what we will try to amend by updating it. That unevenness is revealed through something as simple as the usage of the terms themselves, for while grammar and logic are both represented as possessing a negative threshold (a statement can be

ungrammatical, for example, or illogical), rhetoric is not.[9] There is no statement that is "arhetorical" or "unrhetorical."[10] Although this has at times
been considered a weakness of rhetoric, I would contend that, in fact, the
absence of an analogous threshold for rhetoric is one of the features that
makes it amenable to an ecological approach, one that I would like to
extend to the other two realms as well. This is part of the reasoning behind
my practice of renaming them for our purposes here. The rules by which we
might decide that a particular utterance is ungrammatical are part of the
ecology we understand as grammar; statements that would be deemed
illogical by the rules of formal logic may seem eminently reasonable to the
person making them if that person is drawing on a different set of cultural
resources. However, rather than trying to undo millennia of usage and
encouraging the kind of "free play" misreading that has plagued deconstruction (among other critical projects), it will be more fruitful to consider the
ecologies of code, practice, and culture as the background of this project.

I discuss each of these ecologies momentarily, but it is worth being
explicit about the relationships between code and grammar, on the one
hand and logic and culture, on the other hand.[11] Much like the shift I outline in my explanation of the canons, what I have in mind with respect to
the trivium is a fairly subtle shift in orientation. Rather than imagining
grammar, for instance, as a set of components and rules for the production
of linguistic discourse, I suggest that an ecology of code is comprised not
only of grammar, but also of all of those resources for the production of
interfaces more broadly construed, including visual, aural, spatial, and textual elements, as well as programming codes. To speak of an ecology of
code makes it no more nor less appropriate to write with sentence frag-
ments. Rather, it is an attempt to acknowledge a broader range of
resources on which we draw in the production of interfaces. A second point
worth mentioning is that viewing the trivium ecologically entails seeing
each area as *structurated* (in the sense that Anthony Giddens [1983]
defines the term). That is, shifting our focus from grammar, rhetoric, and
logic (as subjects to be mastered by a student) to code, practice, and culture (as ecologies that we both contribute to and are surrounded by)
implies that we both construct and are constrained by these terms. At each
scale of activity, we acquire the proverbial hammers that extend our capabilities, but predispose us to perceive nails.

As I explained earlier, the *ecology of code* is my designation for the var-
ied communicative and expressive resources we draw on when we produce discourse, regardless of medium. In other words, both the rules and
objects of grammar are located within this ecology, but language is one
among many media whose elements participate in it. Gunther Kress and

Theo Von Leeuwen's (1995) *Reading Images: The Grammar of Visual Design* is one example of scholarship that contributes to this ecology, as the authors submit dozens of images to an analysis that breaks them down into irreducible components. As I discuss next, this irreducibility is less substantive than it is operative, and so different writers' ecologies of code will differ. The most important thing to note at this point is the expansiveness of the term *code* as I use it here. We are accustomed to thinking of code more exclusively as the set of different languages and commands for computers, and the ecology of code extends this usage to discursive production in general.[12]

Much of my definition of the *ecology of practice* is implicit in my redescription of the canons, but a couple of points are worth repeating. Practice implies conscious, directed activity, the explicit combination of elements from the ecology of code to produce a particular discursive effect. As with the ecology of code, I am working with a fairly expansive definition of practice, however. For example, one's choice of medium (or media) I would include as part of the ecology of practice. Ecologically, practice includes all of the "available means" and our decisions regarding which of them to pursue. In the case of interfaces, this ecology also includes not only those practices involved in the production of a particular interface, but those made possible by it. The ability to select books based on the relevance of aggregated user data, for instance, is part of the ecology of practice at Amazon (and many other sites). But it is also important to acknowledge those practices that may be unintended—users may take up and repurpose interfaces, expanding their ecology of practice beyond a designer's intentions. In other words, I envision this ecology as largely descriptive even as there exist intentions and motives behind the practices gathered within it.

Of these three designations, the *ecologies of culture* are perhaps most appropriately thought of in the plural because it is this category that operates at the broadest range of scales, from interpersonal relationships and local discourse communities to regional, national, and even global cultures. Any act of discourse is going to be constrained in various ways by cultural assumptions; similarly, such acts intervene simultaneously at several levels. It would be no exaggeration to suggest that, from the perspective of ecologies of culture, discourse is necessarily multiple. A site like Amazon, even as it has pioneered several customer-oriented practices that carry no direct benefit for the company, is only successful insofar as it successfully competes in the marketplace. Every interface strikes a similar balance among various constituencies, competing ideologies, and multiple contexts. Although they are less the focus of this book than are ecologies of practice, ecologies of culture provide a corrective to what could be perceived as a more formalist orientation in ecologies of code and practice.

I close this section with a more detailed consideration of how these ecologies fit together. However, before I offer that explanation, it is worth briefly noting some of the precursors for my own updated trivium in the work of other rhetoricians. For example, the attentive reader may note some of the similarities between my treatment of the trivium and that of Kenneth Burke (1969), who, in his *Rhetoric of Motives*, articulates his own trivium of "positive, dialectical, and ultimate terms." Positive terms, which would correspond to grammar, are for Burke, expressed in terms of a "physicalist" vocabulary, those terms that name the concrete objects of existence. Dialectical terms are those for which we have no "positive referent," and in fact, Burke cites *positivism* as one such term. Rhetoric is for Burke the site of dialectical action, an order that "would leave the competing voices in a jangling relation with one another.. . . ." They are the terms over which we wrangle. The final category of terms for Burke are ultimate terms, which "place these competing voices themselves in a *hierarchy*, or *sequence*, or *evaluative series*." Ultimate vocabularies are contrasted with dialectical terms insofar as they foreclose on the debates that characterize the latter. The parallels with my own trivium are apparent, particularly as concerns the relationship between the ecology of code and Burke's positive terms, both of which name concrete, irreducible phenomena. Where Burke suggests the difference between dialectical and ultimate vocabularies, however, I see variations within ecologies of culture. Burke's categories, particularly the latter two, are products of particular interpretations. That is, they describe patterns of usage rather than static categories; what stands as an ultimate term for one person may be entirely dialectical for another. Yet there is an exclusivity to Burke's categories that, as I explain shortly, marks a significant difference between his terms and my own.

A second, more recent precursor can be found in David Kaufer and Brian Butler's *Designing Interactive Worlds With Words* and their discussion there of what they call "representational composition." Kaufer and Butler find in representational composition a middle ground located between two more conventional approaches to writing: structural composition and genre theory. Structural composition, they argue, has dominated writing instruction and focuses on the grammatical "principles of writing [that] could lawfully turn smaller structures into larger ones, words into clauses, clauses into sentences, and up the linguistic food chain" (p. 5). At the other end of their spectrum lie genres, "the cultural, historical, and sociological specifications that have led to the settling in time and place of one or another family of representations as an object of sufficient recurrence and cultural visibility to be named" (p. 12). As a bridge from the former to the latter, they advocate training in representational composition, a sort of "pattern language" for writing, comprised of "basic element patterns" that can be adapted to a broad range of external circumstances and generic demands.[13] Again, there are obvious parallels between their work and my own, not the least reason for which is that new media provides part of the exigence for Kaufer and Butler's project. If Burke's latter two terms collectively correspond to my notion of ecologies of culture, I would argue that ecologies of practice include Kaufer and Butler's representational composition and genres as well. However, I am hesitant even to imply that this is a shortcoming given that their purpose is chiefly pedagogical.

A third site of parallels for my project is Clay Spinuzzi's (2003) *Tracing Genres Through Organizations*. Unlike my own approach, Spinuzzi's is largely inductive, drawing on fieldwork to arrive at a formal model informed by activity theory. Spinuzzi's model has three parts, also described as scales or levels of scope: operations (which are unconscious and habitual), actions (which are conscious and goal-directed), and activities (which are unconscious and cultural-historical). The "three levels of scope complement each other" (p. 36), intertwining to form, along with other factors, what Spinuzzi ultimately describes as *genre ecologies*. Spinuzzi's is perhaps the closest model to what I have in mind here, even as our approaches differ. One insight in particular from his book that is important for my purposes is the degree to which the different scales interpenetrate, resulting in operational rather than substantive distinctions among them. For example, he explains that operations are also called operationalized actions "since they begin as conscious goal-directed actions that are then made automatic" (p. 34). Think here of macros or templates for a word processor, which are pre-designed forms that free a user from having to format a conventional document from scratch. Actions also can become activities, as a conscious action made in a particular organizational context becomes part of that organization's traditional or customary way of doing things even after the context no longer holds.

Although I share Spinuzzi's willingness to treat these categories as flexible and context-dependent, there are a couple of important differences between his model and my own. Like Burke's three-part scheme, Spinuzzi's categories are exclusive. A particular phenomenon may move from one category to another over time, but at any given moment, it occupies only one—a fact reinforced by the use of micro-, meso-, and macroscopic to describe the different scales. This difference is not necessarily a crucial one, coming as it does from the different purposes behind our respective projects. But the labels for the different scopes raise a second difference, one that is fairly important. Although I have described code, practice, and culture as operating at different scales, I hope to do so without necessarily assigning them a corresponding sizing. It is customary to think of the classical trivium in differently sized scales, but, if possible, this is a custom worth resisting. One way of describing the relationship among these three ecologies is to see practices as combining various elements of code to produce a statement or action, one of many such that then combine and contend to produce a particular culture. However, this notion is not entirely inaccurate, but such an account ignores the degree to which each of these three ecologies can be more or less present in even the most irreducible element. The use of the word *terrorist* (code) to describe someone (practice) carries heavily charged ideological implications (culture) at this point in our history, for instance. Or consider Nietzsche's (1998) infamous claim that "we are not getting rid of God because we still believe in grammar" from *Twilight of the Idols*.

In other words, I am offering this update of the classical trivium neither as categories nor as a progression so much as another "light structure" with which we might triangulate those analyses that the canons make possible. There are elements of code, practice, and culture in each of the interfaces that we might read or write with the canons, and those elements will add texture to our discussions as we consider the canons in more detail. Although this project focuses specifically on ecologies of practice, distinguishing them from the ecologies of code and culture can only ever be a temporary, conceptual maneuver—one that does not translate into actual usage. In other words, there is no "pure" zone of practice distinguishable from either code or culture. Yet ecologies of practice also carry a certain limited amount of autonomy, shaped but not determined by ecologies of culture and capable of reframing ecologies of code in unforeseen ways.

TRACKBACKS AS AN ECOLOGY OF PRACTICE

Before turning to the individual chapters, and hence the individual canons, it is worth our time to clarify a couple of points about the framework I have developed in this chapter. Each of the canons can be described as an ecology, a complex system of people, sites, practices, and objects; taken together, the canons form what I am describing here as an ecology of practice, within which the canons operate. As such, the canons occupy a space that overlaps with ecologies of code and theory, but that is nonetheless distinct.

The chapters that follow treat each canon more or less independently of each other, but it is important to acknowledge that the distinctions among them are far less certain than the chapter structure of this book implies. Just as a single discursive event can be read productively across the ecologies of code, practice, and theory, it is not unusual to locate particular practices within more than one of the ecologies designated by the canons. I want to close this chapter with a brief demonstration of this claim, by examining the trackback link (Fig. 2.2).

Trackbacks are a feature of weblogs, although not all blogging platforms support this feature. Although we typically speak of a trackback in the singular, it normally involves multiple steps. The standard link on a webpage allows a user to move from one page to a second page, but that link is unidirectional unless the owner of the second page has linked back to the first. Trackbacks provide a protocol for establishing both links at the same time, functionally creating a bidirectional link between two weblog entries. These two entries supply part of the trackback's *ecology of code*, as does the HTML that enables the first writer to create a link to the second weblog. For the trackback to work, however, the second weblog must first be published with a platform that allows trackbacks. Then that weblog owner must enable a CGI script, which will, once the first writer sends a "ping," rewrite the relevant page on the second weblog, adding a link to the first weblog (and usually the title and a brief excerpt of the entry being linked). From the perspective of the first writer, the process is much simpler than this. Each entry on a weblog has a unique trackback URL, and all that is required of the writer is that she copy and paste this URL into a window on her composing interface. Some weblog platforms even provide "auto-discovery," where the software will follow each of the links in an entry, determine whether any of the pages are trackbackable, and automatically ping them if they are.

From the perspective of *ecologies of culture*, trackbacks represent a step toward a more open, collaborative web, in no small part because trackbacks allow other people to make changes to a small portion of a weblog entry without the author's express permission. As anyone who has used trackbacks knows, however, this also leaves the weblog vulnerable to spammers, who have exploited trackback links in an effort to boost search engine rankings for their products. Trackbacks thus also participate in the arms race between spam marketing and the people trying to stop it. Finally, they contribute to the perception that weblogs are a conversational space, rather than a purely informational space. They allow bloggers to directly invoke and address a particular audience in a much more immediate fashion than would be possible, say, with a search engine.

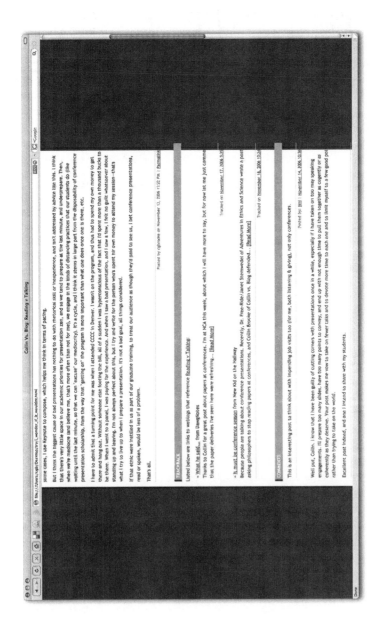

Figure 2.2. An illustration of a trackback link, taken from my weblog

How might we consider the practice of trackbacking? Trackbacks can be read in terms of each of the canons; that is, they provide one example of a site where all five of the canons intersect and overlap. Although they are perhaps not typical in this regard, trackbacks provide an excellent illustration of the claim that the canons are not mutually exclusive categories, but complementary perspectives that allow us to focus on different dimensions of even a single practice.

Invention

In many ways, the motive behind trackbacks is an inventional one. Weblog entries frequently link to other sites, and such links are implicit endorsements of the sites to which they link. But a trackback link also places a link on the object site, and there is a certain obligation built into this practice. By placing a link to one's own weblog on someone else's site, the blogger is suggesting that the other person's audience will find something relevant on her site as well. Often this will take the form of response, critique, or elaboration, but the basis of the trackback link is the idea that one's own site will supply some *new* information in addition to the *given* of the other writer's entry, whether it is new evidence, a different perspective, or a reinterpretation of material from the original.

Arrangement

By placing links to each other on pages at two different sites, the trackback also serves an arranging function. Anjo Anjewierden and Lilia Efimova (2005) pioneered a method whereby they use links (trackback and otherwise) to map out the relationships pertaining to specific social networks and to weblog conversations (Fig. 2.3), even going so far as to suggest how link patterns reveal different participants' centrality or marginality in a particular network. Although it makes intuitive sense to say that there would be a denser pattern of linkage among the members of a social network, trackback links contribute to the process of making that linkage visible and measurable.

Style

Although trackbacks may not make an intrinsic contribution to the style of a given weblog entry (considering that their most significant change occurs

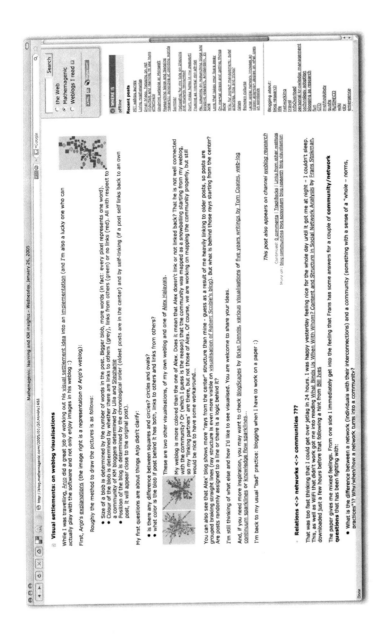

Figure 2.3. A weblog conversation mapped by Anjewierden and Efimova

on someone else's page), they do alter the form of a weblog in slight ways. One of the factors distinguishing weblogs from online journals, as Will Richardson (2004) explains, is the author's willingness to engage with other blogs and sources. An online journal is often insular in style, recounting events and thoughts from a particular writer's life, whereas blogs engage each other, in part, through the practice of linking. The presence of trackbacks on a blog entry may not have an effect on the diction or word choice in that entry, but the broader form of the weblog is rendered more open to interaction and connection than it would be otherwise.

Memory

Much like their contribution to arrangement, trackbacks make the associations generated by a particular writer both visible and archivable. Unlike a face-to-face conversation, where we might recall the general tenor of a conversation, or a particular position adopted by one of the participants, trackbacks archive the conversation, storing the connections as well as the participation. This is particularly significant considering how quickly individual entries are consigned to the archives by most blogging platforms. Weblog conversations can be recalled months after the fact, a process made much easier by the presence of trackbacks.

Delivery

Similarly, trackbacks aid in the process of circulation if we draw on the metaphor of the web as a place where we move from one site to the next. As frequently updated sites, weblogs do not encourage their owners to update the links within a particular entry once it is published. Enabling trackbacks allows a writer's audience to do the updating, making it easier for readers to follow a particular conversation and offer their own contributions in the form of trackbacks, even when a conversation has "finished."

In suggesting that each of the canons plays some role in our understanding of the trackback link, I have relied here on fairly traditional understandings of the canons, understandings that in some ways the subsequent chapters challenge or augment at the very least. I hope that this underscores my belief that the version of the canons offered here is not intended as authoritative or correct in any way. One of the central premises of this project is that the canons are mutable and dynamic, that they shift with changes in our discursive technologies as those technologies constrain particular strategies and make others possible. It also is the case that different interfaces will combine and mingle the canons in various ways. In the case of the trackback, for example, it is fairly clear that spammers are interested almost exclusively in increasing the circulation (*delivery*) for their own sites, while I myself have used them to assist in the organization of a blogging "carnival," a distributed conversation about common topics occurring on multiple blogs, where my chief intention was to use them as a means of *arrangement*. The value of the canons, as an ecology of practice, lies in their ability to help us distinguish these various uses and to imagine yet others. To arrive at that point, however, we need to consider the canons in more depth and complexity than has been commonplace in our field, and it is to such a consideration that this project now shifts.

NOTES

1. See, for example, Jennifer Edbauer's (2005) "Unframing Models of Public Distribution: From Rhetorical Situation to Rhetorical Ecologies."
2. See, for example, J. Fred Reynolds' (1993) *Rhetorical Memory and Delivery*, or more recently, Kathleen Blake Yancey (2006), *Delivering College Composition: The Fifth Canon.*
3. I am not arguing here that rhetoric is *primarily* technology to the exclusion of its other intrinsic qualities, although I would contend that many in our field who are comfortable describing rhetoric as intrinsically social and cultural, for example, overlook its necessarily technological dimension.
4. Access is a particularly interesting case in point. With few exceptions (e.g., Banks, 2006), access is treated as a problem endemic to technology, meaning computers, as if access to public forums in ancient cultures (or to printing presses in early Modern Europe, or to means of distribution in contemporary societies) weren't similarly restricted. In 2005, on one of our disciplinary list-servs, in response to an NPR story about musicians who were circumventing the highly restrictive and exploitative recording industry by composing music and distributing it online, several writers accused these artists of elitism simply because they were using computers to do this.
5. The Address was published in the December 2004 issue of *College Composition and Communication* as "Made Not Only in Words: Composition in a New Key."
6. I use the word *tend* here advisedly. In the example that follows, I would not describe Aristotle's *pisteis* as a "theory" per se, but because the proofs are near universal, they *can be used* to build theories, such as the notion that a truly "good" argument is one that uses a balance of the three types of proof, rather than, say, appealing exclusively through *pathos*. I disagree with this application

of the *pisteis*, but my broader point is that the canons cannot be "applied" in this fashion.

7. To my mind, the pervasiveness of the theory/practice split in composition and rhetoric goes without citing. Nevertheless, Lisa Ede's *Situating Composition* is one of the most recent in a long history of texts that addresses it. See in particular her 15-year bibliographic "compilation of research on theory and practice in composition" on pp. 122-123.

8. Interestingly enough, a search on the trivium will reveal a range of resources for home schooling based in whole or in part on the classical trivium, sometimes mapped across similar frameworks from the Bible.

9. Although this discussion is perhaps not as clear-cut as I have presented it; the debate over Ebonics, for example, is in part a debate over the value of a negative threshold for grammar. Nevertheless, I would argue that this is still a widely held position, particularly outside of the academy.

10. This claim is more controversial, perhaps, for scholars outside of the discipline of rhetoric than it is for those of us inside. For a discussion of the "rhetoric of no rhetoric," see Valesio (1980).

11. As I explained previously, I take the shift from rhetoric to practice to be a much more modest shift than the other two.

12. There is overlap here between my own adoption of the term code and that of Katherine Hayles' (2005) latest book, *My Mother Was a Computer*. For Hayles, code encompasses the prior regimes of speech and writing, but she also situates code at the same conceptual level as the other two.

13. This is a reference to Christopher Alexander's (1977) *A Pattern Language*.

3

PROAIRESIS

---

inventio, by its nature, calls for openness to the accumulated resources of the world a speaker lives in, to its landscapes, its information, its ways of thinking and feeling...

—Jim Corder (1995)

I think every writer carries in him or herself as a particular temptation the weakness or the possibility of ignoring that he or she is committed to a *je ne sais quoi* . . . the "evidence" that we have to take on the burden of the linkages between thoughts or phrases does not mean that we ever master them.

—Jean-François Lyotard (1988)

Of the five rhetorical canons, invention is without question the one to which rhetoric and composition has attended most frequently in its disciplinary history. Memory and delivery, considered largely irrelevant to the production of print texts, have been dismissed, whereas arrangement and style take their place in the writing process only when invention has begun. Decades of research on invention in the field serve to assist the writing instructor in guiding his or her students through the process of creating something (a polished essay) from nothing (the empty page or blank screen). Millions of those students, faced with the daunting prospect of writing, have asked themselves (or their teachers, or their handbooks), "How do I start?"

The question of where to begin a piece of writing is so central to our field's understanding of invention, in fact, that Irene Clark's (2003) *Concepts in Composition* devotes almost as much space in her chapter on invention to the problem of writer's block as she does to invention's roots in classical rhetoric. Although our handbooks are careful to explain that invention is ongoing, most focus on invention as "prewriting" or "planning," to be executed prior to the production of the formal essay. When that formal essay serves as the basis for evaluation, the process leading up to it is likely to acquire secondary status, regardless of teachers' theoretical adherence to process pedagogy. Reflecting on his own training in writing, Scott Lloyd DeWitt (2001) observes, "Invention, exploration, and topic development were viewed as skills that follow or are secondary to proficiency in form and structure and, therefore, don't necessitate instruction" (p. 31).

This reduction of invention is, in part, intrinsic to the process model, despite the various pedagogical strategies that attempt to mitigate it (e.g., asking students to submit prewriting along with the essay). Students have a limited amount of time to produce written work, and those limits play some role in the writer's block that plagues them. Despite what we know about writing, we also are constrained by some of the same attitudes that Sharon Crowley (1990) aptly critiques in *The Methodical Memory*, that invention processes represent the intellectual quality (or lack thereof) of the writer's mind, and that the written essay represents the quality of those inventional processes. Within the classroom, at least, traditional forms of assessment reflect these attitudes, and a broader understanding of invention, one that includes more than prewriting, is frequently one of the casualties.

These restrictive cultural attitudes toward invention—invention's ecologies of culture—are tied closely to the modernist figure of the author as well as a fairly limiting model of textual economy. Rehearsing the features of this model is almost unnecessary; one of the defining missions of rhetoric and composition is its insistence on the social, cultural, and contextual position of the writer; the participation of readers and audiences in the construction of meaning; and the necessary imprecision of language—all positions that refute the traditional notion of the author/inventor. As we consider rhetoric and composition's approach to invention, then, it is unsurprising that these themes would emerge and come to dominate our discussions of this canon. A brief review of that approach comprises the first section of this chapter. The section that follows looks more closely at a parallel approach, early hypertext criticism's consideration of authorship. Although hypertext critics were often working from a different set of assumptions and writers, the claims they advance on behalf of hypertext bear a strong resemblance to rhetoric and composition's take on invention. Neither of these approaches, however, ultimately manages to escape a print-based model of authorship; each ends up focusing on the generation of textual objects, hyperlinked or not.

In the third section of the chapter, I introduce a distinction between *hermeneutic* and *proairetic* invention, named thusly after two of the codes that Roland Barthes (1974) introduces in *S/Z*. Hypertext criticism in particular depends on the insights of Barthes, the French literary critic who is perhaps best known in this country for his essay proclaiming the "death of the author." But in our focus on that idea (and on the distinction between *readerly* and *writerly* texts), we have overlooked (I contend) the extent to which *S/Z* is a book that signals the transition from literary/textual object to interface. It is possible to read Barthes' reading of a Balzac short story as the attempt to render it as a cultural interface, and the "codes" that Barthes uses to do so are exemplary literary practices, unearthed through his reading.

The remainder of the chapter attempts first to articulate what a specifically *proairetic* practice of invention entails and, second, to offer a couple of examples of this practice. In the context of Barthes' analysis, the hermeneutic and proairetic codes complement one another, as they must necessarily do to produce a satisfying textual object. However, when we shift our attention to interfaces, I would argue that proairesis takes precedence under certain circumstances, and that it is this type of invention that our discipline must account for as it considers new media.

A DISCIPLINARY ECOLOGY OF INVENTION

I began this chapter referring to the reductive approach to invention that was, at one time, commonplace in the writing classroom. No disciplinary account of invention would be complete, however, without acknowledging the strong, even dominant, thread of scholarship that calls this impoverished notion of invention into question. One of the longest lasting works in this tradition is Karen Burke LeFevre's (1987) *Invention as a Social Act*. Written nearly 20 years ago, LeFevre's book remains influential, if not foundational, for any study of invention. In it, she articulates the range of disciplinary and historical forces that have contributed to the prevalence of what LeFevre describes as a Platonic view of invention, one that includes a solitary author/inventor, abstracted from society, participating in a closed, one-way system (cf. LeFevre, chap. 2). Arrayed against this view of invention, LeFevre outlines several alternatives, placing Platonic individualism on a continuum that includes internal dialogue, collaboration, and social collectives. More important, LeFevre rescues invention from the tendency to think of it as either something that necessarily "begins" with the individual writer or that ceases with the final revision of a particular product.

In a section that recalls Kenneth Burke's (1969a, 1969b) conversational parlor, LeFevre (1987) explains that "a view of invention as an act emphasizes that inventing, whether in a rhetorical or a generic sense, often involves a series of social transactions and texts that may extend over time" (p. 40). LeFevre argues for a conception of invention that extends synchronically beyond the individual author and diachronically beyond the present moment, although she would argue that this is less a matter of extending invention, perhaps, than it is a matter of undoing our disciplinary restrictions. Toward the end of her book, LeFevre recommends that "we should study the ecology of invention—the ways ideas arise and are nurtured or hindered by interaction with social context and culture" (p. 126). Restoring invention to its fully ecological status, according to LeFevre, would challenge some of our most basic assumptions about education, knowledge, and society, not to mention the classroom.

In challenging those assumptions at the level of our cultural beliefs about invention, LeFevre offers what I described in chapter 2 as an *ecology of culture*. One of the more recent books to take up LeFevre's ideas, Anis Bawarshi's (2003) *Genre and the Invention of the Writer,* provides an excellent complement to *Invention as a Social Act,* one that locates itself in *ecologies of practice.* Bawarshi cites LeFevre's call for the study of ecologies of invention approvingly, adding, "In the years since, scholars have taken up this call by examining the interpersonal, textual, material, and ideological nature of this ecology" (p. 71). Bawarshi does likewise, through the study of genre as a crucial element in an ecology of invention. If, for LeFevre, invention must be redefined as "social act," then for Bawarshi, genres provide the "sites of action" that correspond to those acts. Bawarshi also increases the reach of the term *ecology,* defining genres as "rhetorical ecosystems":

Our interactions with others and with our environments, therefore, are mediated not only by physical conditions but also by rhetorical conditions that, in part, are ideologically and discursively organized and generated through genres. Genres—what Catherine Schryer defines as "stabilized-for-now or stabilized-enough sites of social and ideological action" (1994, 108)—thus constitute typified rhetorical sites or habitations in which our social actions and commitments are made possible and meaningful as well as in which we are rhetorically socialized to perform (and potentially transform) these actions and commitments. (pp. 81–82)

This definition is important for a couple of distinct reasons. First, Bawarshi redescribes a crucial element of LeFevre's understanding of invention, her inclusion of audience as part of the invention process. LeFevre argues that, in the social view, the inventor "requires the presence of the other. . . . It may be a collaborator with whom one invents or a reader whose participation in constructing a text 'finishes' the enterprise" (p. 39). LeFevre certainly does not suggest that collaborative or collective invention is unmediated, but Bawarshi offers specific and concrete examples of precisely how they are mediated. In other words, one of Bawarshi's contributions to the study of invention is its distribution; although it may seem self-evident to note that our social interactions are mediated and that this mediation is significant, I return to this point momentarily.

My second observation here is related to the first. One of the theoretical implications of LeFevre's position is the decreased distance between the author and reader, and Bawarshi's (2003) work serves to close that gap even further. Genres, as rhetorical ecosystems, are sites where we both act and are acted on. The idea that they are "stabilized enough" suggests that they carry sufficient order, custom, and/or inertia to constrain our acts, while retaining enough flexibility to change over time and to accommodate generic violation.[1] Bawarshi combines Michael Halliday's semantic and actualized potentials with Anthony Giddens' theory of structuration to arrive at a description of genre that accounts both for its effects on writers as well as their ability to act. He explains:

Genres are structures in that they maintain the ideological potential for action in the form of social motives and the typified rhetorical means of actualizing that potential in the form of social practices. Genres are ideological concepts and material articulations of these concepts at once, maintaining the desires they help individuals fulfill. (p. 90)

Any act of invention, then, involves reading and writing insofar as we engage in both sets of practices almost simultaneously. We read the potentials provided for us in the form of genres, internalize them as motives, and enact them as social practices (i.e., we write in ways that confirm, resist, and/or negotiate those structures). For Bawarshi, we have internalized most genres to the degree that we naturalize their ideologies as our own, without realizing that our agency is distributed well beyond our own particular articulation of it.

In considering invention as a distributed practice, our scholarship frequently runs the risk of treating that distribution as immaterial. In other words, if we are to treat our social interactions as mediated, we must consider information technologies in the process. Lloyd Scott DeWitt's (2001) *Writing Inventions* aims, in part, to address the dearth of work on invention and technology. DeWitt addresses LeFevre's continuum only briefly and maps her continuum across terms (*cognitive* and *social*) made popular in discussions of pedagogical theory. His argument, then, is that networked technologies allow for the kind of dialectical model of invention recommended by LeFevre:

> Network-supported writing facilities provide access to particular emerging technologies that allow for a blending of the cognitive with a social vision of invention. . . . Because of the dynamic nature of the computer and its ability to branch information interactively, the Web and other types of hypertext enable students to access and construct texts in an associative, intuitive way. (p. 49)

Students in networked classrooms, DeWitt argues, are able to access not only the Web, but each other (and each others' texts), in a way that works directly against the notion of an individual, abstracted inventor.

At times, as in the passage quoted previously, DeWitt (2001) treads dangerously close to the fallacy of assuming that these technologies somehow more faithfully model our mental processes. Ultimately, however, DeWitt pulls back from this position by refusing to treat technology autonomously. Drawing on Catherine Smith's (1991) distinction between hypertext as information system and as facilitation, DeWitt places his own work squarely within the context of the latter, explaining, "we are less concerned here with hypertext as a system than with how it might facilitate learning for the user" (p. 126). As I hope to demonstrate later in this chapter, there is some value to considering hypertext (or weblogs or wikis) as systems; DeWitt's approach risks reducing the technologies he considers to mere tools. For the moment, however, it is sufficient to note that DeWitt focuses, almost microscopically, on the invention processes of individual users.

DeWitt's (2001) model of invention complements both LeFevre's and Bawarshi's in its emphasis on both internal and external connections. Writers, he explains, engage in the practices of active noticing, of connecting the things that they have noticed, and of tolerating disorder as they work with complex bodies of information. "I see invention," he writes,

> as a layering of episodes, with each episode becoming what I will refer to as a "moment of invention." These moments occur when students notice something and when they see relationships and make connections. Furthermore, when students make connections between two or more moments of invention, they experience yet another, richer moment of invention as they create a mental text of sorts, that begins to pull together their fragmented experience. (p. 24)

DeWitt is careful to explain how these connections are the results of both internal and external exposure, rather than one or the other. Connections between two pieces of "internal" information are typically prompted by something external, and connections among "external discoveries" are driven, at the very least, by internal interpretation.

Modeled this way, it is relatively easy to see how various hypertext platforms or knowledge management tools might aid in the invention process for the students that DeWitt (2001) describes, despite his qualification that "this theory is, on the surface, not necessarily grounded in technology" (p. 15). As the model is developed, however, legitimate questions arise as to its endpoint. DeWitt begins by stressing the importance of tolerating disorder and complexity, of complementing more systematic invention strategies "with more whimsical, haphazard, at times playful, accidental, and random methods of discovery" (p. 23), but there is a limit beyond which these complements do not go. "As ideas are superimposed and layered," he writes, "they reshape and reform, they adapt and respond until the mental text, the invention, is solid, dense, sturdy" (p. 74). At some point, in other words, the ecology of invention starts to grind to a halt, and a product, a textual object, results.

This contrast between the disorder of invention and the sturdiness of the object of invention is not unique to DeWitt's (2001) description. Artifacts are always subject to interpretive drift, and thus there is a degree to which they are never quite "finished," but there is some point at which invention shuts down. An individual writer's articulation for Bawarshi becomes part of the motive potential for other writers; despite her attempts to close the distance between writer and reader, LeFevre can not avoid at least some separation between them.

I would argue that this is an effect of blurring the difference between what I will define next as *hermeneutic* and *proairetic* models of invention. Hermeneutic invention relies on the relative sturdiness of a final object and the negotiation of meanings within it. In other words, much of our theorizing about invention in rhetoric and composition remains bound by the particular media for which we invent, and for the most part we invent (and ask our students to invent) for the printed page. When the final products of our invention are judged, in part, by their solidity or sturdiness, it makes perfect sense that we theorize invention to arrive at such goals. If those goals continue to function naturalistically in our classrooms, then such theorizing will be sufficient. It should be noted that this is less a critique of LeFevre, Bawarshi, and DeWitt than it is an acknowledgment of the institutional context from which their work necessarily emerges. In many ways, each of the three contributes valuable insights to our discussion of invention that need not be forgotten in a discussion of new media, only augmented. Before I move to discuss that augmentation, however, I want to turn to what I see as a parallel development in authorship/invention theory—hypertext criticism from the 1990s.

THE DEATH OF THE HYPERTEXT AUTHOR

> From the vantage point of the current changes in information technology, Barthes's distinction between readerly and writerly texts appears to be essentially a distinction between text based on print technology and electronic hypertext . . .
> —George P. Landow (1997)

Although there are some distinctions we might make between invention as a rhetorical canon and authorship or the figure of the author, they are deeply intertwined.[2] The attitude that invention is the province of the solitary, socially abstracted genius carries a great deal of social inertia, and much of the work done on invention in our field can be read, in part, as an attempt to undo that attitude in our classrooms. Pedagogically, this attempt frequently takes the form of collaborative work and an enforced recursivity in the writing processes of our students. We ask them to perform a different model of invention than most of them likely possess on entering the

writing classroom; in other words, rhetoric and composition has attempted to challenge the inertia of the modernist author at the level of practice.

Early hypertext criticism shares these same concerns, but the
approach embodied in this criticism differs substantially. Rather than focusing on the practices of individual writers, hypertext criticism is an interven-
tion in ecologies of culture, claiming that hypertext was inherently incompatible with the traditional figure of the author. George P. Landow (1997),
in particular, argues that hypertext offers an instantiation of various poststructuralist theories of language, most notably Roland Barthes' "death of
the author" and the distinction between readerly and writerly texts as theoretical precursors to what hypertext accomplishes technologically:

> First of all, the figure of the hypertext author approaches, even if it
> does not entirely merge with, that of the reader; the functions of read-
> er and writer become more deeply entwined with each other than ever
> before. . . . Hypertext, which creates an active, even intrusive reader,
> carries this convergence of activities one step closer to completion; but
> in so doing, it infringes upon the power of the writer, removing some
> of it and granting it to the reader. (p. 71)

Hypertext, Landow (1997) argues, narrows the "phenomenological distance" between author and reader, an assertion that bears some resemblance to the claim offered earlier by LeFevre. But where LeFevre asks us
to bring our perceptions in closer alignment with the reality of
author–reader interaction, Landow asserts a change in that reality. The
transformation he describes as a "near merging" provides the primary warrant for his argument that the author is reconfigured under hypertext. Once
the privileged term of the author–reader binary, the author is decentered;
hypertext "does do away with certain aspects of the authoritativeness and
autonomy of the text, and in so doing it does reconceive the figure and
function of the author" (p. 72).

This series of claims, taken in their milder form (reconfiguring the relationships among authors, texts, and readers), provides a useful starting
point for thinking about authorship and invention in the context of new
media. Critical response to the work of Landow and others has not pro-
ceeded in that fashion, however. Most frequently, critics have taken one of
two paths: Either they have dismissed this work out of hand for its technological determinism or they have simply repeated it and distanced themselves from the claims. A passage from the introduction to John Barber and
Dene Grigar's (2001) collection *New Worlds, New Words* illustrates this second tendency:

Indeed, much of the research literature on hypertext and other current forms of electronic writing suggests that these new communication media will potentially deconstruct the sense of stability surrounding the notions of author, reader, and writing that have long accompanied linear text. (p. 12)

Passages like these, through qualifications ("suggests," "potentially") and citational distancing (attributing these conclusions to the "research literature"), avoid directly reinforcing Landow's claims, but neither do they challenge them. With few exceptions, the scholarship that followed the initial wave of hypertext criticism has engaged in this type of mild qualification. Mark Poster (1990), whose *Mode of Information* was as ambitious as Landow's work in terms of blending poststructuralist thought with technology, also is instructive in this regard. His latest book, *What's the Matter with the Internet?* (2001), repeats claims from his earlier work, but qualifies those claims almost beyond recognition; the transition from the "author function of modernity to a multiple, unstable author of postmodernity" is characterized as a "horizon of visibility" that is "plausible" at best. Furthermore, Poster explicitly addresses his process of revision, visibly altering his text "in order to avoid any hint of technological determinism" (p. 91). In other words, Poster combines the two critical trends mentioned earlier.

The end result of both strategies has been to stall the attention paid to authorship in new media. The fear of being labeled technological determinists or technophiles has slowly eroded whatever critical momentum existed in the earliest work on hypertext. Some of this erosion has been appropriate. For example, the assumption that escape from what Robert Coover (1992) called the "tyranny of the line" would necessarily be liberating invested hypertext with political connotations that have proved problematic to say the least.[3] Richard Grusin's (1996) critique of the "discursive logic" surrounding "articulation[s] of electronic authorship" provides a necessary corrective to the notion that technologies exist independently from their material, social, and cultural contexts. However, as important as these critiques have been, they have forestalled much of the discussion that surrounded early hypertext scholarship. It is almost painful to read Poster's various disavowals of technological determinism, and I would suggest that this constant concern with avoiding impropriety affects his ability to recapture the momentum of his earlier work. In a similar fashion, there has been little scholarship that has advanced our understanding of electronic authorship in the wake of these critiques.

Yet there is little question that, with a turn to new media, practices of invention, writing, and reading do indeed differ from those associated with print technology. But those practices also differ *within* new media, just as they differ from genre to genre within print. Critics have not completely rejected claims like Landow's because there is some dimension to them that corresponds with the experiences that we have when we read or use new media. Elevating that dimension, however, to the level of theory (as Landow and others do) is misleading. Espen Aarseth (1997) writes:

> But the politics of the author-reader relationship, ultimately, is not a choice between paper and electronic text . . . but instead is whether the user has the ability to transform the text into something that the instigator of the text could not foresee or plan for. This, of course, depends much more on the user's own motivation than on whatever political structure the text appears to impose. These transformations may occur in any medium and are not governed by the "laws" (technical and social conventions) of that medium. . . . (p. 164)

To put it another way, and a way that should be familiar to us in rhetoric and composition, reading and writing are practices; although we are certainly constrained by theoretical "laws of media," our practices are not completely determined by them. The modernist figure of the author, for example, is a concept that emerged at a particular historical juncture. Although it has a clear influence on our institutions and perceptions of writing, it also is possible for us to resist that influence and to practice writing in ways that are incompatible with it.

Treating invention as a practice allows us to recognize some of the limitations and shortcomings of the work on electronic authorship, but I would argue that it is equally (if not more) useful as a perspective from which to reexamine that work. At the beginning of this section, I cite Landow's (1997) equivocation of hypertext with Roland Barthes' (1974) notion of the "writerly text." At first glance, Barthes' description of the writerly appears quite relevant to hypertext:

> Why is the writerly our value? Because the goal of literary work (of literature as work) is to make the reader no longer a consumer, but a producer of the text. Our literature is characterized by the pitiless divorce which the literary institution maintains between the producer of the text and its user, between its owner and its customer, between its author and its reader. This reader is thereby plunged into a kind of idleness—he is intransitive; he is, in short, *serious*: instead of functioning himself, instead of gaining access to the magic of the signifier, to the

> pleasure of writing, he is left with no more than the poor freedom either to accept or reject the text: reading is nothing more than a *referendum*. Opposite the writerly text, then, is its countervalue, its negative, reactive value: what can be read, but not written: the readerly . We call any readerly text a classic text. (p. 4)

Although we may disagree with the scope with which this equivalence (hypertext = writerly) has been applied, the comparison makes a certain amount of sense. Landow (1997) explains that the reader's ability to choose particular paths through a body of information represents a "clear sign of such transference of authorial power" (p. 71), and this coincides with Barthes' suggestion that the reader of a writerly text is not simply the consumer of a predetermined set of meanings. The choices present at any point in a hypertext require both material and cognitive efforts that exceed those traditionally associated with print; the reader is ultimately responsible for her own version of a hypertext. Furthermore, as Landow and others following him have noted, Barthes' (1974) vocabulary itself—he speaks of a "galaxy of signifiers," multiple "networks," and "several entrances" to the writerly text, none of which are privileged over the others (p. 5)—seems eerily prescient. Regardless of whether this warrants the conclusions that Landow offers, the fit between hypertext and the writerly seems a secure one.

Yet Barthes' (1974) ideal text and active reader are postulated within a particular technological context—the discursive economy of print. Although that does not present Barthes with any trouble, hypertext criticism has ignored that context, an unusual strategy given its goals. It is instructive in this regard to turn to a defender of that context for an idea of how important it can be. In *The Gutenberg Elegies*, Sven Birkerts (1995) offers a commonsensical description of the relationship between reading and writing, one typical of both print technology and the modernist figure of the author:

> We might reach a more inclusive understanding of reading (and writing) if we think in terms of a continuum. At one end, the writer—the flesh-and-blood individual; at the other, the flesh-and-blood reader. In the center, the words, the turning pages, the decoding intelligence. (p. 96)

Birkerts' "continuum" represents a fairly typical understanding of the discursive economy of print (and a fair approximation of the communication triangle, for that matter). The transaction represented by this continuum, in the minds of most people, is relatively transparent, and this is the same transparency that disciplinary work on invention has struggled against. Although no act of reading or writing can be fully divorced from its context, Birkerts' work is testimony to the suasive force of the illusion that it can.

There are many problems with this kind of model. However, for our purposes, the most relevant of them is that Birkerts (1995) makes reading and writing into a zero-sum proposition. Birkerts continues, "Writing is the monumentally complex operation whereby experience, insight, and imagination are distilled into language; reading is the equally complex operation that disperses these distilled elements into another person's life" (p. 96). Although Landow, following Barthes, posits the relation between these operations as asymmetric, he does so without questioning the assumption that this relation is zero sum;[4] a change on one side of the binary triggers a corresponding (inverse) change in the other. If electronic writing requires a more active, involved reader, one that produces the text as she reads, then it stands to reason (in this model) that the author's responsibility for and control over the text are proportionally less.

We can see this logic functioning in the passage from Landow (1997) cited in the beginning of this section. The "convergence" of the activities of reading and writing are brought "one step closer" by "removing" some of the writer's authority and giving it to the reader (p. 71). As long as the relationship between author and reader is a closed system, this explanation does make sense. Like LeFevre, however, Barthes is specifically arguing against closed systems; for him, "the writerly text is not a thing" (p. 5). Just as LeFevre works against a particular perception of invention, Barthes attempts to combat the discursive economy typified earlier by Birkerts. It is not that some texts are readerly and some are writerly; rather, individual works occur within the "galaxy of signifiers," and reading that focuses on the isolated works and attempts to "give it a (more or less justified, more or less free) meaning" (p. 5) is the kind of activity that Barthes resists.

What does it mean, then, to describe a text as writerly? To put it another way, what does labeling a text as writerly tell us about the text? According to Barthes, very little. Instead, it tells us how the reader behaves with respect to a text, a focus appropriate to Barthes' concern with language *practice*, rather than specific works of literature. It is not difficult to imagine the ways a given text (or hypertext) might influence this practice in different ways, but it would run counter to Barthes's distinction to suggest that the text itself determines the reader's approach.[5] The best that we might say is that certain texts encourage readers to take the sort of initiative suggested by the writerly. This "encouragement," however, ultimately depends on the reader, not the text. This claim can be extended to Michael

Joyce's (1995) parallel categories—constructive and exploratory hypertexts correspond to writerly and readerly texts respectively—and points out a relatively obvious problem. If we define texts according to how they are used, then the only way those definitions can have any meaning or utility is if audiences approach the text in the same way every time, which runs counter to the way that hypertext was theorized by this first wave of scholars.

To put it another way, although Aarseth (1997) does not really spend time discussing Barthes, he comes closer to Barthes' work than Landow when he explains that the politics of the relationship among authors and readers "depends much more on the user's own motivation than on whatever political structure the text appears to impose" (p. 164). Like Barthes, Aarseth's work tends away from the referential, asking instead what practices are encouraged or enabled by a particular text, practices that include interpretation, but are not limited by it.[6] This is the value of considering invention ecologically; as LeFevre (1987) explains, invention is not simply the process by which a writer creates a text whose meaning is received by a reader. The ecology of invention includes the practices of writing and reading, but the relationships among those practices are not closed, idealized, and privatized transactions. The complexity of invention is one of the most relevant pieces missing from the puzzle of electronic authorship, at least as early hypertext critics approached it.

HERMENEUTIC AND PROAIRETIC INVENTION

To get at that complexity, I leave the parallel approaches of invention and hypertext theories momentarily and return to them in the following section. For the moment, however, I wish to consider more closely the source for the distinction between readerly and writerly texts, a distinction that occupies such a prominent place in hypertext theory. Barthes' (1974) discussion of those terms takes place over a relatively small stretch of pages in *S/Z*, in a theoretical aside to the primary thrust of that book, an exemplary performance of the kind of reading that Barthes is advocating when he turns to the readerly/writerly distinction.

S/Z is a prime example of a text that operates almost exclusively at the level of ecologies of practice; although his argument is mostly implicit, Barthes' book is a direct refutation of the assumption that realist literature simply reflected reality, as faithfully as possible, to its readers. Although he could have made this argument more concisely and theoretically, Barthes' text is an analytic *tour de force*, instead subjecting a Balzac short story ("Sarrasine") to a painstaking explication. Barthes breaks the text into 561 *lexias*, or units of reading, sometimes composed of a few words and sometimes several sentences. His broader point is that what some readers may take as realistic, natural, or reflective of reality in the work of Balzac (a realist *par excellence*) is in fact carefully constructed to appear that way, no more nor less natural than any other literary style.[7] Another way to consider Barthes' performance of reading here is in terms that my own project sets forth: In many ways, Barthes argues that any individual literary text is an interface, an individualized interaction with a "galaxy of signifiers" and literary strategies.

How does he accomplish this? To perform a "writerly" reading of Balzac's "Sarrasine," Barthes (1974) outlines five codes.[8] "Without straining a point," he explains, "there will be no other codes throughout the story but these five, and each and every lexia will fall under one of these five codes" (p. 19). Listed in "order of appearance" rather than importance, Barthes identifies them as hermeneutic, semantic, symbolic, proairetic, and cultural. Of these five, there are three (cultural, semantic, and symbolic) that Barthes labels reversible; in other words, these codes make reference to extratextual ideas, associations, or references, and their presence within a text then becomes part of the extratextual field for subsequent works. We are concerned here, rather, with the irreversible codes—the hermeneutic and the proairetic.

According to Barthes, the two irreversible codes function to make a text readerly—to reduce its plurality by forcing it to adhere to a particular "logico-temporal order" (p. 30). The hermeneutic code operates through the establishment of an enigma, void, or mystery—an absence—that will be fulfilled eventually, but is held in suspense. The hermeneutic marks the goal(s) toward which the reader (and the plot and characters) are headed. The proairetic works in concert with the hermeneutic, but from the other end of things. Barthes uses the proairetic to indicate actions or events— "whoever reads the text amasses certain data under some generic titles for actions (*stroll, murder, rendezvous*), and this title embodies the sequence" (p. 19). Within the context of a murder mystery, for example, the discovery of a corpse might serve as an example of each code. On the one hand, it establishes an enigma (who did it? how did this happen?) that such a story will eventually resolve. On the other hand, it is an irreversible action that precludes some actions and predisposes the character(s) to others (who could have done it? what will we do next?). Between the "truth" of the hermeneutic and the "empirics" of the proairetic, "the modern text comes into being" (p. 30).

The interaction between these two codes is likely so familiar to us that it may seem unusual to consider them separately. The simultaneous push of action and pull of meaning combine for us in the desire for closure. Jane Douglas (2000) accounts for this desire in her description of reading:

> Reading is, more than anything, an act of faith, belief that, by the time we reach the ending, everything we have witnessed will at last make perfect sense, all our nagging questions will have been answered, all disputes settled, all the wayward thread corralled into a tidy unity: something we can lay to rest before comfortably turning our backs on it. (p. 90)

As Douglas demonstrates in *The End of Books—Or Books without End? Reading Interactive Narratives*, closure is not a single, unified phenomenon, and yet it rests heavily on the side of the hermeneutic. As in the previous example, an event may serve both functions; it is not difficult to imagine any number of actions that raise "nagging questions" that will be answered by the end of a given text. The closing implicit in "closure" is a closing off of alternatives, the reduction of a text's plurality. To borrow from Pierre Lévy (1998), whose work we consider in the next section, the hermeneutic code temporarily virtualizes a situation as a means of heightening our expectations (and narrative pleasure) until the point where the enigma (or set of enigmas) is resolved, actualized into a "tidy unity."

Hermeneutics, as resolution or actualization, is in fact probably more familiar to us as a centuries-old tradition of textual reading and understanding, and, as such, it is relatively simple to imagine what it might look like separated from the proairetic. Within a particular text, the hermeneutic combines with the proairetic to generate what we might call textual momentum, with the understanding that this momentum is directed at a specific end, the resolution of the enigma. Elevated to the level of theory, hermeneutics simply assumes systemic enigmas, such as the establishment of genre or the demonstration of a theoretical insight. The quest for meaning takes place both within the logico-temporal order of a given text and amid the network of textuality in general.[9] This model of reading is so common, in fact, that it all but overwhelms the proairetic, which is ultimately judged in the context of the hermeneutic. Actions or events that fail to move the reader toward the resolution of the hermeneutic enigma are quite literally extravagant: They are off-track and may even be resented as wasteful or distracting.

What would it mean, however, to focus on the practice of proairesis and to do so without subordinating it to hermeneutics? Barthes (1972) suggests a similar tactic in his essay "To Write: An Intransitive Verb?" when he considers the "middle voice." Eric Charles White (1987) describes it as follows:

> The task, he says, is "to rethink the lost category and to take it as a metaphorical model . . . to reclaim it by raising it to the level of discourse." The loss at the grammatical level can thus be compensated for at the rhetorical level in an activity of invention that continually recurs to its own occasion, a practice of speculative thought in which subject and object are engaged in an endless process of mutual transformation. (pp. 53–54)

White's name for this activity is *kaironomia*, an inventional practice that locates itself not within repetition (the demonstration of topoi) or difference (the myth of the originary genius), but in the dynamic between the two. This dynamic, for White, represents a "contradictory injunction," he explains. "At the same time that it programmatically denies the possibility of definitive truth, it will nevertheless dream of once and for all deciphering the meaning of the world" (p. 72). In a sense, then, it is difficult to isolate the push of proairesis from the pull of hermeneutics, the temptation of meaning. But proairesis reintroduces what Lyotard describes (in one of this chapter's epigraphs) as a commitment to the *je ne sais quoi*. White explains that such a commitment "will issue, then, in an endlessly proliferating style deployed according to no overarching principle or rational design" (p. 21) because it is contingent on the present moment, the constantly changing conditions to which it responds. Much like DeWitt's emphasis on the ongoing process of drawing connections (or linkages, in Lyotard's parlance), White would have us see invention as a practice that constantly generates "point[s] of departure for further acts of rhetorical invention" (p. 81). Unlike DeWitt, however, the results of the "will to invent" are successful when generative. For White, it is not about reaching a solid or sturdy endpoint or object. Instead, it is "a practice of rhetorical invention that permanently resists closure" (p. 57).

VIRTUAL(IZED) AUTHORSHIP

As I explained earlier in this chapter, much of our field's work on invention makes certain assumptions about the final result; even if we wished to "permanently resist closure," our institutions impose it on us. As a consequence, and much like Birkerts' (1995) "monumentally complex operation" of authorship, what we often mean by invention is necessarily hermeneutic, assuming a particular resolution. We may remove the capital A from Author, but even the most socially informed theories of invention, if they are targeted at static artifacts, can only do so much.

Hypertext criticism carries some hints of the change that new media offers for the dynamics between writers and readers. However, because much of it is concerned with differentiating electronic discourse from print, those hints remain buried at the level of theory. For example, one of the most frequent analogies offered for the link is the footnote from print texts.[10] Footnotes, of course, are subordinate to the main text; we might even describe them as subordinate to the main *texts* because they often contain references to other works. When we come across a footnote as readers, we either read it and return to the main text or we ignore it. Landow (1997) writes that "This kind of reading constitutes the basic experience and starting point of hypertext" (p. 4) and follows by asking his readers to imagine being able to follow the links in a footnote to other works as well. According to Landow, this scenario demonstrates the blurring of writer and reader, but it bears a strong resemblance to LeFevre's inclusion of the audience in the ecology of invention.

More accurately, the footnote example demonstrates a process of (academic) reading, suggesting nothing that is especially new to those who write academic prose. With its emphasis on citation, academic writing brings the *practices* of reading and writing more closely together, certainly, and this proximity is something that most academic writers struggle with at one point or another in their careers. But it is also counterbalanced with heavily articulated intellectual property and/or plagiarism standards that suggest that the distinction between writer and reader is not quite as blurry as Landow (1997) would have it. Most important, however, what Landow describes as the basic experience of hypertext corresponds more closely to a specific—academic—practice of reading. Academics are trained to read networks of scholarship that, even in a print context, are densely interlinked and connected, if not digitized. We learn to situate our own work within those networks, providing links in the forms of citations, foot- or endnotes, and bibliographic entries. The texts that we produce bear a strong resemblance to individual readings of a hypertext: We choose particular paths through webs of scholarship, keep track of those paths, and account for them by publishing essays and books that then occupy a place within the webs that we have engaged.

My description of this process should be recognizable, both as an account of scholarly work and also as a parallel to Bawarshi's (2003) description of genre in the first section of this chapter. In other words, it is possible to read a given discipline, subdiscipline, or topic area as a "motive-potential which frames the possible ways of acting and meaning in any given time and space" (p. 89). Regardless of whether we are aware of those broader issues, we read and write to actualize that potential. But these content areas, just like Bawarshi's genres, are metatextual; that is, they comprise various works that provide future writers with ranges of possibility for action, intention, and meaning. The question, the starting point, should not be to ask what happens when all of those works are connected digitally because they are already connected in practice, either as members of a stable-enough genre or as examples of a particular field of study. Rather, the question that hypertext poses is what happens when that metatextuality is built into a single work? Hypertext criticism has half of the answer, in its emphasis on the activity of the reader, who actualizes paths within a broader field of content. In this way, it is not unreasonable to suggest that the reader of new media acquires some of the agency of the writer. But as I explained earlier, to assume subsequently that the writer cedes power or agency as a result is to think within the discursive economy of print.

The other half of the answer requires us to think outside of that economy. Invention theory has worked to expand our conception of authorship, seeing individual writers not in isolation, but as localized agents of a much richer, more distributed ecology of connections. In Bawarshi's (2003) model of invention, genres provide a motive potential that is actualized by individual writers exercising intention:

> Intention is where motive-potential becomes internalized by actors and then articulated as agency. Whereas motive is socially defined, intention is an individualized interpretation and instantiation of social motive. Intention is a form of social cognition—an embodiment of desire and the means by which individuals become social agents, interpreting and carrying out the social motives available to them. (p. 90)

Whether formulated as the instantiation of social motive, as before, or as a localization of the "interaction with social context and culture" (LeFevre,

1987), or even the computer-mediated site of "a connection between two or more initial discoveries" (DeWitt, 2001), invention theory still focuses its energies on the individual writer, with her work functioning as product. I want to suggest, however, that new media encourages us to consider a more radical distribution of individual intention, figured less as a decrease in authorial agency or power and more as a different activity entirely, one that exceeds authorship as we experience it in a print context.

Bawarshi (2003) draws on the work of Giddens and Halliday to articulate the relationship between genres and writers—work that can be traced genealogically back to Aristotle's distinction between potential and actual substances. In the case of each of these frameworks, the movement is from potential to actual, simultaneously the narrowing and actualizing of one of many possibilities. In *Becoming Virtual: Reality in the Digital Age*, Pierre Lévy (1998) articulates this movement succinctly, explaining that "Thought is actualized in a text and a text in the act of reading (interpretation)" (p. 56). But Lévy asks us to think counterintuitively when it comes to hypertext:

> Ascending the slope of actualization, the transition to hypertext is a form of virtualization. This ascent doesn't return us to the thought of an author, but turns the actual text into one of many possible figures in an available, mobile, freely reconfigurable, textual field, and thus connects it with other texts, incorporates it in the structure of other hypertexts and the various instruments of interpretation. By doing so, hypertextualization multiplies our opportunities for producing meaning and makes the act of reading considerably richer. (p. 56)

For Lévy, as for Landow, the reader of hypertext occupies a place on the "slope of actualization" that we have traditionally viewed as the province of the author. To the extent that the writer remains at that place, we might say that the "boundaries between the [two]" are indeed blurred. But Lévy's point is that the author, with hypertext, must change the direction of her activity.

If an individual text is the actualization of possible connections, then an individual reading within a network, inventing that network requires what Lévy (1998) describes as virtualization, "the opposite of reading in the sense that it produces, from an initial text, a textual reserve and instruments of composition with which a navigator can project a multitude of other texts" (p. 54). From within a discursive economy of print, this kind of counterintuitive thinking does indeed seem a "minor Copernican revolution." Returning again to Bawarshi, how does one "invent" a genre or the kind of field of inquiry from which academic writers actualize their own scholarship?

The question of virtualization becomes easier to answer if we think of it in terms of proairetic invention rather than the hermeneutic variety, and Aarseth's (1997) ability to think beyond interpretation is of help here. Because he refuses to focus exclusively on literary objects, many of the cybertexts that Aarseth describes, in both print and electronic contexts, give us commonsense examples of virtualized, proairetic inventions. For example, a deck of playing cards yields more than 2.5 million five-card actualizations (hands). Fortune-telling devices such as Tarot decks or the *I Ching* combine a finite series of archetypes with the experiences of an individual interpretant to produce a near-infinite range of actualizations. Taken as "texts," the deck of cards or the *I Ching* combinations represent fairly commonplace examples of what Lévy (1998) describes as textual problematics.

Lévy (1998) notes that "this problematic exists only if we take into consideration the human-machine interaction and not only computer-based processes" (pp. 54–55), an issue I take up in more detail in chapter 7. For the moment, it is important to note that a deck of cards means little outside of a particular set of rules and one or more players. Similarly, there are many new media "texts" that do not "mean" in the same way that we might argue that a particular poem or essay means something. This presents an obvious challenge to our ecologies of invention, which focus almost exclusively on the production and construction of meaning. Part of that challenge is suggested by Lévy, whose distinction between potentialization and virtualization echoes Aarseth's (1997) neglect of the print-electronic distinction. "If we consider the mechanical substrate alone," Aarseth explains, "computer technology provides only a combination of possibles, albeit infinite, and never a problematic domain" (p. 52). It is the human–machine interaction that makes for virtualization. Another way of explaining this idea is to say that a deck of cards yields more than 2.5 million "possible" five-card hands, but an infinite number of "virtual" hands at, say, a poker tournament. Just as the human is a crucial element in moving from possible to virtual, I would argue that the technological, as a site of distribution within an ecology of invention, is important for moving from actual to virtual in our inventional practice. The final section of this chapter attempts to render this claim a little more concrete.

PROAIRESIS: INV-ENGINES

> Rather than calling on a creative inspiration that precedes writing and other *artificial* systems, one can make use of an inventive practice that uses rather than dismisses the artificial.
>
> —Craig Saper 1997)

In the past 10 years or so, any number of media have emerged that allow us to see White's (1987) model of invention as something other than a theoretical abstraction. Closure is not an intrinsic feature of bulletin boards, usenet groups, discussion lists, MOOs/MUDs, databases, weblogs, wikis, and so on. The various writing spaces that we might gather under the heading of new media offer frequent proof in this regard, both for a more social model of invention and for a model that is concerned more with practice than product. In this fashion, those scholars (cf. Ong, Welch) who see in electronic discourse a return to some of the features of orality are not entirely off the mark, for many of these spaces function conversationally. But there is a difference between seeing media such as those listed earlier as spaces that enable peer-to-peer interaction and conversation and seeing them as media that transform the nature of conversation or even participate in it.

Search engines provide a fairly simple example of this difference. Too often they are used (and taught) as a neutral textual apparatus, a source of information, not unlike a table of contents or an index. The advice that our field's handbooks offer frames the search as a purely hermeneutic procedure, advocating a process by which search terms grow ever more precise and results become more and more "accurate." The search engine, used "correctly" in this manner, provides a mirror of the user's interests, one whose imperfections must be minimized. The average search, conducted in this fashion, renders the engine as invisible, leading a writer to her sources as quickly as possible. As such, this conception of searching fits easily into a social model of invention and would cast the search engine as yet another space where interactions take place. We have been slow to acknowledge, however, those ways that even a simple Google search is an interpretation, and as White (1987) asks,

> Rather than asking whether or not a particular interpretation corresponds to the facts, the more appropriate question would be: does it provide a fertile topos or point of departure for further acts of rhetorical invention? (p. 81)

One way we might treat Google proairetically is simply to resist the closure implied in search "results" and to treat that page as a point of departure, even and especially when the results are mixed. The results of a given search provide users with pages and pages of links, of departure points, that bring potentially distant topics and ideas into proximity both with each other and the user.

To be fair, however, Google and other search engines are predicated on a hermeneutic motive on the part of the user; to use Google proairetically is to repurpose it. A better example of a proairetic interface comes from the recent wave of social bookmarking services: del.icio.us, ma.gnolia, CiteULike, Connotea, and so on. (Fig. 3.1). Although each of these services differs from the others in various respects, the basic principles behind social bookmarking services (SBS) are common to each of these alternatives. SBS take the practice of bookmarking, an almost universal feature of web browsers, and transform it in at least three ways. First, SBS are web-based. Rather than storing your bookmarks on a single machine (and in a single browser), these services allow users to store them online, making the bookmarks accessible from any location. Second, although most browsers simply store the URL for a site, many SBS allow their users to provide additional information about the bookmark, in the form of annotations and/or keywords. Finally, and this feature puts the "social" in social bookmarking, these services store the bookmarks from all of its users, making them accessible not only to the original bookmarker, but to the other users as well.

To understand just how these services provide a space for proairetic invention, we might consider just what the interface at a service like del.icio.us permits. With a free user account, and having bookmarked a single webpage, any user can follow that entry to a vast network of other sites. A del.icio.us bookmark contains a relatively small set of information; the service stores the URL, of course, and it records each user who has bookmarked the page, as well as the keywords those users have employed to describe it. So, from a single bookmark, our user can find all the other users who have marked the page and peruse their bookmark collections (portions of which are likely to be related to the original bookmark). From each of the keywords that our user has employed, one can find all of the articles tagged with that term and all of the users who have used that term. Del.icio.us provides a tag list for each bookmark—an aggregation of all the keywords that have been used to describe the page in question. In other words, based on a fairly simple set of rules for drawing connections between users, pages, and tags, del.icio.us (and other SBS) generates an associational network of sources, "endlessly proliferating . . . according to no overarching principle of rational design," to borrow White's (1987) language.

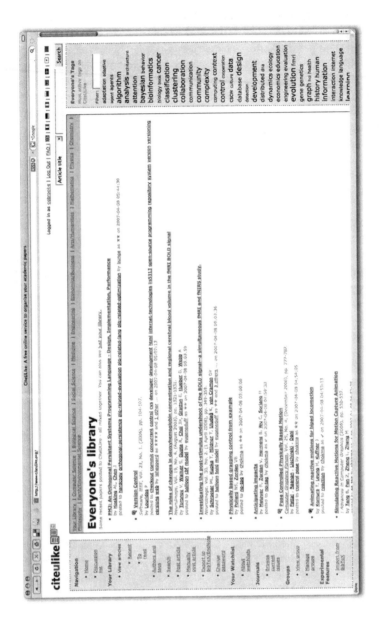

Figure 3.1. A screen shot of the social bookmaking service CiteULike.org

In the first section of this chapter, I mentioned the distinction that DeWitt (2001) endorses, between hypertext as a system and as facilitation; although he elects to focus on the latter, del.icio.us and other SBS provide excellent examples of the former. Although there is nothing to prevent an individual user from putting the results of an exploration of del.icio.us to hermeneutic ends—and it would be both impossible and undesirable to prevent that sort of use—the practice of bookmarking using one of these services is a perfect example of both proairetic invention and how that kind of invention can be intrinsic to a particular interface. The addition of each bookmark changes the site, reinforcing certain connections, adding new ones, and expanding the network in small but important ways. It enables a process of associational research and exploration that resists closure.

Gregory Ulmer's (1994) term for this process is *conduction*, and there is perhaps no better demonstration of a proairetic approach to invention than his book-length mystory, *Heuretics*. Ulmer situates heuretics at the same level as hermeneutics and offers it as a space (*chora*) for experimentation that is the counterpart to analysis and interpretation. As Ulmer (1989) explains in *Teletheory*:

> The "duction" words shared by the fields of logic and electricity, for example, allow the description of a reasoning or generative procedure possessing figura-tively the features of the electronic terms (conduction and transduction). Another way to view the strategy is as a style of thinking by means of an entire set or paradigm, rather than selecting the one unit of the set that apparently (by common sense) would be the "correct" choice. All the terms in the set may be considered relevant to the matter at hand (the invention stage of thought relies on nonsense). (p. 64)

Heuretics is a test or experiment (as opposed to proof) of what becomes Ulmer's injunction to "write the paradigm," that is, to write with sets rather than charting the single, correct path through that set. "The user of a database," he explains, "encounters in principle the full paradigm of possibilities through which a multitude of paths may be traced" (p. 38). In other words, Ulmer's work corresponds almost precisely to Lévy's textual problematic; both are descriptions of the virtualizations possible with electronic writing.

Both Ulmer and Lévy extend our ecologies of invention beyond hermeneutic questions of meaning, as does White for that matter. The question "how do I start?" that dominates pedagogical considerations of invention is more precisely a question of getting to the right answer ("How do I write something that will meet with the approval of my evaluator?"). Lévy, White, and Ulmer each offers insight into what I am calling proairetic invention, a focus on the generation of possibilities, rather than their elimination until all but one are gone and closure is achieved. Closure is no less important now than it ever has been, but with the advent of new media and interfaces that resist closure, proairesis provides an important corrective to the hermeneutically oriented inventional theory that has prevailed in our field to date.

NOTES

1. Bawarshi uses the example of billboards to discuss rhetorical ecosystems, and AdBuster campaigns provide an ideal example of billboards at stabilized enough. AdBusters typically parody well-known advertising campaigns, adhering to visual conventions of the genre while violating their communicative conventions.

2. For example, in her chapter for *Authorship in Composition Studies*, Jonna Gilfus (2006) turns to handbooks' discussion of invention in infer our field's attitudes toward authorship.

3. See, for example, pp. 22-23 of Johndan Johnson-Eilola's (1997) *Nostalgic Angels: Rearticulating Hypertext Writing.*

4. One of the biggest problems with transposing Barthes' work is that few of the scholars who do so are inclined to note its disciplinary context. Barthes' condemnation of "classical texts" is less an argument against specific texts than it is an attempt to dislodge a critical attitude specific to French literary criticism at the time. Phrases like "the death of the author," Barthes' provocative indictment of quasi-biographical literary criticism, have been abused almost beyond recognition in American scholarship. Although the idea of a zero-sum relationship between reader and author can draw on Barthes, I would argue ultimately that it is a misreading to do so.

5. In other words, designating a text as writerly suggests the same relationship that Barthes goes to great lengths to undo in his critique of the readerly. It is not unlike the paradox by which postmodernists, and others interested in subverting canons, have been canonized.

6. Markku Eskilinen (2001), following Aarseth, has repeatedly noted that only a handful of the possible combinations described and taxonimized in Cybertext involve interpretation.

7. S/Z implies an argument familiar to those of us in rhetoric and composition, namely our resistance to the notion that the "truth" is somehow "less rhetorical" than other positions.

8. Because he is identifying their traces within specific text, Barthes uses the term codes; I would argue that the codes he identifies are more accurately termed practices, but I have retained his terminology here for simplicity's sake.
9. In *The Rhetoric of Fiction*, Wayne Booth (1983) suggests that this bifurcation is a normal one, offering it as an analog to his "implied author." See "The Role of Belief," pp. 137-144.
10. See, for example, Snyder (1996), p. 15; Landow (1997), p. 4.

4

PATTERN

That is why, beginning to write without the line, one begins also to reread past writing according to a different organization of space.

—Jacques Derrida (1976)

In the early days of hypertext criticism, if there was a canon of rhetoric that seemed doomed to obsolescence, that canon was arrangement. Most "traditional" definitions of the then-new phenomenon shared the perspective that hypertext had no predetermined order by which it can be read; instead, according to Michael Joyce (1995), "Readers access the symbolic structures of a hypertext electronically in an order that they choose . . . [and those] choices constitute the current state of the hypertext and, in effect, its form" (pp. 20–21). Although any single reader's path through a hypertext may be linear, given perceptual limitations, the text as a whole, they argued, did not privilege any one particular path. Arrangement was no longer a responsibility of the author in such texts; the responsibility for providing order had shifted to the reader.

In an essay explicitly discussing the rhetorical canons, Jay Bolter (1993) went so far as to suggest that hypertext all but does away with arrangement as a practical concern. "Hypertext," he writes, "brings together the canons of delivery and arrangement, in the sense that the arrangement of a hypertext, the order in which the topics appear on the reader's screen, is determined in the act of delivery" (p. 100). To the degree that the reader thus actively selects and shapes a particular reading of a hypertext, Bolter also can write, without any danger of contradiction, that "In a large hypertext with many paths, arrangement is invention" (p. 101). Bolter's collapse of arrangement into invention and delivery is a formation that parallels an earlier subordination to invention and style, one that rapidly became a commonplace among hypertext critics in the early and mid-1990s. Joyce's distinction between exploratory (read-only) and constructive (interactive) hypertexts relies primarily on the difference between invention and delivery, as arrangement is dissolved into them:

> By exploratory use, I mean to describe the increasingly familiar use of hypertext as a delivery of presentational technology. . . . Ideally, an exploratory hypertext should enable its audience members to view and test alternative organizational structures of their own and perhaps compare their own structures of thought with hypertext and traditional ones. (pp. 41–42)

> A constructive hypertext should be a tool for inventing, discovering, viewing and testing multiple, alternative organizational structures as well a tool for comparing these structures of thought with more traditional ones and transforming one into the other. (pp. 42–43)

Insofar as arrangement remained a rhetorical canon in the context of hypertext, then, its influence was subordinated to other canons and rendered largely irrelevant to the writer in an electronic environment. We can perceive this subordination in the parallelism in Joyce's (1993) comments. The "alternative organizational structures" cited by Joyce serve as a given feature of hypertext in both cases. As such, arrangement provides an invisible backdrop for the difference being articulated, the difference between hypertexts that emphasize their inventional capabilities (constructive) or their presentational achievements (exploratory). In other words, any arrangement that the writer of hypertext might practice becomes irrelevant to the reader who can invent, discover, view, and/or test their own forms.

More recently, as hypertext has given way to the proliferation of new media, critical attitudes toward arrangement have shown little improvement. In *The Language of New Media* (Manovich, 2002), for instance, arrangement is no longer the vestigial canon made obsolete. Instead, for

Manovich, it is the *sine qua non* of rhetoric itself, albeit one that simply extends obsolescence to an entire discipline. He explains that "the sheer existence and popularity of hyperlinking exemplifies the continuing decline of the field of rhetoric in the modern era" (p. 77). The modularity of new media textuality, according to Manovich, makes arrangement, and hence rhetoric, unnecessary, although he is willing to grant in a footnote on the following page the possibility that "new digital rhetoric may have less to do with arranging information in a particular order and more to do simply with selecting what is included and what is not included in the total corpus presented" (p. 78).

Joyce, Bolter, and later Manovich all operate with a straw version of arrangement, however. The idea that hypertext, or new media in general, no longer has a use for arrangement is not a particularly persuasive one. In Book VII of Quintilian's (1953) *Institutio Oratoria*, he imports a metaphor from architecture to argue for the importance of arrangement:

> But just as it is not sufficient for those who are erecting a building merely to collect stone and timber and other building materials, but skilled masons are required to arrange and place them, so in speaking, however abundant the matter may be, it will merely form a confused heap unless arrangement be employed to reduce it to order and to give it connexion and firmness of structure. (preface)

To continue Quintilian's metaphor, we might argue that, just because there is more than one way to walk through a building, this does not make its arrangement (architecture) irrelevant. So too with hypertext, and so too with the modular texts that Manovich imagines. He writes that "it is perhaps more accurate to think of the new media culture as an infinite flat surface where individual texts are placed in no particular order" (p. 77), and yet in the process of building meaning out of that surface, he ignores the order that we regularly impose on it. The links that allegedly demonstrate the irrelevance of rhetoric are rhetorical practices of arrangement, attempts to communicate affinities, connections, and relationships.

The mistake that each of these writers makes is to presume that arrangement must be an all-or-nothing affair: Either a text is painstakingly ordered by its producer and passively consumed or new media is the "confused heap" that Quintilian warns of, where, according again to Manovich (2002), "the acceptance of hyperlinking in the 1980s can be correlated with the contemporary culture's suspicion of all hierarchies" (p. 76). Needless to say, there is considerable space to be found between these two options, and this chapter devotes itself, in part, to exploring some of it.

Initially, I take up the issue of discursive space, arguing that with new media the traditional understanding of *arrangement as sequence* is more productively conceptualized as *arrangement as pattern*. This first section takes another look at the work of Jay Bolter and draws on the writing of Mark Bernstein and David Weinberger, among others, to suggest that writing with new media is to engage in the practice of patterning.

The second section of this chapter takes up a question that has provoked a fair amount of discussion, particularly in the wake of Manovich's work—namely, the opposition of narrative and database as cultural forms. As the earlier selections from Manovich imply, he is often credited with posing them in opposition to one another and dismissing the impact of narrative and its cognates in favor of a new media culture dependent on the database. Finally, this chapter turns to a couple of different examples of the practice of patterning that is possible with new media, focusing on the construction of databases at a more personal scale (as collections), as well as a feature common to several new media platforms—the tagcloud. One of the assumptions underlying this chapter is that arrangement, which for a long time has been one of the most visible of canons, must be thought of in terms of *practice* if it is to thrive in the interfaces of new media. Whether a particular textual object evinces signs of arrangement is a question that is left over from print culture; the issue is not whether arrangement predates our textual encounters, but rather what practices we might develop with new media to make sense of them.

FROM SEQUENCE TO PATTERN

Each technology gives us a different space.
—Jay David Bolter (1991)

It is a fairly modest claim to assert that the canon of arrangement is the one where concerns of discourse and space interact. As Nedra Reynolds (1998) has observed, it is difficult (if not impossible) to talk about writing without relying on a wealth of spatial metaphors. According to Reynolds, they "have long dominated our written discourse in this field because, first, writing itself is spatial, or we cannot very well conceive of writing in ways other than spatial. . . . To control textual space well is to be a good writer . . ." (pp. 14–15). However, we tend to see through these metaphors. We do so because "the property of the sign is not to be an image" (Derrida, 1976, p. 45), that is, because print texts, for all that they standardize and make visible a certain spatial relationship, do so only so that this spatiality becomes transparent to us. As Bolter explains, print is a technology that depends on such transparency; the "visual minimum" of the printed page allows us to engage more single-mindedly with the text.

But one of the accomplishments of new media has been to problematize that visual minimum. In an issue of the *Iowa Review Web* devoted to "reconfiguring place and space in new media writing," Scott Rettberg (2006) offers the following overview:

> In most hypertext fiction, the role of chronology in structuring the narrative is greatly diminished in comparison to print fiction conventions. In the absence of chronology, the authors of fragmented multilinear narratives need to offer their readers other tools for navigating the text. In an environment described as *cyberspace*, developed with *home* pages on web *sites*, geographical metaphors make almost intuitive sense. ("Editor's Introduction")

Manovich (2002) suggests that this privileging of geography over chronology, of space over time, is a case where the effects of postmodernism on our culture have been made literal by new media. Any new aesthetic or rhetoric, he explains, "may have less to do with the ordering of time by a writer or an orator, and more with spatial wandering" (p. 78). It is tempting to follow Manovich and to see the binary of space and time (as they relate to discourse) as an opposition. Rettberg's claim is more modest because he understands each as a solution to the navigational challenges faced by readers of *any* text, and it is this latter position that is ultimately more fruitful. We encounter all texts in the context of space and time; it is not especially productive to imagine some as spatial and others as temporal. We should instead amend Bolter's comment to read that every technology gives us not only a different space, but a different time as well.

It is in the strategies that we develop as readers and writers that the differing times and spaces generated by various technologies are achieved. Hence, for the purposes of this chapter, it is worthwhile to ask what kinds of spatial practices we engage in with print and how those practices might change as we encounter new media. New media writing subverts the expectations that we have for print texts. According to Darsie Bowden (1993), those expectations (particularly in rhetoric and composition) have taken the form of containerism, a set of metaphors that posit the discursive space of writing as a container into which we pour content (from the containers that are our minds). One of the primary implications of containerism, according to Bowden, is the establishment of an in/out distinction that corresponds to our notions of subjectivity and identity and, as such, appears quite natural to us. Discursive space is reified, external, and prior to the process by which we fill it in this model. The text as container is generic until it is filled with content and achieves some sort of meaning, a metaphor that relies heavily on classical understandings of space, which, as Victor Burgin (1996) explains,

> . . . is still predominantly an amalgam of Newton and Aristotle—"places in space," a system of centers of human affairs (homes, workplaces, cities) deployed within a uniformly regular and vaguely endless "space in itself." (p. 42)

To read a print text is to exist in this a priori space, then, but it is to do so within the safe boundaries of the container text, which "limits and restricts forces within the container" (Bowden, 1993, p. 368). According to Bowden, "Because of this restraint of forces, the contained object gets a relative fixity of location" (p. 368). We are conditioned to place ourselves within the container text when we read, to the extent that when our texts fail to provide containment, our fixity of location turns to disorientation, one of the reasons that Rettberg suggests that geographical metaphors provide such an intuitive fit with new media writing.

Within the context of containerism, the canon of arrangement is not particularly dynamic. In fact, as Jeanne Fahnestock (1996) has observed, "there is an inevitable tendency in the manuals and pedagogical tradition for arrangement advice to become fixed rather than contingent" (p. 35), a tendency that Erika Lindemann and Ann Berthoff, among others, have attempted to resist in their work with an emphasis on form as opposed to formula. Within the text as container, the space presents the illusion that the full meaning of a text can be captured in linearity—a phenomenon that Derrida (1976) describes as "the repression of pluri-dimensional symbolic thought" (p. 86). Regardless of how intricately or complexly interwoven a set of topics may appear to us, the text as container both allows and encourages us to accomplish it through sequentiality—we also might say that it requires us to do so. As Peter Elbow (2006) explains it, somewhat more colorfully,

> When we read a text, we are like the ant. The text is laid out in space across multiple pages, but we can only read one small part at a time.

We may jump around the text, grasshopper-like—especially with long texts—looking at chapter titles and other headings, browsing the openings and closings of chapters, looking for "perspective." Some texts lead off with an abstract—as this journal now asks. Books have tables of contents. But still we can take in relatively few words at a time. (p. 621)

Elbow's solution to the sequentiality of the printed page is to explore other means of "good organization for events that take place in time," such as music, but such exploration ignores the proliferation of new media forms that carry with them different conceptions of space than are provided by printed pages.

According to David Weinberger (2002), the first step in acknowledging the different space(s) of the Web is to shed the metaphor of the container. "Real-world space is a preexisting container in which the things of the world exist," he explains. "Web space is created by the things in it" (p. 44). One example of the kind of misunderstanding Weinberger wants to correct comes from the world of e-commerce. He is critical of "traditional" companies that design their web presence as containers (often represented as "silos"), whose goal is to keep customers from ever finding what they need and ever leaving the site. By locking visitors into the site, or at least making it difficult for them to leave, such companies assume that they have a better chance of making sales. But this kind of design runs counter to one of the distinct advantages of the Web—the ability to visit a competitor's site without having to drive across town. The Web feels spatial, explains Weinberger, "because it's 'place-ial' and, because until now all our places have been in space, when we see a place we assume it must exist in space" (p. 50). This goes some distance toward explaining the behavior of many commerce sites, which attempt to replicate the "stickiness" of bricks-and-mortar sites. Most consumers are not going to want to spend the time to visit competitors' stores in an effort to find the best price; visiting competitors' sites on the Web is a much more convenient process.

Weinberger (2002) goes so far as to explain that the Web is, in fact, the opposite of a container, "explosive, outbound, digressive" (p. 55). One of the things that this means for a revised canon of arrangement is that we can no longer rely on the formulae that Fahnestock describes. Weinberger describes a "sense of place that creates its own space" in his discussion of the Web. Although there is nothing to stop us from replicating sequence online (indeed, many of our discipline's electronic publications do just this), it would be somewhat absurd to stop there. The model of space that Weinberger describes is an active one when compared to the passive conception of space "as a container, as the grand 'outside' of everything that exists." In other words, as he explains, "If I write a page, it becomes part of the Web, and thus extends the Web place" (p. 51). Although we are not necessarily well equipped to understand this distinction, the Web offers us what Weinberger calls "places without space." Ideally, this means that we should be able to find some middle ground between the sequentiality of the printed page and the "confused heap" that Quintilian warns against.

There are some places in hypertext theory where linearity is not offered as an all-or-nothing concern. For example, in the essay "Socrates in the Labyrinth," David Kolb (1994) explains,

> We need to understand better the ways in which links and paths can enact forms and figures (intermediate between the lexia and the whole document) that bring pressure to bear upon the "internal" being of the individual lexias . . . because we must avoid the temptation of seeing hypertext either as a collection of atomistic information units or as an infinite play of signifiers. (p. 336)

Kolb calls here for us to attend to the spaces that we build through the creation of place, forms that lie somewhere in between the containers that print has encouraged and the paralyzing freedom of an infinitely open space. One of the writers to take up Kolb's challenge was Mark Bernstein (2006), of Eastgate Systems, who delivered a talk on "Patterns of Hypertext" for the Hypertext '98 conference. His essay suggests a number of intermediate forms (cycles, counterpoints, mirror worlds, tangles, sieves, montages, neighborhoods, split/joins, missing links, and feints), patterns that demonstrate a variety of rhetorical effects that are possible if we think beyond the container model, effects not unlike those proposed by Winston Weathers (1980) in his work on "Grammar B." For example, the following is a portion of his discussion on the Cycle:

> In the Cycle, the reader returns to a previously visited node and eventually departs along a new path. Cycles create recurrence and so express the presence of structure. Kolb's *Socrates In The Labyrinth* discusses the role of the Cycle in argumentation, showing how hypertext cycles emerge naturally from traditional argumentative forms. Cyclical repetition also modulates the experience of the hypertext, emphasizing key points while relegating others to the background. Writers may break a cycle automatically by using conditional links, or may use breadcrumbs to guide the user to depart along a new trajectory. Relying on breadcrumbs to break cycles is common on the Web. ("Cycle")

In another essay, Bernstein (1998) offers some of the conceptual underpinning behind the attention he pays to these patterns, returning to a geographical metaphor. Bernstein compares new media writing to the creation of gardens and parks—spaces that provide balance between the notion of indoors and outdoors, between the intentionality of design and the chaos of nature. In a section called "The Virtue of Irregularity," he explains that, "in a hypertext, as in a garden, it is the artful combination of regularity and irregularity that awakens interest and maintains attention." Bernstein's remarks provide an interesting echo to Weinberger (2002), who says much the same thing: "The real stickiness on the Web isn't inconvenience but interest" (p. 55).

One approach to arrangement in the context of new media, then, is to work ourselves free of the regularity of sequential media, to invent the kinds of intermediate forms and figures that Kolb calls for and that Bernstein exemplifies in his essay on "Patterns." At the same time, this approach runs the risk of falling into the formulae that Fahnestock offers—of setting the boundaries of the container a little more expansively, yet leaving them in place. Indeed, this is one of the weaknesses of much of the hypertext theory that celebrates the radical nonlinearity of that textual form. As Johndan Johnson-Eilola (1997) puts it in *Nostalgic Angels*, "Dismantling the technology of the print book does not necessarily remove the social forces that articulated the classic book text" (p. 137). Too often hypertext theory assumed that a change in medium automatically entailed leaving the features of other media behind. In the next section of this chapter, we leave behind containerism for good, turning to the "infinite flat surface" of the database as Manovich articulates it. One of the questions we attempt to answer is whether there is space for the canon of arrangement in that model.

DATABASES, DATA MINING

Therefore, database and narrative are natural enemies.
—Lev Manovich (2002)

One of the lasting contributions that Lev Manovich's (2002) *The Language of New Media* has made to the study of contemporary information technologies is his elevation of the database as an important cultural form. This elevation follows an important thread in the study of technology, one that leads away from hypertext to new media more broadly and that includes, among others, Johnson-Eilola's (1997) critique of the arbitrary distinction between literary and more functional hypertexts (such as help menus), as well as Espen Aarseth's more expansive definition of cybertext, which spoke to the "chauvinism" of technology theories developed by English studies scholars. Too much of the early criticism of discursive technologies presumed a universality on the part of narrative. Counter to this presumption, as Manovich (2002) explains,

> Many new media objects do not tell stories; they do not have a beginning or end; in fact, they do not have any development, thematically, formally, or otherwise that would organize their elements into a sequence. Instead, they are collections of individual items, with every item possessing the same significance as any other. (p. 218)

From the perspective of this definition, it is not difficult to see how the field of rhetoric might seem less than relevant to Manovich. Without sequence, order, development, or causality, the database as a cultural form would not seem to lend itself to the kind of discourse that we typically treat to rhetorical analysis.

Before we speculate about what role rhetoric, and more specifically the canon of arrangement, might play in databases, it is worth our time to be a bit more precise. As Katherine Hayles (2005) has observed, Manovich could be clearer about the relationship between narrative and database, or at least more consistent. At one point he writes,

> As a cultural form, the database represents the world as a list of items, and it refuses to order this list. In contrast, a narrative creates a cause-and-effect trajectory of seemingly unordered items ([or] events). Therefore, database and narrative are natural enemies. Competing for the same territory of human culture, each claims an exclusive right to make meaning out of the world. (p. 225)

At another point, however, Manovich suggests that they are "competing imaginations" that have been with us since the ancient Greeks. At yet another point, he implies that narrative represents a special case, and thus a subset, of database. For Hayles, who acknowledges the value of his work, "[Manovich's] construction of the narrative/database dyad is nevertheless plagued by certain intractable problems" ("Narrating"). These problems arise for her from the "slippages" in the way the terms are deployed.

It is this last definition that I want to take up because I find it one of Manovich's (2002) clearer articulations of the relationship. One of the places that he turns for an analogy to this relationship is Saussurean linguistics. Database and narrative correspond, he writes, to the paradigmatic and syntagmatic dimensions of language, or to *langue* and *parole*. With traditional media, the syntagmatic dimension, the utterance, is the dimension that is present to us, whereas the linguistic paradigm, the sum total of possible choices that we could have made, is virtual. "New media reverse this relationship," according to Manovich. "Database (the paradigm) is given material existence, while narrative (the syntagm) is dematerialized. Paradigm is privileged; syntagm is downplayed. Paradigm is real; syntagm, virtual" (p. 231). Manovich's claim that these dimensions are reversed in the form of the database is a compelling one, but Manovich does not really explore this analogy as fully as he might. In the case of language, it is true that an individual utterance has the advantages of presence and materiality, but it necessarily depends on the paradigmatic resources available to a particular speaker or writer. What is more, that utterance feeds back, however minutely, into the paradigm. Those available resources differ from location to location, in the case of regionalisms, and they differ across time, as usage patterns change. The relationship between the paradigmatic and syntagmatic dimensions of language is more complementary than it is a competition.

If we develop this analogy more fully and move back to Manovich's database-narrative pairing, I think that it helps make more sense of that relationship. At one point, Manovich cites Amazon.com's database of millions of books, for example, but at no point did their database serve simply as paradigm (Fig. 4.1). The motives behind amassing that database were economic—Amazon's database has little meaning unless we also consider the uses to which it is put. Although "customer X buys a book" is not the most exciting narrative, perhaps, it is one that is both enabled by Amazon's database and that feeds back into the database, potentially contributing to the creation of another person's spending narrative. This is to say nothing of the various narratives that have gone into the creation of the book that each customer buys, the narrative of authorship, the review process, the publishing process, the various encounters they have with the book before they purchase it, like friends' recommendations, for instance. What this suggests is that database and narrative are no more "natural enemies" than are *langue* and *parole*, no more than a dictionary and novel are "enemies," although they serve different purposes.

Just as there are hybrids of these print exemplars (Bierce's *The Devil's Dictionary*, Milorad Pavich's *Dictionary of the Khazars*, and Barthes' *A Lover's Discourse* come to mind), it is not difficult to find examples in new

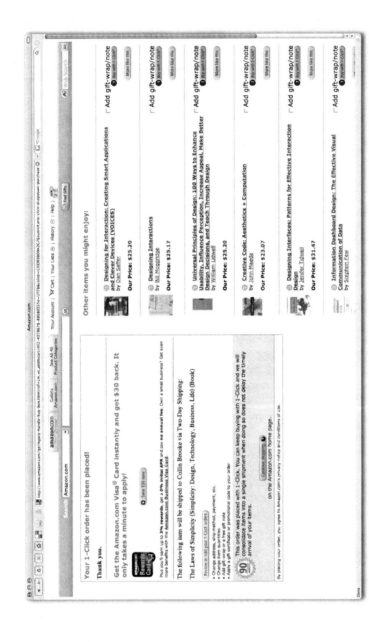

Figure 4.1. Screenshot of Amazon purchase page

media of the different strengths of narrative and database being combined to produce rhetorical effects. Sites like Amazon's are one class of such hybrids, but as we look at the various forms that have emerged in recent years—weblogs, wikis, Web 2.0 sites like Flickr, and so on—it is actually more difficult to locate sites that are purely one or the other (Fig. 4.2). Most important, perhaps, the analogy between narrative/database and *parole/langue* tells us that the key to the relationships between each of these dyads is to be located in *practice*. In itself, language does not actually *mean* anything; it is only when it takes the form of utterance, when it is put into practice, that meaning is generated. The same thing is true of databases; at one point, Manovich (2002) acknowledges this:

> New media objects may or may not employ these highly structured database models; however, from the point of view of the user's experience, a large proportion of them are databases in a more basic sense. They appear as collections of items on which the user can perform various operations—view, navigate, search. The user's experience of such computerized collections is, therefore, quite distinct from reading a narrative or watching a film or navigating an architectural site. (p. 219)

This definition of database as a cultural form, one that shapes our experience as it is used, is more useful than treatments of databases in the abstract. Furthermore, it reopens the door for us to consider rhetoric in the context of databases.

Although databases may contain no predetermined order, they are useful to us to the degree that they provide some sort of order when they are acted on by users. To continue the previous example of Amazon, when we visit that site and search for a particular book, we are imposing a certain amount of order on the database that underlies their site, even if it is an order as minimal as asking the site to display the books by a particular author or on a specific topic of interest. The page for an individual book also contains several different tools for finding books, each of which assumes that all of their products are in fact *not* of equal significance once a search has been initiated. There are often links to other users' ordered lists if the book in question appears on them. Amazon uses aggregated purchase information to offer educated guesses about the kinds of books that a user might be interested in following up on. It would be hard to extend a user's encounter with Amazon into something resembling a full-fledged narrative, but at the same time, the site is designed to respond accurately and *meaningfully* to such encounters—a response that is not accounted for in descriptions of database that stress its utter randomness.

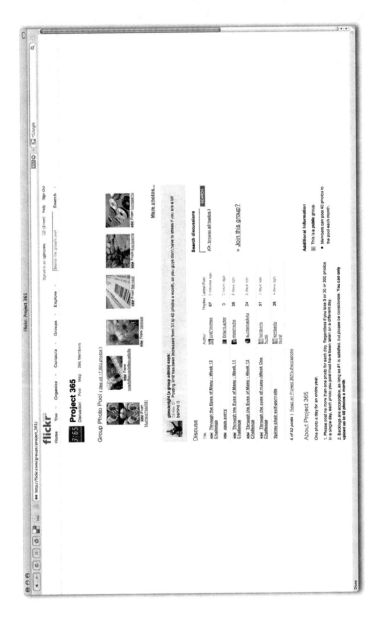

Figure 4.2. Screenshot of a Flickr "365 Days" project

This may seem like a trivial example of the canon of arrangement, but it is only so from the perspective of the individual user. Each purchase that we make at sites like Amazon feeds into the patterns and associations that guide subsequent users' searches, which do the same. When these purchases are aggregated, they become remarkably useful and accurate. If we return briefly to Weinberger's discussion of the Web, it is this kind of shaping implied by his explanation of "places without spaces." The books on Amazon do not exist in "sections," rest on "shelves," or occupy any physical space whatsoever. Much of the data that appear on the page for any individual book are constructed relationally based on the interactions and choices of other site visitors. The patterns that emerge are sets of associations among texts that the site reinforces through visibility, potentially becoming less contingent or temporary as future visitors act on the recommendations generated at the site. As I discuss later, these patterns can acquire significance beyond the collected record of purchases.

We can extend our experience at sites like Amazon to the practice of search more generally, which is in some ways nothing more than the imposition of a particular pattern on a database. It is a pattern that we are familiar with from journalism—the inverted pyramid. Search engines allow one to view and navigate small portions of the colossal database of the Web based on a small set of instructions that we provide in the form of search terms. As best as they are able, search engines locate the sites most relevant to our queries and present them to us in the form of a list ordered from most relevant to least. Again, our own contributions to the database as individuals are small ones. By linking to certain pages and not to others, we fuel the algorithms that search engines' use to determine relevancy. As Ebrahim Ezzy (2006) writes of the latest generation of search tools, however, our own ability to influence the results and affect the patterns may soon grow:

> Third-generation search technologies are designed to combine the scalability of existing internet search engines with new and improved relevancy models; they bring into the equation user preferences, collaboration, collective intelligence, a rich user experience, and many other specialized capabilities that make information more productive. ("Search 2.0")

Tools like those that Ezzy describes make Manovich's diagnosis for rhetoric—that it may simply involve "selecting what is included and what is not included in the total corpus presented"—take on a much more central cultural role when combined with the ubiquity and prevalence of search engines.

If the search tools at a given site like Amazon represent a fragment of what is possible with engines like Google, search represents only a portion of a larger set of practices known as *data mining*. As its name suggests, data mining is a process involving sorting through massive amounts of data to locate information, typically in the form of trends, relationships, and patterns, which is valuable. The kind of information retrieval that Google supports has become ubiquitous to the point of entering our everyday vocabulary, but retrieval is only a small part of what is possible with databases. Unsurprisingly, the most compelling descriptions of data mining come from the business world, where consumption patterns are used to build demographic profiles, to target marketing to the likeliest consumers, and to model trends in an attempt to predict successes and failures.[1] The advantage of data mining is that it provides access to trends and patterns that might not otherwise be perceptible; corporations spend a great deal of time and energy in attempts to find those variables that will give them an advantage in marketing products and services, and data mining is one of the processes by which they locate them.

There is more to data mining than the profit motive, however. Valdis Krebs (2004) is the author of both InFlow, one of the leading applications for network mapping, and a number of different studies conducted with that software. In one such study (repeated three times over the course of about a year), Krebs took the top 100 best-selling political books on Amazon and plotted them onto a network (Fig. 4.3). Each of the books is a single node connected to other books based on whether they appear on the "People who bought this book also bought. . ." feature at Amazon's site. In other words, books were linked in the network when they were purchased together. The results of this study are not particularly surprising: Despite the presence of a handful of "boundary-spanning" books,

> The division between left and right remains strong—polarization and the political food fight continues. Social network metrics, as well as the visuals, show two dense clusters with high preference for homogeneous choices. Echo chambers, on the right and left, remain amongst book readers in America. (Krebs, 2004)

The polarization of the political landscape, Krebs argues, is reflected in these purchase patterns because the patterns themselves hold strong despite the release of two "popular middle books." Lada Adamic and Natalie Glance (2005) later performed a similar analysis (and arrived at similar conclusions) of the political blogosphere by collecting data on the linking patterns of explicitly political weblogs. Both analyses pointed to the kind of polarization that was articulated in mainstream media in the months leading up to the 2004 presidential election in terms of red and blue states. Both projects scale down a large dataset into quickly discernable patterns and turn relatively innocuous data (purchases on Amazon and links on blogrolls) into culturally relevant conclusions.

The advantages of data mining in the academy may not be as obvious to those of us who are not accustomed to handling large sets of quantitative data. The final section of this chapter offers a couple of smaller scale examples of this work, but it is worth calling attention to the work of Franco Moretti (2005), whose *Graphs, Maps, Trees: Abstract Models for a Literary History* attempts to revitalize literary history through data mining. Moretti argues that approaching literary history from the perspective of individual texts is unsystematic to the point of being random. Another example of data mining, one that operates at a smaller scale, is an essay from Anne H. Stevens and Jay Williams (2006) entitled "The Footnote, in Theory." Stevens and Williams tabulate the footnotes from 30 years worth of the journal *Critical Inquiry* and, among other things, present tables of the most frequently cited thinkers, offering Top 10 lists for each of six 5-year periods, as well as an overall list of the top 95. This information provides Stevens and Williams with a place from which to speculate about trends in critical theory, about the rise and/or fall of particular writers, and about the disciplinary role and identity of the journal. Attempts like these to translate the work of humanities scholars into quantifiable data may have their limitations, but increasingly work like Moretti's or Stevens and Williams' is providing interesting avenues of inquiry into scholarly practice. These writers are working with patterns in a way that traditional approaches to the canon of arrangement can only hint at.

PERSONAL PATTERNS: MAPPING AND MINING

In chapter 3, I suggested the social bookmarking service del.icio.us as one example of a proairetic practice of invention, but del.icio.us also serves as an example of the kind of database that operates at a more personal scale than sites like Google or Amazon. There is a case to be made that even something as simple as a purchase at Amazon carries unforeseen rhetorical consequences in the form of the patterns that it contributes to, but the significance of individual purchases is minimal. Amazon's automated recommendation system, which allows individual users to customize their

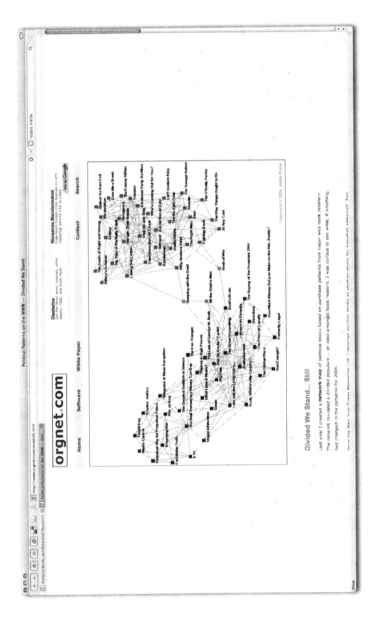

Figure 4.3. Visualization of book network from Krebs

preferences and the results, is closer to an example of a database on a personal scale, one that permits the kind of patterning we are associating in this chapter with the canon of arrangement. A site like del.icio.us, where profit motives do not interfere with the assembly of a personal database, provides an even better example, however. It has the added benefit of allowing users to construct them from the ground up, which offers more control over what is included and excluded. In the previous section, the discussion of data mining might lead us to conclude that our focus on pattern is a focus primarily on the practice of *reading* databases and locating patterns therein. There is equal value in the writing of databases, as Stevens and Williams do in preparation for their essay or as Moretti does in his work. The construction of small-scale databases can create the conditions of possibility for the kind of pattern and relationship analysis carried out under the umbrella of data mining.

It would be more accurate, however, to think of database construction in the proairetic sense discussed in chapter 3. Rather than attempting to record particular patterns (as we do in the structure of a printed essay), building a database of related items allows patterns and relationships to emerge. The extended example I use to describe this process is my own work as the Associate/Online Editor for *College Composition and Communication* (*CCC*), our flagship journal in rhetoric and composition. In 2005, I assumed responsibility for the journal's online presence and, with the help of a few other people, reconceived the mission of the site, turning it into a bibliographic database of the journal's content. Although journal content remained (and remains) password-protected for subscribers only, my team and I began the process of entering metadata (information about the articles, rather than the articles themselves) into a content management system (a software platform used to produce weblogs) and designing multiple navigation points into the database that resulted.

Because the site is attached to a specific journal, the question of what to include and exclude is basically moot. Where Stevens and Williams basically tabulate names in their own study, we were faced with the broader question of what kinds of information to supply at our site. Each entry in the database contains:

- The full (MLA) citation for each article
- A timestamp corresponding to the publication date
- An abstract of the article
- The article's full bibliography
- A list of 10–15 keywords or tags

Additionally, each entry is bookmarked in a del.icio.us account set up exclusively for the site. Much of this information is simply provided in the text of the entry; only the timestamp (which is used to preserve publication chronology) and the keywords (which also are links) are separate. But there also is a set of relationships that we use the software to chart:

- Entries contain links to the pages of articles they have cited
- Entries contain links to the pages of articles who have cited them
- The keywords are links to del.icio.us pages for that keyword

We also supply a link to the original, NCTE-housed content, of course. With these types of relationships included in our database, what begins to emerge is the network of published scholarship that the journal makes visible. In addition to being able to tabulate the number of times particular articles and authors are cited in the journal, we are able to trace the conversations that those citations represent.

Opening the site to del.icio.us has enabled us to provide a keyword index of the journal as well. Each entry lists the keywords for that article, and each keyword is a link to a del.icio.us page that compiles all of the *CCC* articles tagged with that keyword. Del.icio.us creates a separate listing of "related tags" as well so that visitors can do faceted index searches; for example, going to the "technology" page allows a user to click on "pedagogy" and bring up a page listing all those articles tagged with both keywords. As I explain later, the simple presence of keywords/tags generates a variety of patterns that are all but indiscernible otherwise.

Visibility is one of the crucial ways that databases assist our capacity for perceiving these patterns. In many cases, the patterns are already there; to a degree, becoming acclimated to an academic discipline is an apprenticeship in the ability to see them. Where databases contribute is in allowing us to quantify and qualify the relationships among texts (in this case), to spatialize them in such a way that the "perspective" that Elbow writes about earlier is possible. New media interfaces such as blogs and wikis—platforms that allow us to interact on a more intimate scale with databases—make this practice much more accessible than they were even a decade ago. The site for *CCC* requires a small set of specialized scripts, but otherwise it is the same interface that thousands of bloggers use on a daily basis to update their weblogs, and the site is designed to emphasize the collection rather than its weblog-like qualities.

I use the word *collection* consciously here because, rather than offering a choice between narrative or database (as Manovich sometimes implies), new media provide the means of bridging the two productively, allowing us to switch back and forth. One metaphor for this bridge is the collection, the individual assembly of a large group of whatever items we might choose to collect; many of us in academia have massive collections of books, for instance. In the collection *Illuminations*, there's a short essay by Walter Benjamin (1978) called "Unpacking my Library." Benjamin begins this essay with his books in boxes: "The books," he writes, "are not yet on the shelves, not yet touched by the mild boredom of order." What begins here as a database, however, becomes for Benjamin a collection. For Benjamin, the existence of the collector is tied

> to a relationship to objects which does not emphasize their functional, utilitarian value—that is, their usefulness—but studies and loves them as the scene, the stage, of their fate. The most profound enchantment for the collector is the locking of individual items within a magic circle in which they are fixed as the final thrill, the thrill of acquisition, passes over them. Everything remembered and though, everything conscious, becomes the pedestal, the frame, the base, the lock of his property. (p. 60)

There are echoes of Manovich in this passage, the construction of narrative, of narratives plural, from the raw, syntagmatic materials of the database.

Much of Benjamin's (1978) essay is composed of these echoes, but toward the end, he offers some hint as to movement in the other direction. "One thing should be noted," writes Benjamin. "The phenomenon of collecting loses its meaning as it loses its personal owner. Even though public collections may be less objectionable socially and more useful academically than private collections, the objects get their due only in the latter" (p. 67). Once a collection loses the intimacy felt for it by its owner, we might argue that it has drifted back toward the database end of things. We may remember where, when, and how we acquired each of the books on our shelves, but a visitor to our home will experience the collection as database. More generally, we might argue that the relationship between database and narrative is not simply a matter of whether there are patterns among the items collected. I might look at a book on my shelves and recognize it as a purchase belonging to a certain phase in my intellectual development, either ongoing or in the past, and place it into a narrative of that development. Someone coming to that book without my context may connect it with other concerns entirely, based on where it is shelved, what books surround it, and so on. The collection is a quasi-genre that allows different patterns to emerge depending on one's perspective.

In terms of *CCC Online*, weblog software allows us to approach the journal as a collection in Benjamin's sense. Users might trace a particular conversation by consulting each of the articles that cites Maxine Hairston's "Diversity, Ideology, and Writing" or the Elbow/Bartholomae debate, for instance, performing a search that is guided by disciplinary narrative. It is no less possible, however, to treat the journal as a database and search for the term *diversity*. The search results overlap, but are by no means identical. This is consistent with Benjamin's characterizations of the collection in general, whose quality is in part determined by the particular affective investments that one has in relationship to it. The more intimately we are involved in the assembly of a collection, the more likely we are to perceive it incrementally and narratively, while different patterns may emerge in a casual encounter of someone else's collection.

Although the construction of small-scale databases represents one side of the practice of arrangement for new media, I want to close this chapter by describing an emergent new media practice that is more directly involved with patterning—the tagcloud. Tagclouds are weighted lists of keywords extracted from a body of material, whether the back issues of a journal or the entries on an individual weblog. Typically, the terms are presented in alphabetical order, but what adds dimension to the list is that color and font size are often used to display frequency. Although a standard index might simply list keywords, tagclouds allow for users to access terms according to popularity as well. Most important, for this chapter, tagclouds provide the kind of perspective that Elbow describes. Although a tagcloud is no substitute for actually reading a text, it is a snapshot in the same way that tables of contents, indices, and bibliographies often are. Yet tagclouds embody the idea of a collection by offering some idea of the investment attached to particular terms. In a bibliography, a print version of a database, entries are listed with equal significance whether they receive a single, footnoted mention or focus the discussion of an entire chapter. Tables of contents sketch out a more linear approach to a given text. Indices come closer to tagclouds than either of these other forms of metadata, but even then the role of an index is search and retrieval, rather than the representation of the text.

The tagcloud for the 11 most recent volumes of *CCC* articles (Fig. 4.4), which aggregates just over 200 articles' worth of keywords, may not hold many surprises for experienced scholars in rhetoric and composition. In part, this is because the journal expresses a set of core issues that is common to much of our practice—concerns such as language, writing, pedagogy, literacy, community, and culture. We expect, as we move deeper into the archives adding back issues, that the *CCC* tagcloud will remain fairly

Figure 4.4. A tagcloud representing keywords appearing in *CCC* articles, Vols. 47–57

static. But it also provides a synoptic view of the discipline's flagship journal, one that may be of use to someone new to the journal or the discipline.

Tagclouds also can be used to reflect more contingent trends and patterns, however.[2] Many weblogs now feature tagclouds, but often the clouds only reflect a portion of the blogger's activity, such as keywords from the last 3 months' worth of entries. Such a cloud, then, would change along with the blog, reflecting changes in its author's priorities over time and introducing new readers to those priorities. For instance, an academic blogger's tagcloud, if it encapsulates 3 months, might be weighted heavily toward more academic concerns in November than it would be in August. As I explain in chapter 6, this practice also can be considered in terms of memory because it allows bloggers to see patterns that they are enacting, whether consciously or not.

As I hope is clear by this point, the tagcloud is a form of automated data mining that does not require the kind of data collection implied by the work of writers like Krebs, Moretti, or Stevens and Williams. The tagcloud is not as extensive or detailed a model as is generated by the projects of these writers, but, much like weblogs or CCC Online, such clouds represent this practice of patterning at a smaller, more personal scale. The tools necessary for generating a tagcloud are accessible to anyone with a collection and a basic knowledge of HTML. They open up a number of possibilities that take the canon of arrangement beyond the sequentiality of print texts. Rather than seeing arrangement as a canon that is divided into categories like narrative and database, it is possible to reconceive it as a practice that mediates those categories.

NOTES

1. Two relatively recent books that contain examples of data mining are Malcolm Gladwell's *Blink: The Power of Thinking Without Thinking* and Michael Lewis' *Moneyball: The Art of Winning an Unfair Game*, which looks at data-mining techniques applied to baseball scouting.
2. I discuss some of these uses in chapter 6.

5

PERSPECTIVE

The passionate visualist, roaming the labyrinth of the postdisciplinary age, is haunted by the paradoxical ubiquity and degradation of images: everywhere transmitted, universally viewed, but as a category generally despised.

—Barbara Stafford (1998)

To date, style has probably been the most productive canon for explorations of new media; since McLuhan's aphoristic pairing of medium and message, a pairing that maps across the much older opposition between form and content, to speak of media is to speak of forms of expression, the traditional province of the canon of style. Indeed, a great deal of scholarship on new media has taken as nearly tautological the relationship between media and style. More than any other potential site of inquiry, this scholarship has focused on the inextricable combination of visual and verbal elements within new media. Although the relationship between the visual and the verbal certainly did not begin with their copresence on our computer screens, there is a prevailing sense that, somehow, new media have intensified that relationship or, at the least, made our understanding of that relationship more pressing.[1]

It would be nearly impossible to account sufficiently for the relationship between the visual and the verbal in a single chapter, particularly when there are entire books on the subject (e.g., Mitchell's [1995] *Picture Theory*). But it is important to ask exactly what new media bring to that relationship, if anything. It is equally important, in the context of this project, to consider what style might look like when we consider it in terms of interfaces rather than static texts. The answers to both of these questions, I argue, comes from the paradox of *perspective*—a term that, as Keith Moxey (1995) notes, can mean "either one point of view among many, or *the* point which organizes and arranges all the others" (p. 779). In short, I argue here that one of the things that new media interfaces do stylistically is to help us move from the abstracted, single perspective of the reader of a static text or the viewer of a painting to the multiple and partial perspectives necessary for many forms of new media. New media do not somehow abolish mathematical perspective, as if such a thing were even possible. I would argue, however, that they can loosen the hold that perspective has held on our discipline (and many others) for quite some time.

This chapter opens by considering recent attempts to establish a framework for looking at visual rhetoric—efforts that seem to reinscribe the visual into terms and strategies more appropriate for print-based textuality. I contend that much of what has passed for the examination of "visual rhetoric" in our field is more accurately described as "visual grammar." In other words, there are parallels between recent work on the visual in our field and the reduction of style to grammar that we find as far back in our disciplinary histories as Aristotle. The following two sections explore this parallel, finding in Aristotle's treatment of style and metaphor the beginnings of a critical stance that culminates in mathematical perspective. Ultimately, I draw on Friedrich Nietzsche to suggest that we restore style to its place in our ecology of practice, rescuing it from its classical banishment to the ecology of code.

The final two sections offer specific suggestions for achieving this restoration. First, I argue that we need to be wary of calls for the establishment of various synoptic "literacies" that would gather together the visual, verbal, and other forms of meaning-making. Just as chapter 1 suggests that the traditional critical stance is insufficient to account for interfaces, this chapter argues that our field needs to resist the tendency to collect nonverbal media under the banner of literacy. Second, I briefly examine Richard Lanham's (1993) classic *at/through* distinction, laid out in *The Electronic Word*, and argue that a third preposition, *from*, needs to be added to his "bistable decorum" to account for the partiality of new media. This section of the chapter closes with a couple of concrete examples of how this addition might enrich our understanding of style as it applies to new media interfaces.

UNDERSTANDING (VISUAL) RHETORIC

It would not be far from the truth to suggest that rhetoric and composition has undergone a "turn" to the visual over the past 5 years or so. In addition to a great deal of scholarship on the visual, there are several composition readers on the market that take the visual as their focus (e,g., *Picturing Texts, Illuminating Rhetoric, Seeing and Writing*). It would be oversimplifying to suggest that all of this work takes the same approach, and yet there is a strong tendency in our discipline to approach the visual in a somewhat territorializing fashion. For example, in "Understanding Visual Rhetoric in Digital Writing Environments," Mary Hocks (2003) offers rhetoric as her genus, with visual rhetoric as a differentiated subset. Although she critiques visual communication theories for their tendency "to draw too easy a parallel between visual grammar and verbal grammar" (p. 630), that parallel seems implicit in the discussion that follows. "Critiquing and producing writing in digital environments," she writes, "actually offers a welcome return to rhetorical principles" (p. 632), which suggests that the principles in question exist prior to any attempt—verbal, visual, or hybrid—to instantiate them.

Indeed, her article is less about generating strategies than it is about locating these principles as they appear in online texts.[2] "To explain visual rhetoric online to our students, we can begin by carefully articulating the rhetorical features we see in various interactive digital media" (p. 631). Hocks identifies three such features—audience stance, transparency, and hybridity—and proceeds to locate them in three separate web-based documents. There is nothing incorrect with proceeding in this fashion—indeed, this kind of rhetorical analysis is one of the cornerstones of much of our disciplinary activity, but this kind of analysis has its roots in a technologically specific version of rhetoric. The ability to pore over a static document (or hyperlinked set of lexias) and identify specific features presumes both a catalog of preexisting rhetorical features that can be isolated, as well as a static object from which one can achieve critical distance. In short, the model of rhetorical analysis being proposed here by Hocks, and elsewhere in our textbooks and scholarship, is a model we have grown accustomed to through print literacy. Barbara Stafford (1998) attributes this kind of approach to the "linguistic turn" of post-structuralism, explaining:

> Modeling comprehension as a kind of ascetic, even anesthetic, information processing allowed influential academic areas such as semiotic and deconstructive literary theory or interpretive anthropology to reconceive the material subjects of their inquiry as decorporealized signs and encrypted messages requiring decipherment. So Clifford Geertz's narrational view of ethnography as "thick description"—influential on new historicist tendencies in recent scholarship—treated artifacts, behavior, and culture as if they were layered pages in a book demanding sustained decoding. (p. 211)

Hocks (2003) is well aware that "Any rhetorical theory works as a dynamic system of strategies employed for creating, reacting to, and receiving meaning" (p. 632), but the method she outlines in the paragraph that begins with this statement is guilty of the asceticism that Stafford (1998) decries. Her "dynamic system of strategies," which hints promisingly at an ecology of practice, ultimately turns to a grammar for its analysis.

This strategy, locating style grammatically, is so familiar to us as rhetoricians in the late age of print that we frequently take it for granted. Our contemporary understanding of style treats it as sentence-level syntax, catalogs of tropes and figures, and commonplace injunctions (e.g., avoid the passive voice; use specific, concrete language), reducing it to a series of localized, conscious choices. Translated into reception, as Stafford suggests, this model of style allows others' conscious choices to be deciphered, documented, and decontextualized. But this articulation of style is the result of a great deal of misinterpretation.[3] One such misinterpretation is widespread enough that Edward Corbett (1999) begins his chapter on style in *Classical Rhetoric for the Modern Student* with it:

> One notion about style that needs to be erased at the outset is that style is simply "the dress of thought." . . . [A]ny true understanding of the rhetorical function of style . . . precludes the view that style is merely the ornament of thought of that style merely the vehicle for the expression of thought. Style does provide a vehicle for thought, and style can be ornamental; but style is something more than that. (p. 338)

The belief that style is merely or primarily decorative is a persistent one. In "Representing Macbeth: A Case Study in Visual Rhetoric," Hanno H. J.

Ehses (1989) cites Corbett's admonition of this belief, but in the paragraph before he does so, in a discussion of rhetorical figures, Ehses explains that, "The essence of a rhetorical figure is an artful departure from the ordinary and simple method of speaking" (p. 166). In other words, despite his confirmation of Corbett's position, Elses violates it, identifying figures as "artful" deviations from an "ordinary" norm.

Ehses (1989) neglects the possibility that our contemporary understanding of style might have its roots in the position(s) that Corbett urges us to abandon. The result is Ehses' insistence on portraying figures as "departures" and "substitutions" throughout the remainder of the essay—choices that undermine its avowed position. Paul Ricoeur (1977) interrogates this portrayal in the first "study" of his *The Rule of Metaphor* and links it to the decline of rhetoric:

> Indeed, since the Greeks, rhetoric diminished bit by bit to a theory of *style* by cutting itself off from the two parts that generated it, the theories of *argumentation* and of *composition*. Then, in turn, the theory of style shrank to a classification of figures of speech, and this to a theory of tropes. (p. 45)[4]

Ricoeur's study of metaphor begins with Aristotle, but he observes that, by that time, "rhetoric is already a domesticated discipline" (p. 10), having been pacified by Aristotle to preserve it against Platonic critique. Plato dismisses the discipline of rhetoric altogether; in response, Aristotle reconfigures it by rendering it supplemental to philosophy or dialectic.

Ricoeur's (1972) analysis of metaphor is instructive in this regard because much of what he has to say about metaphor can be extrapolated both to Aristotle's treatment of style and to his domestication of rhetoric. Ricoeur identifies a tension in Aristotle's definition of metaphor in the *Poetics*. Aristotle (1991) identifies *lexis* as something that occurs at the level of discursive practice, but this identification is quickly abandoned in favor of a definition of metaphor that occurs at the level of grammar: "Metaphor is the movement of an alien name from either genus to species or from species to genus or from species to species or by analogy" (p. 295). As a result, according to Ricoeur, "the destiny of metaphor is sealed for centuries to come: henceforth it is connected to poetry and rhetoric, not at the level of discourse, but at the level of a segment of discourse, the name or noun" (p. 14).

For Plato, the persuasive qualities of style, and their capacity for abuse, are ultimately blamed on the discipline. Aristotle's reconfiguration of rhetoric allows this blame to be shifted to individual rhetors, those who do the abusing, by making rhetoric instrumental. In effect, for Aristotle, (1991), rhetoric does not mislead people; people mislead people. This attitude appears explicitly in Aristotle's definition of rhetoric, the ability to see the available means of persuasion (p. 36), as well as in his treatment of *lexis*. If rhetoric is merely the art of finding or seeing available means of persuasion, the responsibility for deploying them rests with those who actually speak (or write). In this configuration, rhetoric yields its epistemic force and becomes a more pragmatically oriented, instrumental discipline. The guiding value for rhetoric and, more specifically, for *lexis* becomes appropriateness.

Aristotle is careful not to deny the occasional usefulness of stylized language, but usage that "deviates" from the ordinary is much less appropriate than it is in poetry. In the *Rhetoric*, Aristotle (1991) offers the first formulation of the notion that "authors should compose without being noticed and should seem to speak not artificially but naturally" (p. 222). Although metaphor and style may sometimes serve to enliven discourse, they call attention to it and run the risk of excess for Aristotle. The responsibility for avoiding that risk, for maintaining appropriateness, falls to the rhetor, and it is a responsibility that persists to the present day in our attitudes toward language—from word choice at the barest syntactic level to issues of intellectual property and authorship on the cultural level.

Perhaps most significant for our purposes, however, is the implied distance that Aristotle (1991) establishes between language and its users. One of the sources for Plato's antipathy to rhetoric is its ability to overwhelm (and/or deceive) an audience. In *Preface to Plato*, Eric Havelock (1986) explains the immersive qualities that language held in a predominantly oral culture. Aristotle's answer to this is to provide a theory of rhetoric that places crucial distance between language and those who use it; the Aristotelian rhetor reflects on subject matter, audience, style, and so on, making conscious, rational choices according to criteria that are independent of any specific rhetorical context, but designed to optimize each context. If this is a description of Aristotle's rhetoric at a theoretical level, his definition of metaphor provides an instance of it at the level of code.

It is not as if rhetors did not choose particular words instead of others prior to or following Aristotle. But Aristotle formalizes criteria for making that choice, designating particular names, nouns, or terms as "ordinary" and all others as deviations, substitutions, and/or borrowings. He asserts a positive relationship between the noun and the thing(s) it names, and that relationship provides a measure for metaphor. "Ordinary" language for Aristotle possesses both ontological and rhetorical priority, whereas poetic language represents a conscious change that individual rhetors perform.

Ordinary language provides a kind of zero degree of rhetoric, the unmodified, minimally mediated access to the things. Much like the belief that any sort of literary language is "ordinary language plus," for Aristotle, metaphor (and style and rhetoric more generally) are variations and deviations performed on the clarity of ordinary language.

THE EMERGENCE OF PERSPECTIVE

When Hegel summed up the perfect alphabetism of his time, he called it spirit. The readability of all history and all discourse transformed man or the philosopher into a god.
—Friedrich Kittler (1999)

Although he cites Aristotle's theory of metaphor as one of the origins of rhetoric's decline, Ricoeur (1977) is careful not to place all of the blame on the *Rhetoric*:

> Now this is not to say that Aristotle can be accused of having reduced the fuller scope of rhetoric to a theory of style, much less to a theory of figures of speech, nor that the vitality of his analysis is dissipated in purely taxonomical exercises. . . . If, then, Aristotle is the father of this model, it is not at all because of his definition of the field of rhetoric, and thus of the place of *lexis* in it, but solely because of the central position accorded the noun in the enumeration of the parts of *lexis* and the reference to noun in the definition of metaphor. (p. 47)

Ricoeur's analysis here differs from my own slightly because I would argue that the nominalization of metaphor is part of a broader pattern of instrumentalization—one that does connect the fates of *lexis* and rhetoric more directly than he allows. It is no accident that Aristotle's (1991) exhaustive descriptions and analyses of rhetoric adopt the critical distance that his account of rhetoric encourages. Aristotle is the first to ask and answer thoroughly the question "What is rhetoric?", and his answers have been both persuasive and pervasive, enduring to the present day. With Aristotle, rhetoric acquires the contours of a discipline that can be examined from a distance, as Aristotle demonstrates.

Ricoeur (1977) is correct to avoid laying all the blame for this reduction at the feet of Aristotle, however. Thousands of years and countless choices have elapsed since Aristotle (1991), both figuratively and literally, wrote the book on rhetoric. But it is important to acknowledge those ways that Aristotle both performs and lays the ground for a distanced, analytical perspective, one that prepares future rhetoricians for the kind of critical mastery that we take for granted today as one of the goals of literacy. This perspective, although not necessarily foreign to the oral culture of ancient Greece, becomes far simpler with the emergence of writing:

> It is important to realize that a close textual analysis cannot be performed on a spoken text unless that text is preserved for repeated scrutiny. Analysis proceeds from some kind of preservation, an act that brings with it repeatability. (pp. 85-86)

In *Electric Rhetoric*, Kathleen Welch (1999) adds to the issue of repeatability the technological construction of audience. Although she is dealing there with the intended audience for the transcribed speeches of Isocrates, more generally, she raises the question of the role that technology plays in the construction of author, text, and audience. More specifically for our purposes, she suggests a link between Aristotle and contemporary, impoverished accounts of *lexis*.

The emergence and eventual primacy of writing or literacy is a well-worn topic in technology studies, and I will not rehearse it here except to note that the connection I wish to draw between Aristotle's rhetoric and the development of literacy is meant to be more suggestive than exhaustive. Needless to say, there are many other factors—social, cultural, political, religious, and so on—that play a role in both the development of literacy as well as the people and societies who have practiced it. We are more interested here in the establishment of the critical perspective, which locates the reader outside of the text and elevates her, as Kittler notes of Hegel, to near divine status. Although we have linked Aristotle's rhetoric and the technology of writing to that perspective thus far, the connections extend beyond those two.

The invention of the book coincides roughly with the development of perspective in the visual realm, for instance. Perspective is a method for displaying three-dimensional objects and/or scenes on a two-dimensional space.[5] Much like the technology of writing exteriorizes the reader, perspective presumes a viewer whose physical position mirrors the vanishing point. Robert Romanyshyn (1989) draws a similar conclusion about the relationship between print language and visual perspective:

At approximately the same time that Alberti's procedures are mapping the world as a geometric grid, laying it out in a linear fashion, the book will be introduced and mass produced. The linearity of the geometric world will find its counterpart in the linear literacy of the book, where line by line, sentence by sentence, the chronological structures of the book will mirror the sequential, ordered, linear structure of the sciences. In addition, the interiorization of individual subjectivity within the room of consciousness will find apt expression in the private act of reading and in silence, unlike the manuscript consciousness of the Middle Ages, where reading was done aloud. (p. 351)

Peter Cresswell, (1998), likewise, identifies perspective as one of the "founding regulations" within the history of Western painting and analogous to the rules with which one must become familiar to learn language and to communicate with it. Like the textual standardizations that emerge with the printing press, such as margins, spaces between words, and a relatively narrow range of acceptable font shapes and sizes, perspective involves the disciplining of the eye to the point of transparency.

Erwin Panofsky (1991) identifies the minimal necessary conditions for perspective as an "immobile eye" and a material surface that is, through the application of perspective, rendered effectively transparent. These minimal conditions strongly resemble Don Ihde's (1993) description of the physical, perceptual process of reading:

With reading there is *always perception*, but a particularly structured perception. It is a perception which, normally, carries with it a dampening of bodily motion, a fixed place for its object, an enhancement of the visual, and the privileging of an elevated or overhead position. (p. 86)

Ihde distinguishes between microperceptions, which are bodily and/or sensual, and macroperceptions, which are hermeneutic and/or cultural. The structuring (or disciplining) of perception marks a transition from microperception to macroperception; in other words, the transparency of the printed word renders our physical perceptions of the text, as we are reading at least, minimal to the point of nonexistence.

We take the establishment of "critical distance" for granted, frequently treating it as little more than a hermeneutic category, a warning against becoming too involved or invested in a particular object of study. But as Ihde asserts, critical distance requires a transition, one that in some cases is literally movement. Michel deCerteau (1988), in his section on "Spatial

Practices" from *The Practice of Everyday Life*, dramatizes this movement in the form of a trip to the top of the World Trade Center:

> To be lifted to the summit of the World Trade Center is to be lifted out of the city's grasp. . . . An Icarus flying above these waters, he can ignore the devices of Daedalus in mobile and endless labyrinths far below. His elevation transforms him into a voyeur. It transforms the bewitching world by which one was "possessed" into a text that lies before one's eyes. It allows one to read it, to be a solar Eye, looking down like a god. (p. 92)

In other words, while perspective emerges as a property of visual art during the Renaissance—much like verbal style is commonly conceived as a property of a written text—it disciplines us, predisposing us toward what deCerteau describes as "the exaltation of a scopic and Gnostic drive" and "the lust to be a viewpoint and nothing more" (p. 92). Perspective, when not built into a particular text, can be achieved through the literal achievement of distance (and, in the case of the city, elevation).

DeCerteau (1988) attempts to account for the will to perspective in his discussion of strategies and tactics,[6] and that discussion allows us to circle back to Aristotle's treatment of metaphor and style and to see perspective as the broader framework to which that treatment contributes. DeCerteau describes strategies as the calculations or manipulations of power relationships, and he notes three effects of a strategy in particular:

- "The 'proper' is a *triumph of space over time*."
- "It is also a mastery of places through sight. The division of space makes possible a *panoptic practice* proceeding from a place whence the eye can transform foreign forces into objects that can be observed and measured, and thus control and 'include' them within its scope of vision."
- "It would be legitimate to define the *power of knowledge* by this ability to transform the uncertainties of history into readable spaces. But it would be more correct to recognize in these 'strategies' a specific type of knowledge, one sustained and determined by the power to provide oneself with one's own place." (p. 36)

DeCerteau's (1988) descriptions make it difficult to perceive Aristotle's appropriation and exposition of style as anything other than strategic in the sense with which deCerteau defines the term. With Aristotle, style (and subsequently rhetoric) is assigned to its own specific place in the taxonomy of knowledge, and his exhaustive definitions of rhetorical figures transforms an oral and temporal verbal practice into a catalog of objects that, as Ricoeur (1977) observed, later becomes the restricted scope of rhetoric as a whole. The definition of metaphor as a departure or deviation from the "proper" name of a thing is a crucial step as well, turning variation (the uncertainties of *langue*) into deviation from a norm.

In short, although the *Rhetoric* prefigures the development of mathematical perspective by many centuries, it is possible to see Aristotle's work on *lexis* as one of the precedents for that development. Pinning down the historical trajectory of perspective, however, is less important for our purposes here than simply understanding how the practice of style has come to be defined in a range of domains. That definition provides the backdrop against which we might begin to explore what art historian James Elkins describes as "the practice of perspective"—a practice that has been subsumed by mathematical perspective and one that will prove important for reconceiving style for the interface.

AN OLD PERSPECTIVE ON METAPHOR

But there is no "real" expression and *no real knowing apart from metaphor*. But deception on this point remains, i.e. the *belief* in a *truth* of sense impressions. The most accustomed metaphors, the usual ones, now pass for truths and as standards for measuring the rarer ones. The only intrinsic difference here is the difference between custom and novelty, frequency and rarity.

—Friedrich Nietzsche (1990)

Writing in the narrow sense—and phonetic writing above all— is rooted in a past of nonlinear writing.

—Jacques Derrida (1976)

Tracing the irony of "diminishing returns" of style from Aristotle to the present day is a perversely satisfying activity because it allows rhetorical scholars the mirror pleasures of both establishing our discipline's roots in antiquity and breaking from that tradition in an enlightened fashion. But the path from Aristotle to the present is not as uncomplicated as we sometimes make it seem; there are a number of thinkers who have refused Aristotelian conceptions of metaphor and language, and those thinkers provide us with alternative source for developing stylistic practices. Given the unrelenting iconoclasm of his thought, it should be no surprise to find that Friedrich Nietzsche supplies just such an alternative.

Although he is not alone in suggesting a relationship between metaphoric and (so-called) nonmetaphoric (or "ordinary") language that differs from Aristotle's, Nietzsche's account of that relationship is one of the most insistent and vivid. In "On Truth and Lies in a Nonmoral Sense," Nietzsche (1990) provides his famous definition of truth, calling it

> A movable host of metaphors, metonymies, and anthropomorphisms: in short, a sum of human relations which have been poetically and rhetorically intensified, transferred, and embellished, and which, after long usage, seem to a people to be fixed, canonical, and binding. (p. 84)

It is this definition (which Jacques Derrida [1992] later picks up in his essay "White Mythology") where Nietzsche compares truth and proper meanings to coins that "have been drained of sensuous force" and "have lost their embossing." Significantly, Nietzsche's account of the passage from metaphor to the "lie" of clarity resembles the discussion about the establishment of perspective, which also involves the draining of sensuous microperception to arrive at a "pure" hermeneutic viewpoint.

It is equally important to understand that Nietzsche's revaluation is not simply an account of this process; it is a wholesale reversal of the priorities that Aristotle (1991) assigns in his exposition of *lexis*. For Aristotle, metaphor is the substitution of an "alien name" for a thing's proper name; according to Nietzsche, all names are "alien." There is no particular privilege accorded to a so-called proper name. Rather, the proper is simply that which a group of people has agreed on. The contingent, consensual qualities of that agreement are eventually forgotten, leaving a normed or proper name for which metaphors are described as deviations. According to Nietzsche, the first extramoral "lie" is the translation of a signified into language, but it is a necessary one for discourse to take place. To suggest that certain translations are inherently more proper than others ultimately compounds that lie, but again, for discourse to extend beyond the private or individual, it is a necessary move. Nietzsche's scorn is reserved not for those who have forgotten that lie—it is a near-universal and necessary forgetting—but those for whom this illusion is accorded the force and privilege of truth.

There are strong ties between this attitude toward truth and language and the deconstructive reading practice associated with Derrida. In fact, Nietzsche is one of the sources for Derrida's skepticism with regard to binaries, hierarchies, and the assertion of singular, proper meanings. One of Derrida's most frequent strategies is to identify key terms within a text and to tease out the various connotations, associations, and connections that surround the word—those that the author must neglect, ignore, or forget to achieve a particular meaning.[7] Although Derrida takes issue with Nietzsche's elevation of metaphor, both in *Of Grammatology* (1976) and his essay "White Mythology" (1982), it is nevertheless possible to suggest that one potential description of deconstructive practice is that it attempts to restore the embossing on certain crucial, philosophic terms.

Restoring some of the embossing on Aristotle's use of the word *metaphor* reveals some interesting connections—connections suggested both in the transmedial development of perspective and in more recent attempts to gather media under the umbrella of polymorphic or multiliteracies. Aristotle's definition of metaphor as a departure or deviation from ordinary language creates a tension that seems almost too obvious to mention. If we have at our disposal ordinary or proper terminology, what is to be gained by deviating from it? Why sacrifice clarity? Aristotle's answer is quite what we would expect in a book about persuasion: Sometimes it is necessary to depart from standard usages to achieve various rhetorical effects that a clear or ordinary style might not. In his description of this process, however, Aristotle (1991) drifts from a purely verbal account of what metaphor can accomplish:

> To this same characteristic Aristotle attributes another feature of metaphor that has not appeared before, and that seems somewhat disconcerting at first glance. Metaphor, he says, "sets the scene before our eyes" (1410 b 33). In other words, it gives that concrete colouration—imagistic style, figurative style it is called now—to our grasp of genus, of underlying similarity. (Ricoeur, 1977, p. 34)

In other words, even as Aristotle defines metaphor as a type of lexical substitution, he also explains it (particularly in chaps. 10–11 of Book 3 of the *Rhetoric*) as a "bringing-before-the-eyes." Ricoeur explains that metaphors can therefore "carry both the logical moment of proportionality and the sensible moment of figurativity" (p. 34).

Nor does Aristotle's description stop there. Etymologically, *metaphor* is defined as a movement (*epiphora*) or displacement, from one term to another. "To explain metaphor," Ricoeur (1977) writes, "Aristotle creates a metaphor, one borrowed from the realm of movement; *phora*, as we know, is a kind of change, namely change with respect to location" (p. 17). The metaphor of movement does not stop there, either. Aristotle's (1991) explanation of what it means to bring-before-the-eyes is tied up with motion as well; he opens Chapter 11 of Book 3 by explaining that "I call those things 'before the eyes' that signify things engaged in an activity (*energeia*)" (p. 248). Further into the chapter, praising Homer, Aristotle explains that "[Homer] makes everything move and live, and energeia is motion" (p. 249).

It is ultimately difficult to take issue with Aristotle's definition insofar as it operates at the level of grammar or code. But the instant that Aristotle attempts to articulate what metaphor accomplishes in practice, he is forced to both turn to metaphor and draw on resources that are extraverbal. Part of the reason for this is that what style *does* exceeds what it *is* and what style does extends beyond the verbal. As the development of perspective demonstrates, and despite the material differences among media, there are stylistic practices that cross the boundaries that separate them. Mathematical perspective, and the critical distance that accompanies it, is one example of such a practice, but it is hardly the only one.

LITERACIES OF STYLE?

At the same time that we attempt to move style away from its place in an Aristotelian ecology of code, it is important to be wary of the tendency to abstract it beyond practice. Returning momentarily to the strategies offered by Anne Wysocki (2004) and considered in chapter 1, if the attempt to identify a visual grammar focuses on individual texts, the attempt to establish an umbrella literacy that encompasses the visual and the digital is the corresponding attempt at generalization. In this regard, the following claims from J. L. Lemke (1998) and Gunther Kress (2000) are typical:

> There was a time perhaps when we could believe that making meaning with language was somehow fundamentally different, or could be treated in isolation from making meaning with visual resources or patterns of bodily action and social interaction. But today our technologies are moving us from the age of writing to an age of multimedia authoring in which voice-annotated documents and images, and written text itself, are now merely components of larger meaning objects. (Lemke, 1998, pp. 72–73)

> The semiotic changes which characterize the present and which are likely to characterize the near future cannot be adequately described and understood with currently existing theories of meaning and communication. These are based on language, and so, quite obviously, if language is no longer the only or even the central semiotic mode, then theories of language can at best offer explanations for one part of the communicational landscape only. (Kress, 2000, p. 153)

Faced with an array of new opportunities for expression—in 1992 Myron Tuman described it as an "onslaught"—we must develop, according to both Lemke and Kress, new literacies—frameworks for both understanding and producing these new messages. Lemke, Kress, and the countless others who deploy this particular gambit offer something of a variation on the traditional academic progress narrative, temporarily reversing it. The static styles and literacies with which we have worked are no longer sufficient, the argument goes, and so we must disrupt them, eventually rethinking our approach to a "communicational landscape" that is populated by "meaning objects" larger than, or at least different from, the products of the printing press. We must, therefore, unlearn the habits of thought and expression developed for that more restricted landscape.

This argument makes a great deal of sense, but it frequently relies on assumptions about "currently existing theories," treating them more narrowly than they deserve. For example, new media scholars are often guilty of characterizing the users of older media as straw people—as "passive" consumers of works forced on them by "tyrannical" authors/designers/artists. The move to new media, and to users who are much more "active" by contrast, ends up appearing (and is sometimes characterized as) liberatory. This *faux* politicization of the medium has been thoroughly discredited, as I mention in chapter 3, but the argument, built on a sloppy, overgeneralized contrast, persists in some accounts to this day. The strategy, drawing arbitrary boundaries that can then be crossed, continues to be effective. In his essay "Visualizing English," Craig Stroupe (2000) offers another variation of the argument that Lemke and Kress make:

> As more information is shared and cultural work performed via electronic environments—in June 1999, the size of the Web passed 300 million publicly accessible pages—English studies will find its stock-in-trade of verbal rhetorics and literacies increasingly in competition and combination with extra-verbal codes and languages. (p. 607)

Stroupe opens his article by revisiting a passage from Landow's (1997) *Hypertext*—one where Landow dismisses a distinction between the terms *hypertext* and *hypermedia*. Landow ignores this distinction because "hypertext, which links a passage of verbal discourse to images, maps,, diagrams, and sound as easily as to another verbal passage, expands the notion of text beyond the solely verbal" (p. 4). Landow's expanded notion of text is one that he clearly inherits from French poststructuralism.[8] Early in *Of Grammatology*, for instance, Jacques Derrida (1976) anticipates Landow's arguments by some 30 years:

> And thus we say "writing" for all that gives rise to an inscription in general, whether it is literal or not and even if what it distributes in space is alien to the order of the voice: cinematography, choreography, of course, but also pictorial, musical, sculptural "writing." One might also speak of athletic writing, and with even greater certainty of military or political writing in view of the techniques that govern these domains today. (p. 9)

Derrida declares "the end of the book," much to the delight and citation of technology scholars, but the second half of his chapter title, "the beginning of writing," fails to receive as much attention.[9] In the case of Landow's expanded notion of text, Derrida remains invisible for the sake of contrast, just as Landow's argument serves Stroupe less as a point of contention or inquiry than an argumentative foil.

There is something at play in the strategies of both Landow and Stroupe, something structural that requires Derrida (among others) to remain invisible. Even as new media scholars draw on this scholarship to make their arguments, they end up neglecting some of the premises that lead to the conclusions we are fond of citing. Derrida (1976) follows the list of "domains" offered previously with a remark about the scope of "writing," which he uses "to describe not only the system of notation secondarily connected with these activities but the essence and the content of these activities themselves" (p. 9). One of the primary goals of *Of Grammatology* is the deconstruction of the binary between speech and the more narrow, technologically specific form of writing, a binary on which an entire metaphysics of presence is constructed in Western philosophy. For Derrida, the "death of the book" is not the harbinger of new textual objects,[10] but rather a metaphorical call to "think of a new situation" for a broader definition of writing, one less focused on those "secondarily connected" systems of notations.

The difference between the analysis that Derrida performs and much of the new media scholarship that draws on his work is a subtle one. His argument is that there is a practice, an activity, that he calls writing, and it is a root activity on which various notation systems and domains have been elaborated. Once elaborated, writing was characterized as a supplement to the more primary system of speech (itself a supplement of thought). Derrida's concern is not with denying the obvious differences between speech and writing, but rather with challenging the metaphysics grounded in the relationship between them. To do so, he focuses on crucial writers and texts, repeatedly demonstrating that these key works fail to seal themselves off from the play of signification, among other things. More important, however, Derrida's (1976) project is not to build a better "writing." After outlining the nexus of implications that the Western sign carries with it, he explains that "it would be silly to conclude from [the sign's] placement within an epoch that it is necessary to 'move on to something,' to dispose of the sign, of the term and the notion" (p. 15). The subtlety of this position is frequently lost on those who appropriate Derrida on behalf of new media; he attempts to break from a tradition that he fully admits he cannot truly break from as he relies on that tradition for the discursive tools with which he critiques it.

This careful mix of critique, respect, and invention that Derrida (1976) brings to bear on the texts that he reads stands in stark contrast to the dismissals that characterize many of our contemporary announcements of a transformed communication landscape. It is difficult to imagine, with Kress (2000) that anyone has argued that language is the "only semiotic mode." Similarly, except for early to mid-20th-century New Criticism (and then only to a degree), the notion that language has been studied in stark isolation from other forms of meaning-making is debatable at best. New media: In these accounts, are represented to us as decisively breaking from old media; in Derrida's terms, the focus tends to be placed on these secondary systems without a great deal of concern for those ways in which our understandings of new media are necessarily bound by the traditions we are allegedly "breaking" from.[11]

The distinction I attempt here is the difference between Derrida's ability to read *within* and *against* the traditions he examines and our contemporary tendency to locate ourselves outside and/or above the objects of our own critique. To put it more starkly in terms of this chapter, I attempt to draw a contrast between Derrida's ability to acknowledge the partiality and the various perspectives from which he works, on the one hand, and our contemporary desire to reach an absolute perspective from which we might understand new media, on the other hand. The result of that desire, when we survey the scholarship, is a dizzying array of metadiscursive terms intended to fully comprehend the "larger meaning objects" of which

Lemke speaks. For Lemke, we should be working towards "metamedia literacies." Kress (2000) speaks of *design* as an umbrella term for the "multiliteracies" of the New London Group; Stroupe (2000) suggests a "hybrid literacy" of the visual and verbal. They are by no means atypical; having concluded that new media are the next big thing, we have engaged in repeated attempts to name the "something" to which we should be moving on. Faced with the opportunity to develop new practices and/or rethink our current practices, too often our response has been to search for terms that can comfortably encompass them all.

There is a certain degree of "kitchen sink-ism" in this attempt. Although she is not writing specifically about new media in this instance, Kristie Fleckenstein (2004) tries to fuse the visual and verbal into what she describes as a "polymorphic literacy." Her description of polymorphic literacy resonates to a degree with Derrida's definition of *writing* when she explains that "It emphasizes the reality that meaning shapes itself in response to the dictates of different media, modes, and contexts of representation" (p. 615). This focus on the activity of meaning, however, finds itself at odds with the attempt to establish the umbrella term *literacy*. Drawing on George Herbert Betts' work on mental imagery, Fleckenstein proposes to subsume verbal literacies within a much broader category, one "characterized by its multimodality, which means it contains within it aspects of various physical experiences of reality, including visual, auditory, cutaneous, kinesthetic, gustatory, olfactory, and organic images" (p. 623). When she provides specific instances of meaning-making interactions, Fleckenstein's account of a literacy that ranges beyond the verbal is convincing, but where Derrida turns to the practice of meaning, Fleckenstein attempts to gather her exhaustive list of activities into an umbrella term, a genus, that ultimately encompasses all forms of meaning-making. According to Fleckenstein, "Polymorphism underscores the flux between meaning and literacy, binding us philosophically and ethically to that fluidity and to the factors arresting fluidity" (p. 617).

Unfortunately, literacy ultimately makes for a questionable choice if our commitment is to multiplicity, to media in general, or to fluidity. As Anne Wysocki and Johndan Johnson-Eilola (1999) observe in their essay "Blinded by the Letter," literacy carries with it implications, both of a specific technology (the book) and a particular approach to meaning ("a basic, neutral, contextless set of skills") (p. 355). As they explain:

> When we discuss "technological literacy" or "computer literacy" or
> "[fill in the blank] literacy," we cannot pull "literacy" away from the two
> bundles of meaning and implications we have described. We may

> argue that we want to use "literacy" because it is a handy shortcut for covering a wide range of skills and procedures and practices. . . . But we are still using "literacy," which, unless we deny our histories, comes to us in the bundles we have just begun to unpack. (pp. 359-360)

They explain that literacy implies a relationship to its objects that is "externalized, linear, private, visual, static, and authoritative" (p. 360), features that run counter not only to Fleckenstein's bond to fluidity, but to the goals set forth by Kress, Lemke, Stroupe, and many others who attempt to answer the questions of new media with an answer of literacy or literacies. Answers like these are bound to fail because "No single term—such as 'literacy'—can support the weight of the shifting, contingent activities we have been describing" (p. 366).

For Derrida, the focus on those "shifting, contingent activities" entails keeping the discussion at the level of activity, avoiding what he describes as "the instituting question of philosophy: 'what is . . .?'" Derrida advocates "challenging the very form of the question," which cannot be done with the kind of metadiscourse so many technology critics advocate. The first question provoked by these neologistic literacies is that "what is": What is computer literacy? Technological literacy? Polymorphic literacy? Metamedia literacy? Wysocki and Johnson-Eilola (1999) suggest instead that we pursue "productive ways of questioning our current positions," rather than casuistically stretching them to accommodate new media. Rather than cataloguing the various expressions that new media make possible and gathering them together under a single heading, we should be trying to work from the ground up, much as Derrida does with "writing." In many ways, this is simply another argument in favor of what I describe in chapter 2 as "light structure," and there are similarities. In the following section, I try to take one of the defining frameworks in computers and writing for the past decade and open it up in just this fashion.

INTERFACIAL PERSPECTIVES

Since speech is made up of nouns and verbs...
—Aristotle (1991)

Do you notice that, in relation to other parts of speech, the preposition has almost all meaning and has almost none? It

> simultaneously has the maximum and minimum of meaning,
> exactly like a variable in classical analysis.

—Michel Serres (1995)

More than 10 years after its publication, Richard Lanham's (1993) *The Electronic Word* remains one of the most persuasive accounts about what happens to language when it passes from print to screen, but Lanham has been thinking about style from a range of perspectives for much of his career. In addition to his book about digital style, he is the author of an "anti-textbook" on the subject, a handbook of rhetorical tropes and terms, and in *Eloquence of Motives* he offers a history of the relationship between philosophy and rhetoric—one that relies heavily on various historical attitudes toward style. In fact, it is almost impossible to ignore those ways that the *electronic word* represents the proper domain for *homo rhetoricus*, Lanham's term for the "rhetorical stylist" who "feels at home" in a broad range of roles and who feels comfortable switching among them at will.

According to Lanham (1993) and many others before him, print text aspires to the ideal of transparency, minimally mediated access to the ideas expressed in language. Language on the computer screen, in contrast, is subject to so many different kinds of transformation by the user (size, font, color, layout, etc.) that Lanham argues we are often encouraged to consider the textual form as expressive. With electronic text, he explains, we often toggle between looking *through* text and looking *at* it. "Such and oscillation between looking AT the expressive surface and THROUGH it seems to me the most powerful aesthetic attribute of electronic text" (p. 43).

Lanham's (1993) at/through distinction has proved to be almost prescient because he makes this claim well in advance of the explosion of the Internet and graphical web browsers. In fact, this distinction has become so diffuse that Jay David Bolter and Diane Gromala (2005), in their recent book on interface design *Windows and Mirrors*, effectively allude to it in their title. Although they do not cite Lanham, the at/through distinction (renamed as states of transparency and reflectivity) is one of the central theoretical tenets of their text. Good designs "oscillate" between the two states, which exist on a continuum.[12] Much like Lanham locates this oscillation at the heart of a resurgent interest in rhetoric, Bolter and Gromala use it to mediate the conflict in interface design between structuralists (such as Jakob Neilsen) and designers (such as David Siegel), arguing that both elements are crucial for good design.

One of the important dimensions of Bolter and Gromala's work is the extent to which their "states of transparency and reflectivity" can be read across a range of media. Because Lanham (1993) is working from and in a more strictly verbal tradition, his at/through distinction is frequently mapped across the visual and verbal, respectively. Lanham refers to them as "two kinds of syntax" between which "we have to learn to alternate" (p. 77). As we observed earlier, however, the transparency of perspective is not limited to the printed word. Mathematical perspective has disciplined our eyes to read visual artifacts just as strictly as we have come to ignore the nonverbal elements of the printed page. As Bolter and Gromala demonstrate, there are any number of objects that instantiate various transparency/reflectivity ratios. If, in fact, as Mitchell (1995) argues, all media are mixed media, then the at/through distinction becomes a crucial framework for working with and in media of all kinds.

If there is a weakness with this distinction, however, it is one with a lengthy pedigree. In examining metaphor and style at the level of the word/name, Aristotle (1991) ushered in a particular approach to style, one that Lanham has devoted several books toward undoing. Yet in a similar fashion, the at/through distinction encourages us to treat interfaces as static objects, rather than dynamic practice. Just as metaphors may lose their "embossing" and become ordinary language, even the most reflective interface tends toward transparency as a user becomes accustomed to it. When I finally made the switch from one Macintosh operating system to another (from OS 9 to OS X), I spent the first couple of months relearning a variety of processes (opening and closing documents, accessing functions in different pulldown menus, etc.). During that time, I was extremely conscious of the interface, looking *at* it with some frequency. Six months later, I accessed a machine running the old operating system and found that it was foreign to me, despite the years I spent working on variations of it. This is a minor example, certainly, but it is representative of our experiences with interfaces in general. Transparency and reflectivity do indeed exist on a continuum, but our own position along that continuum is never static. To paraphrase Heraclitus, we never use the same interface twice.

To take a macroperceptual example, consider Cynthia Selfe and Richard Selfe's (1994) classic essay, "The Politics of the Interface: Power and Its Exercise in Electronic Contact Zones." Selfe and Selfe offer a critique of the desktop metaphor common to most graphical user interfaces (GUIs), concluding that many of the metaphors that condition those interfaces (files, folders, trash cans, or recycling bins) are, in fact, "sites within which the ideological and material legacies of racism, sexism, and colonialism are continuously written and re-written along with more positive cultural legacies" (p. 484). Even in an example as apparently obvious as the computer desktop, the idea of the desk as a primary and portable interface makes assumptions about the cultural background of the user. Is the desktop, then, something that we look *at* or *through*? The obvious answer is that it is going to depend on our level of comfort with the various metaphors operating there. It depends on where we look *from*. It may well be that the desktop has diffused sufficiently into our culture so as to become invisible, that it has become *the* perspective, but even this view assumes a stability on the part of the desktop that may be assuming too much. The point is that we as users participate in the construction of our interfaces.

Another more elaborate example comes from the interface for *World of Warcraft* (WOW), a Massively Multiplayer Online Role Playing Game (MMORPG). Whereas the desktops on our computers change at a relatively slow pace, interfaces like the one that governs play in WOW exist at several points along the continuum from transparency to opacity simultaneously, and the customization of the interface is one of the hallmarks of gameplay.

Figures 5.1 and 5.2 offer two examples of the WOW interface: one taken from a low-level character and the other taken from a character that is significantly more advanced. Although there are obvious discrepancies, consider first the similarities between them. There are at least three different perspectives that are melded into the WOW interface. The first is an over-the-shoulder "camera" shot that allows the player to perceive what his or her character perceives in the game world. WOW allows a player to zoom the camera in, simulating the view from the character's eyes, or out, producing an even more distant third-person perspective. This is the default perspective of most players because it bears a great deal of similarity to our experience of the world. But there are two other perspectives represented in the interface as well. In the upper right-hand corner of the screen, the character is represented at the center of an overhead map not unlike a radar screen. At various times, hostile creatures, treasure, quest goals, and other game components might appear on this overhead view, along with a character. The other perspective embedded in the standard interface is the dashboard of controls for the game, which includes not only controls for accessing the world map, quests, and game controls, but also customizable "action bars" that are arranged and populated by the character's various skills, spells, and inventory items. As a character gathers items and increases in level, the number of game actions that can be placed in the action bars necessarily increases, and that is one of the important differences between Figs. 5.1 and 5.2. A final perspective that is practiced regularly in the WOW interface appears in Fig. 5.3, the World Map, which allows players to see their characters in a broader geographic context, much like drivers use atlases to plan and track their trips.

Figure 5.1. The World of Warcraft interface for a beginning character

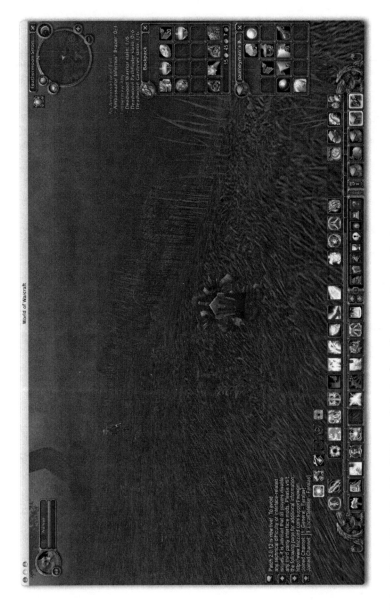

Figure 5.2. The World of Warcraft interface for an advanced character

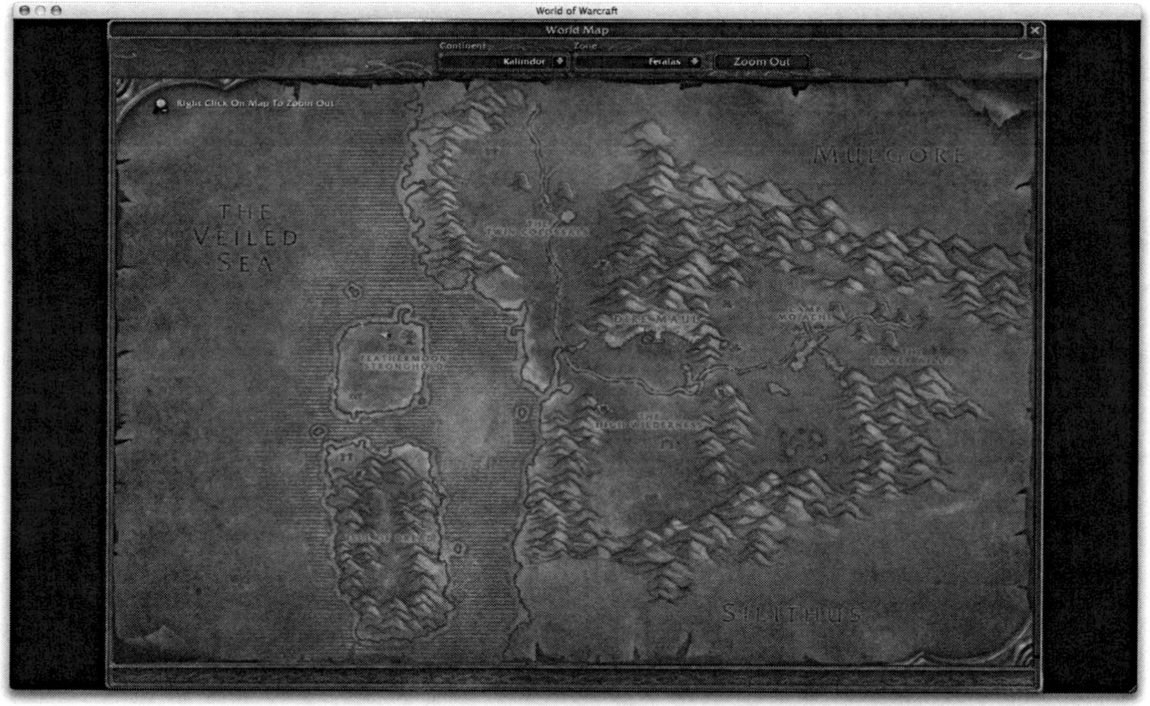

Figure 5.3. The WOW World Map

On the one hand, it would be relatively easy to rank these different per-spectives according to their relative transparency during gameplay. The first-person default seems necessarily more immersive than the dashboard, which is both layered on top of it and used by players to interact with the game.[13] From the position of a player new to the WOW interface, this might even be correct. But it also can be argued that an implicit part of the gameplay is the gradual immersion that one experiences with the entirety of the interface—nor is it simply a matter of getting used to the interface and taking it for granted. Certain action bars are keyed to the top row of numbers on the keyboard, allowing players quick access to certain actions, whereas others must be activated with the mouse. As players develop dif-ferent combinations of actions as part of their strategy during gameplay, they immerse themselves not only microperceptually, but macroperceptu-ally as well. Changing the interface does not simply change the "look" of the game, although it does do that as well; it also affects the physical actions (keyboard and mouse manipulation) used to trigger game actions. Much like one might recall a phone number through the physical pattern used to dial it, the dashboard in WOW conditions the player to particular keystroke and mouse combinations. The interaction is so elaborate, in fact, that there are specific keyboards designed to support the large set of com-mands and actions necessary (Fig. 5.4).

From the other end of the spectrum, the default perspective is not always the object of looking through, either. Often a particular quest requires a player to choose a path through the landscape with caution, making that default a perspective that must be treated less immersively. My point here is that, although each element of the interface combines interaction and immersion—looking at and through—in different ways, those combinations change over the course of gameplay and cannot be taken as static. Nor do the various perspectives encompassed by the inter-face add up to omniscience. Players must move their characters through a large world, interacting with other players as well as obstacles, and their knowledge of the world is limited by both their geographical position and the qualities of their character, including race, class, level, and so on. WOW, like many other games, encourages players to progress through its world by making exploration one of the goals. Looking at and through its inter-face is important, but equally crucial is the heavily articulated position *from* *which* a player engages that interface.

In his *New Philosophy for New Media*, Mark Hansen (2004) makes this feature (looking from) one of the signal differences between new media and old:

Figure 5.4. Ideazon's WOW keyboard

> Moreover, the viewer must participate in the process through which the mediated digital data is transformed into a perceivable image. . . . We could say, to put it in simple terms, that it is the body—the body's scope of perceptual and affective possibilities—that informs the medial interfaces. This means that with the flexibility brought by digitization, there occurs a displacement of the framing function of media interfaces back on to the body from which they themselves originally sprung. (p. 22)

With interfaces, it is no longer sufficient to speak simply of an at/through distinction that leaves the position of the viewer, user, or reader unexamined. Just as we look *at* and *through* interfaces, we also look *from* a particular position, and that position is *both* macro- and microperceptual. It is important to acknowledge that interfaces position us perceptually and that our sensual experiences of interfaces are often as customizable as our hermeneutic approaches to them. That capacity, perhaps more familiar to us from video games and DVD special features than more traditional media, is only increasing.

One of Ricoeur's (1997) conclusions about metaphor is that it both destroys an old order of relations among ideas and creates a new one. "Pushing this thought to the limit," he writes, "one must say that metaphor bears information because it 'redescribes' reality" (p. 22), a claim we might easily transpose to the interface, except to add that interfaces redescribe our perspectives. In this fashion, they take advantage of the ambiguity of the term *perspective*, which, as I noted at the beginning of this chapter, can signify "either one point of view among many, or *the* point which organizes and arranges all the others" (Moxey, 1995, p. 779). In new media, one place that style is practiced in the creation of perspective, an emergent quality of a specific interaction among user, interface, and object(s), drawing on each without being reducible to any of those factors.

NOTES

1. See, for example, Carolyn Handa's (2004) "Placing the Visual in the Writing Classroom," her introduction to the collection *Visual Rhetoric in a Digital World: A Critical Sourcebook*.
2. To be fair, Hocks's approach in this article is constrained by the fact that it was prepared for a print journal, a fact that carried certain evidentiary expectations. The same also might be said of many, similar instances of this sort of analysis.

3. In some ways, the history of rhetoric is a history of style. Rhetoric still connotes "style without substance" in popular parlance, and style is widely regarded as a secondary concern.

4. Ricouer lays this decline out on pp. 45-46 as a detailed series of postulates.

5. One of the classic introductions to perspective is Erwin Panofsky's (1991) *Perspective as Symbolic Form*. In it, he explains: "For us, perspective in the strict sense is the capacity to represent several objects in one area of space so that the appearance of a material surface is entirely displaced by the appearance of a transparent plane, beyond which we believe we see an imaginary space . . ." (p. 292)

6. It is tempting to adopt deCerteau wholesale here and to argue that interfaces are necessarily tactical. Although the connection is certainly suggestive and potentially productive, I take strategies and tactics to be different practices, each of which a particular interface design might aspire toward. Perspective as I describe it in this section is both strategic and interfacial.

7. Perhaps the most familiar of these, for those of us in rhetoric, is Derrida's examination of the Greek word *pharmakon* in Plato's *Phaedrus*. *Pharmakon* is used to denote "poison," in keeping with Plato's opinion of rhetoric, but it also connotes "medicine," a meaning that Plato must ignore ("Plato's Pharmacy," *Dissemination*).

8. That inheritance is explained extensively in John Mowitt's (1992) *Text: The Genealogy of an Antidisciplinary Object*.

9. Gregory Ulmer's (1994) work is an important exception to this. It is worth noting that Stroupe compares the ways that Ulmer and Landow handle the visual and the verbal, and that Ulmer provides a better model for the dialogic relationship between the two.

10. Too much hypertext criticism treated hypertext as a result of a Hegelian synthesis of book (thesis) and poststructural criticism (antithesis).

11. One obvious exception to this particular strategy comes from Jay Bolter and Richard Grusin's (1999) *Remediation*, discussed in chapter 1.

12. The parallels between Bolter/Gromala (2005) and Lanham (1993) are, in fact, striking in places. Compare, for instance, the chart on p. 67 of *Windows* (where Bolter and Gromala use the words *at* and *through*) to Lanham's p. 14. Even their language—oscillation, continuum, and the association of transparency with "serious" work—is similar.

13. At one time, *interactive* and *immersive* were treated as poles of activity not unlike *at* and *through*, respectively, although they are more recently considered as different dimensions of a single, interfacial encounter.

6

PERSISTENCE

. . . after rhetoric came to be concerned mainly with written discourse, there was no further need to deal with memorizing. . . . There will be no consideration in this book of this aspect of rhetoric.

Edward P. J. Corbett (1999)

No, the technical structure of the *archiving* archive also determines the structure of the *archivable* content even in its very coming into existence and in its relationship to the future. The archivization produces as much as it records the event.

—Jacques Derrida (1996)

The traditional approach to memory in our field, typified previously by the excerpt from Corbett (1999), has been to adopt an almost McLuhan-esque attitude toward it, relying on the commonsense assumption that books (and various other technologies) function as extensions of our more limited individual memories. Memory in this approach is something less than a practice; accounts like Corbett's reduce memory instead to a question of storage, as if memory simply signified the retention or location of quantifiable amounts of information. It is in this sense that we speak of a computer's memory—its capacity for storing a finite number of kilo-, mega-, and gigabytes' worth of information.

Needless to say, this chapter aligns itself more closely with Jacques Derrida (1996) who, in *Archive Fever*, writes of the effects that changes in archival technology have on both what is being (and can be) archived, as well as on the people doing the archiving. Although many of the practices of memory outlined in this chapter are not intrinsic to new media, I suggest by the end of this chapter that they acquire particular forms in new media that would be difficult to approximate in more traditional media. This chapter begins by considering in some detail the implications of positions like Corbett's; in particular, I return to the Platonic attitude toward writing and memory discussed briefly in chapter 2, arguing that this attitude has left us with a legacy of considering memory in terms of absence and presence. Even attempts to account for distributed cognition, itself a particular form of memory practice, still retain the Platonic tendency to spatialize memory. The second section of the chapter borrows from N. Katherine Hayles' (1999) "semiotics of virtuality" in an attempt to move beyond the presence/absence account of memory. I argue that we need to think of memory not simply as the storage of data, but also in terms the construction of pattern, an argument that recalls chapter 4.

The following two sections suggest one place where Hayles' (1999) axis of pattern/randomness might hold some relevance for the practice of memory in new media. The third section, working from Scott DeWitt's (2001) critique of the "feed-forward" impulsiveness of the Web, suggests that perhaps there is a form of cognition (and memory) that can take advantage of the quality of the Web that would seem to militate against reflection and thought. In short, I argue that there are tools that make it possible to achieve *persistence of cognition*—a term I coin in analogy with the cinematic notion of *persistence of vision*, the quality of vision that enables us to perceive motion from a precession of still images. In the final section of the chapter, I examine two online platforms for processing RSS feeds, paying particular attention to the way that each enacts the presence/absence and the pattern/randomness axes of memory. Finally, I close with an examination of this memory practice applied to a broader dataset of documents, presidential speeches. Perhaps more than any of the other four canons, memory is the one canon whose status as *practice* is in need of rehabilitation. The assumption of memory as storage is an incredibly potent one, but there are new media sites that will enable us to rethink this canon.

MEMORY AS PRESENCE/ABSENCE

In chapter 2, I cite that portion of Plato's (2006) objections to writing that has to do with memory—his conviction that "If men learn this, it will implant forgetfulness in their souls; they will cease to exercise memory because they rely on that which is written, calling things to remembrance no longer from within themselves, by means of external marks" (*Phaedrus*). Although Plato's position is in some ways a precursor to Corbett's, at least insofar as it asserts that memory has nothing to do with writing, there are additional implications to this position worth considering beyond the question of whether memory belongs in the canons. Gregory Ulmer (1985) explains,

> Plato is condemning writing not just as "writing-down" but as a whole theory of the relation of memory to thought. Plato's diatribe against the sophists condemns artificial memory (hypomnesia) in general, including mnemotechnics, the system of topoi, or commonplaces developed for rhetorical training. (p. 69)

The oppositions that animate Plato's rejection of writing include not only natural/artificial and orality/literacy, but also the question of whether knowledge is located inside or outside of the knower. Perhaps most important for the work of writers like Ulmer, Derrida, and Jasper Neel, the binary of presence and absence underlies Plato's position on writing.

The work of Plato (and many other philosophers) has resulted in that feature of our ecologies of culture that Derrida labels the "metaphysics of presence"; much of Derrida's early work, in fact, is devoted to diagnosing and exploring that particular aspect of our culture. Part of that exploration undoes the binaries that Plato articulates; in *Dissemination*, for example, Derrida (1981) writes that "The outside is already *within* the work of memory" (p. 109). But we need not turn to deconstruction to find examples of the effect that Plato's approach to memory has had; his imposition of presence/absence on memory has had far-reaching effects that last to the present day. Although few would be willing to adopt the extreme position his dialogue represents,[1] eschewing all external forms of memory in favor of one's own ability to remember, our commonsense understandings of memory preserve the binaries that Plato introduces there.

In other words, the vast externalization of memory represented by a range of media from page to screen has become an accepted and even integral part of our society, but we still have not shaken the effects of Plato's critique. One implication is that memory, perhaps more than any other canon, has been subject to the polarization that Anne Wysocki describes (cf. chap. 1). On the one hand, we perceive memory as an individual faculty, a quasi-objective measure of the contents of our minds; on the other hand, we perceive it at the collective scale of memorials and monuments in terms of history. Much work has been done in recent years, particularly in transdisciplinary fields such as trauma studies, to complicate the binary of history and memory. For example, in *History and Memory After Auschwitz*, Dominick LaCapra (1998) writes that

> Memory is both more and less than history, and vice versa. History may never capture certain elements of memory: the feel of an experience, the intensity of joy or suffering, the quality of an occurrence. Yet history also includes elements that are not exhausted by memory, such as demographic, ecological, and economic factors. More important, perhaps, it tests memory and ideally leads to the emergence of both a more accurate memory and a clearer appraisal of what is or is not factual in remembrance. (p. 20)

It is notable, however, that this passage comes at the end of a discussion of attempts to assert the primacy of one over the other. Such assertions quickly fall back into the language of absence or presence. Memory and history are each charged with being incapable of providing what its "opposite" does; in each case, there is something absent from the particular account. It is not difficult to see how memory and history might be mapped across other of Plato's binaries, like natural and artificial.

This reductive view of memory, which presumes the individual, mental storage of information, has its roots in attitudes toward rhetoric that Sharon Crowley accounts for extensively in *The Methodical Memory*. Revisiting that account in an essay on "Modern Rhetoric and Memory," Crowley (1993) explains that "Methodical invention privileges unity and coherence. Memory, on the other hand, is associative, global; it privileges disquisition, repetition, digression, allusion, allegory" (p. 43). Modernism, in its valorization of the "sovereign author," occludes what Crowley describes as the shared or communal nature of memory. For the moderns, memory was not the productive storehouse that it was for the ancients, preceding the act of invention. Contrasted with this model, "Modern invention is economical, spare, methodical; the investigator decides on an object of study, investigates its parts in order, and reports results in a discursive order that re-presents the order of the investigation as nearly as possible" (pp. 42–43). Memory, if it enters this model anywhere, comes after the fact, and even then it is subordinated to the emphasis on method. Combined with modern progress narratives, it is not difficult to see how our individualistic sense of memory can only ever achieve approximations of knowledge. It is no accident that the mark of "perfection" is the "photographic memory," which is able to achieve perfect replication of something that its possessor has seen. Photographic memory is a far cry from the rhetorical memory for which Crowley and others argue.

If, at the scale of the ecology of code, memory is reduced to a yes/no question of storage, the canon of memory in ecologies of culture takes the form of history, where, in recent years, it has been treated less reductively. It would be difficult to find those in our field willing to defend a strictly factual and referential model of history; although there are those unwilling to go to the opposite extreme, even relatively traditional historians now acknowledge an irreducible margin of interpretation on the part of historical research.[2] They may still argue for the best possible histories based on fairly conservative criteria for evidence, but it is difficult to wholly dispute the arguments of Hayden White and others, who locate evidence of historians' constructive contributions to the historical work that they do. A similar concern with the scale of practice, or the mix of practice and culture, has dominated discussions of memorials and monuments. In his Introduction to *The Texture of Memory*, James Young (1993) explains that, "For once it was recognized that monuments necessarily mediate memory, even as they seek to inspire it, they came to be regarded as displacements of the memory they were supposed to embody" (p. 4). Later in that book, he discusses the ways that monuments' fixedness in space ensures their "death over time: an image created in one time and carried over into a new time suddenly appears archaic, strange, or irrelevant altogether" (p. 47). Young's exploration of countermonuments and, more recently, Gregory Ulmer's (2005) *Electronic Monuments* have begun to restore both the dialogue surrounding monuments and an explicit focus on the scale of practice. Yet there is still a logic of presence and absence governing much of the discussion of memorials and monuments, particularly outside of academic circles.

Both the question of individual memory and that of its more collective forms are much more complicated than the preceding discussion indicates, certainly. But much of the logic that informs those questions relies heavily on the terms that Plato set for media and memory in ancient Greece. The binary of presence/absence reduces memory to a question of storage, with little thought given to the effects that various media might have on what is being remembered. Over the past century, we have begun to inch away from this legacy, considering not only *whether* we remember, but *how* we remember as well, a shift that begins to raise questions of memory practices. In the next section, we consider N. Katherine Hayles' "semiotics of virtuality" as a framework that might help us think of memory in terms of practice.

MEMORY AS PATTERN/RANDOMNESS

N. Katherine Hayles' (1999) *How We Became Posthuman* is an account of particular developments within the history of cybernetics. Specifically, Hayles characterizes this development in terms of three interrelated stories: the disembodiment of information, the invention of the cyborg as a technological and cultural artifact, and the emergence of the posthuman. In part a call "to contest for what the posthuman means" (p. 291), her book contests the privilege that information has been granted in cybernetics, arguing instead for an understanding of information that is inseparable from embodiment. As part of that understanding, Hayles suggests a "semiotics of virtuality" that maps phenomena along two different axes: absence/presence and pattern/randomness. In part, this suggestion grows out of Hayles' conviction that the dialectic of presence and absence no longer provides us with an adequate epistemological framework, particularly when it comes to the complex relations among bodies and technologies. In discussing the construction of knowledge in virtual reality, Hayles explains,

> Questions about presence and absence do not yield much leverage in this situation, for the avatar both is and is not present, just as the user both is and is not inside the screen. Instead the focus shifts to questions about pattern and randomness. (p. 27)

Pattern and randomness provide Hayles with an axis both complementary and dialectic to presence/absence, and this conceptual maneuver, I want to argue, also helps us at the scale of practice. Hayles puts this semiotic to use in her book by examining several novels that collectively represent the posthuman, but our use of it here is somewhat more modest.

Although memory is a canon that focuses our attention on the relationship between discourse and time, the treatment of memory as storage spatializes the canon, reducing it to the single axis of presence and absence.

Even discussions of distributed cognition, an approach to memory and mind that treats them environmentally rather than individually, still considers memory primarily in terms of location. Information is either located *here* in one's head or *there* in a book, a database, someone else, and so on. The reinscription of the axis of pattern and randomness into memory allows us to retemporalize this canon, a move that highlights memory's status as practice. In an essay of mine entitled "Forgetting to be (Post) Human: Media and Memory in a Kairotic Age" (2000), I argue that we can think of pattern and randomness in terms of the two competing models of time that we have inherited from the Greeks: *chronos* and *kairos*. *Chronos* is the artificial patterning of time, its division into equal, measurable segments— the time by which we set our clocks and watches, conduct our classes, and organize our history. *Kairos* is the time sense at the other end of the spectrum, the opportunities that emerge to be seized in a particular situation, unrepeatable and unsystematizable. If *chronos* represents our triumph over time as a cultural achievement, *kairos* "is tied to a nonrational *physis* that is excessive and unmasterable" (Davis, 2000, p. 28). It is the unwillingness of the kairotic moment to submit itself to our control that has led to its "neglected" status in rhetorical theory, according to James Kinneavy (1986).

In "Forgetting," I turn to two representative anecdotes, two important instances in our recent collective history, that demonstrate the way that media and memory interact along the axis of pattern and randomness. The first was the beating of Rodney King in 1991, and specifically the treatment of that event in the subsequent trial involving the arresting officers. One of the things that went unspoken in the denouement of the King incident was the doubling of the violence made possible by technological advances. Avital Ronell (1992) explains that, "For the duration of the trial, the temporization that reading video customarily entails was halted by spatial determinations that were bound to refigure the violence to which King was submitted" (p. 306). In other words, the experience captured by a home video camera was converted into an extensive frame-by-frame series of still photographs. The defense team in the trial committed a form of interpretive violence on the evidence and ultimately justified, to a jury's satisfaction, the physical violence with which the police responded to King. "No one needs to read Derrida's work on framing," suggests Ronell, "in order to know that justice was not served in Simi Valley, California" (p. 306), but we do need to begin to question the conditions that kept justice from being served. In terms of Hayles' semiotics, the presence of the video footage remains unchanged. One implication of the disembodiment of information, according to Hayles, is the belief that information can be translated from one material substrate to another without alteration. But this ignores the different patterns constructed by the translation of video to still images.

The second representative anecdote involves another earlier trauma in the recent history of our country—the Challenger disaster in 1986. The media coverage of this event was, in some respects, similar to the King incident. Television stations replayed the explosion repeatedly, capturing it in slow motion as if pinpointing the precise moment that the explosion began could somehow supply it with meaning. In his book *Statues*, Michel Serres (1987) likens the Challenger to the ancient Carthaginians' practice of sacrificing humans and animals by burning them alive inside a giant statue of the deity Baal (Lapidus). As Latour (1995) notes in his *Conversations on Science, Culture, and Time*, an extended series of interviews with Serres, it is difficult for us to follow the parallel that Serres sets up:

> . . . to be modern is precisely to accept that the Challenger has nothing to do with Baal, because the Carthaginians were religious and we no longer are, because they were ineffectual whereas we are very effective, and so on. (p. 138)

The media blitz surrounding the Challenger elevated it to the status of national tragedy, in part obscuring the culpability of NASA. As we have since discovered, part of the fault for the Challenger disaster lies with NASA's information design workers, who, had they been attuned to their limitations, could have predicted and prevented the explosion (cf. Mijksenaar, 1997; Tufte, 1983). The cultural investment in the incident prompted by the media helped to obscure the scientific failures that were directly responsible for it. The lack of pattern preceding the Challenger's explosion only serves to heighten the sense of tragic randomness with which the event is viewed historically.

In each of these cases, there is a translation occurring along the axis of pattern and randomness—one that, it might be argued, served to distort the events represented. The police in the Rodney King incident, and subsequently the defense team at the trial, are at least responsible for transforming a kairotic moment by translating it chronologically without accounting for the effect that the medium had on the message. This translation allows the event to be "articulated as a metonymy of the war on drugs" (Ronell, 1992, p. 307), and the event's insertion into that larger pattern enabled the defense to justify the actions of the police. The Challenger disaster signifies a transformation in the other direction. The explosion was predictable and preventable insofar as it was part of the larger pattern of the space program, but it was refigured as *kairos*—a tragedy senseless for the randomness of the event. In each case, certain characteristics of the event in question are obscured, reshaped as they are remembered for us and to us. Neither event was simply made present to a national media audience; both involved the establishment or dissolution of certain patterns within which we eventually came to understand them.

I mean to suggest two overarching conclusions here with my citation of Hayles and these representative anecdotes. The first is that a focus on temporality in the context of memory allows us to examine that canon as practice. Although it may not be particularly controversial to suggest that we construct our memories, construction has not been an emphasis in our considerations of the rhetorical canon of memory. Even the ancient practice of memory palaces combined mental space with the traversal of that space. The second conclusion, which I build on in the following sections, is that the construction (and dissolution) of patterns over time, what I describe later as *persistence*, is a practice for which new media are particularly well suited. In *Ancient Rhetoric for Contemporary Students*, Crowley and Hawhee (1999) speak briefly to the potential held by "electronic memory systems" (p. 273), but that potential is largely conceived of in terms of the storage capacity of such systems. They note that electronic memory represents a "vast improvement," but this improvement is figured as quantitative. In the next two sections, I attempt to demonstrate that new media introduce new qualities to our practice of memory as well.

PERSISTENCE OF COGNITION

One of the prevailing themes with the rise of the Internet over the past 20 years has been the sheer amount of information that we produce and are increasingly called to consume. Although critics have been quick to praise the fact that new media have enabled unprecedented cultural production on the part of users, the "overload" of information thus produced is often cited as one of the downsides. Although his account of it is now several years old, David Shenk (1997) characterized the overload of information "data smog":

> When it comes to information, it turns out that one can have too much of a good thing. At a certain level of input, the law of diminishing returns takes effect; the glut of information no longer adds to our qual-

> ity of life, but instead begins to cultivate stress, confusion, and even ignorance. Information overload threatens our ability to educate ourselves, and leaves us more vulnerable as consumers and less cohesive as a society. (p. 15)

Shenk is writing in 1997, only a couple of years into the Internet's entry into mainstream consciousness; if anything, the anxieties present in his account of information overload have become even more exaggerated. The theme of the 2006 O'Reilly Emerging Technology Conference, one of the bellwether events for the technology industry, was the "attention economy." In the materials for the conference, the organizers hail conference-goers with a passage that sounds similar to Shenk's pronouncements:

> Today's consumer technology breaks focus rather than facilitating it, peppering us with pleas and offerings by dozens of applications competing for our attention. Not to mention the overwhelming amount of data we produce and consume every day. No longer constrained by any virtual limits, we're feeling the effects of this flood of digital assets. It's in our inboxes and news aggregators, on our hard drives and iPods, overloading our very capacity for managing it all. As organic creatures with fallible and finite perception systems, complex desires, and an ever-decreasing amount of time, how do we attenuate the flow to allow for synthesis and reflection? ("An Invitation")

As these two passages suggest, it is not unusual to see the overload of information cast in catastrophic terms, but I want to add a third passage to these two, suggesting that our contemporary problems are not quite as singular as Shenk and the organizers of ETech would have us believe:

> There is a growing mountain of research. But there is increased evidence that we are being bogged down today as specialization extends. The investigator is staggered by the findings and conclusions of thousands of other workers—conclusions which he cannot find time to grasp, much less to remember, as they appear.

This third passage comes from Vannevar Bush's (1945) "As We May Think," published more than 60 years ago. We could easily spend the rest of this chapter reproducing similar passages taken from the last century, penned by writers each of whom was equally convinced of the catastrophic implications of his or her own era's overload of information.

As Bush makes explicit, and both Shenk and the ETech organizers imply, the question of information overload is a question of memory. Cursed with "finite perception systems," when data exceed our ability to grasp them, we find ourselves in the position of overload that each of these writers bemoans. It is not simply a matter of our abilities stopping at some point beyond which data become unmanageable. Shenk (1997) cites the work of memory expert Robert Bjork and explains that the more things we have to remember or learn, "the lower the probability that you'll remember any one of them" (p. 49). Bjork's analysis is almost an analogue for one form of writer's block; like a writer faced with too much to say and who is thus unable to begin, memory is not simply a matter of filling our minds until they are full. The presence of too much information, according to both Bjork and Shenk, "just overloads the system" (p. 49).

In this section of the chapter, however, I want to suggest that perhaps it is not as simple as this—that we do have certain coping strategies for dealing with an abundance of information, memory practices that are not often thought of as such. In the closing section of this chapter, I speak more concretely about how memory is practiced in new media—both the traditional model of memory as *storage* and the model of memory that I will articulate in this section, memory as *persistence*. If, as Ulmer (2005) writes in *Electronic Monuments*, we can understand monuments and mnemonics as practices that respond to catastrophe, then perhaps the catastrophic characterizations of information overload (e.g., smog, flood) will prompt us to consider new models of memory—practices appropriate for the attention economy that is emerging in our era of new media.

One practice that emerged alongside contemporary concerns of information overload, equally likely to produce the kind of hand-wringing, is the colloquialism of "surfing the Web." Although some writers attempted to rehabilitate Web surfing by comparing it to the physical activity of riding waves on a board, the analogy is more frequently made with channel surfing a TV, the frequent changing of channels guaranteed to annoy anyone not actually doing the changing. It is this analogy that prompts Steven Johnson (1997) to bemoan the "terrible injustice [done] to what it means to navigate around the Web" (p. 107). Johnson's answer to the analogy with channel surfing is to suggest that it is a false one, explaining that channel surfing is a sign of boredom, whereas Web surfing is performed out of interest. Web surfers, he explains, move to a new page out of interest in or curiosity of what lies at the end of the link.

Yet Johnson's (1997) distinction does not quite answer concerns over Web surfing. Although the motivation for moving from page to page may differ from that of moving from program to program on the TV, it is debatable whether one accomplishes more than the other. Scott Lloyd DeWitt (2001) takes up this issue in *Writing Inventions*, where he argues that "Web technology abets a rapid, feed-forward motion":

> The rapid succession of the Web is important in understanding students' reading of it, also. . . . In much the same way that we read a newspaper or magazine, students don't always read an entire Web page before they come upon a link that provokes them to move to the next text. (p. 143)

At another point in his discussion, DeWitt describes this as an "Impulsive Model" of reading, where the feed-forward nature of Web reading discourages students from moving "beyond the moment" in their traversal of multiple Web pages. To put it in the terms from the ETech organizers, we might say that the Web actively works against our ability to "attenuate the flow to allow for synthesis and reflection."

DeWitt (2001) contrasts the Impulsive Model of reading with the more deliberative and reflective model characteristic of "proficient readers and writers," concluding that his students' approach to reading the Web "represents an ineffective invention strategy" (pp. 140–143). Although this reading strategy (like the rest of the book) is cast in terms of invention, when it comes to a specific account of the problems that DeWitt sees in his students, he turns to memory:

> The rapid downloading of Web pages also plays a role in the decentering process, which I describe as "a letting go of what was and readjusting to what is." Whereas a quickly downloaded page encourages students to *forget* what they were looking at and focus on what has appeared on the screen, decentering can be prevalent in students' reading of the Web even when the technology is not working quickly, and perhaps even just as prevalent when they are taken rapidly from site to site. (p. 144; italics added)

DeWitt follows this analysis with the vivid metaphor of *cognitive fabric*, the braiding together of multiple threads and texts to achieve a fabric "dense in weave and rich in pattern" (p. 144). Students who succumb to the Impulsive Model of reading the Web, he suggests, suffer from "holes in [their] cognitive fabric." His solution (termed the "Reflective Model") proceeds as we might expect. If the rapid, feed-forward motion of the Impulsive model is responsible for these holes, then the Reflective Model addresses those holes by slowing readers down. Among the features of this model that DeWitt suggests are writing as they read, keeping a running "expectation log," and annotating each site that they visit. DeWitt's sensible suggestions rest on the idea that if browsing speed is making us forget, then slowing down will enable the kind of reflection that we typically hope for from our writing courses.

Analogously, one solution to information overload is simply to take in less information. In many of the arguments decrying information overload, it is not unusual to find writers treating the flow of data as something over which we have lost all control; in the past few years, an entire industry has emerged, typified by sites like *43 Folders* (http://www.43folders.com), dedicated to the application of basic organizational strategies to our e-mail inboxes, for example. Although such sites are clearly useful, much of the advice they proffer amounts to reminding their readers that they can choose to turn off their e-mail during working hours or slow their activity down and restore some sanity to their workload. DeWitt's (2001) solutions for achieving more reflective Web readers are in a similar vein, with the notable exception that the students he discusses are often unaware of the alternative that he is offering. But his Reflective Model for reading also makes particular assumptions about the relationship between reading and memory and about the kinds of proficiency that we should be encouraging our students to acquire. Those assumptions are not problematic; as I mentioned earlier, I find this approach to slowing down Web reading quite sensible. But just as the axis of absence/presence does not exhaust the canon of memory, I suggest that the memory practice represented in the Reflective Model is but one of many.

DeWitt's (2001) Reflective Model is a familiar one because it has much in common with the model that most academics share for textual research. As academic writers, it is almost second nature to us to weave together various and disparate texts and then contribute our own particular approach or perspective, resulting in the kind of "cognitive fabric" that we publish as an article in our disciplinary journals. Yet not every text we come across contributes to the "supertext" that is the end goal of our scholarly endeavors. Although in an ideal world we might have the time and inclination to read, reflect, and synthesize all potential sources in anticipation of writing our own texts, this is neither practical nor realistic. The two models of reading that DeWitt offers do not map cleanly across the print-digital divide, nor does he suggest that they do. Neither, however, does he acknowledge that sometimes we read impulsively and that there is a proficiency required to do so well. We frequently describe this practice among ourselves in terms of the value of learning to skim; faced with our own disciplinary version of information overload, it is not unusual for us to scan a table of contents, bibliography, or index to determine whether a text is likely to be of use to us. Nor is it unheard of that we might scan the first and last few paragraphs of each chapter, hoping to piece together enough of a fabric that we can decide whether to pursue a text further. This is not the rich and dense fabric that DeWitt advocates, obviously, but this is a pragmatic reading practice that most of us resort to at one time or another. It is a practice no less useful than the ability to weave the rich, dense cognitive fabric of the Reflective Model.

Rather than seeing cognitive fabric as a whole from which pieces are missing, this pragmatic alternative works more inductively, connecting smaller pieces, keywords, sources, and ideas, insisting on a *proairetics* of invention (see chap. 3), rather than the synthesis of the Reflective Model. This is not to suggest that, at some point, synthesis would not become appropriate, but DeWitt's suggestions should be tempered with the fact that "whole" cognitive fabric is not always our goal. The memory practice associated with these more modest goals is one that emphasizes pattern over presence, although not to the exclusion of the latter. Skimming requires a reader to be able to piece together information in ways that are *good enough* to gauge a text, perhaps without arriving at a full representation of it. As an analogue for this kind of reading and memory practice, I turn to a concept from visual studies, *persistence of vision*, and suggest an analogue, *persistence of cognition*. In other words, although we are capable of slowing down as readers and building the kinds of mental representations that the Reflective Model calls for, we also might consider what kind of memory practice lends itself to the impulsive reading that the Web seems to encourage.

Persistence of vision is the term for the way that our visual faculties perceive motion when presented with still images. As Anthony Kinsey (1974) puts it in *How to Make Animated Movies,*

> This term describes the way in which an image "burns" itself onto our retina so that it remains with us for a small fraction of time after the source of the image has been removed. This phenomenon is the basis of the cinema film, enabling the succession of projected images to be assimilated without interruption and thereby producing an illusion of continuous and natural movement. (p. 15)

There is an obvious analogy here between the successive still images of analog cinema and the "live for the moment" Web reading that DeWitt (2001) describes (or even the practice of skimming/scanning a text). Therefore, can we speak of a persistence of cognition, one that might be an appropriate memory practice for the impulsive reader? As I explain in the next section, I think that there are certain new media tools that already point us in that direction. Persistence of cognition is more than a neologistic way of describing short-term memory, although it may bear some relation to it. Persistence is the practice of retaining particular ideas, keywords, or concepts across multiple texts, be they websites, journal articles, or chapters of the same book. We also might describe it as an initial step toward the kind of full-fledged reflection that DeWitt argues for because it functions to sketch out an initial outline or shape for a set of texts.

For the moment, it is enough to note that persistence marks a play between presence and absence. Hold on to too many pieces and information overload would be the result; there is a necessary amount of forgetting that takes place. But persistence also names the presence of particular pieces—certain themes persist across a set of texts. Persistence as a memory practice is the ability to build and maintain patterns, although those patterns may be tentative and ultimately fade into the background. To put it in terms familiar to us from socioliterary theory, persistence is a practice of bricolage, one that doesn't necessarily replace the engineering required in DeWitt's (2001) Reflective Model, but that might usefully augment it and arrive at different kinds of knowledges. In the final section of this chapter, I try to articulate these differing models and their benefits more concretely.

PRESENCE AND PERSISTENCE IN NEW MEDIA

The existence of other kinds of memory practices does not invalidate the continued need for memory that is figured simply as storage. There is certainly cultural value to be had in remembering the important events in our shared, social history—making those events present helps to shape our community in desired ways. But there are important differences among the memory practices outlined in this chapter; the reflection prompted by a monument is not an effective strategy for the kind of feed-forward reading that DeWitt (2001) describes or indeed for the glut of information that marks our contemporary circumstances. As I suggested in the last section, I believe that certain new media offer us tools for building persistence of cognition, the inductive perception of connections, and patterns across multiple sources. In this final section of the chapter, I want to draw on an example from my own reading practices, contrasting two forms of reading and memory in which I engage—one that draws on a more traditional understanding of memory and one that demonstrates the potential utility of persistence as a memory practice. I follow that discussion with an analysis of a relatively recent site devoted to applying some of these techniques to a broader corpus of texts.

As blogspace has grown over the past 5 years or so, one of the challenges facing those of us who follow many weblogs is the ability to keep up with them. I track more than 100 sites on a daily basis, and I have heard of colleagues who manage to stay abreast of twice or three times as many. From the perspective of basic web surfing, the time needed for this would be prohibitive. Although weblogs tend not to be graphically intensive (and thus download fairly quickly), the time required to check even a purely textual page regularly for updates—because most blogs are not updated on a strict schedule—would be daunting. The solution for this particular form of information overload comes in the form of syndicated feeds. Much like the Associated Press news wire, which syndicates its writers' stories to news outlets, most weblog platforms now allow their users to publish feeds as they publish entries. Without getting too deep into the history of syndication,[3] as of this writing, there are two primary formats for syndication— Really Simple Syndication (RSS) and Atom—each of which makes part or all of a weblog entry available in XML format. The feeds from many blogs can be collected by feed readers or aggregators, and there are both desktop and web-based versions of these programs (Fig. 6.1). More recently, web browsers have incorporated aggregation into their suite of services. Effectively, aggregators check weblogs and keep track of whether a particular user has accessed the most recent content. They check our blogs so that we do not have to, in the same way that most mail programs can be set to inform a user when there is new mail in the inbox.

The usefulness of syndication has spread well beyond blogspace as well. In late 2002, the *New York Times* began making headline feeds available to subscribers, and, in the meantime, almost every major news organization has followed suit. From weblog aggregators to personalized startup pages, syndication has fueled the boom in recent years of individuated and customized content even when users are unaware that syndication is behind that content. (In 2004, a white paper from Yahoo! and Ipsos Insight suggested that more than a quarter of Internet users were using RSS without being aware of it.) Syndication drives sports scores, weather reports, news headlines, auction bids, and countless other forms of information; it is the idea behind many of the applications that automate the "page-checking" process, freeing us up for other tasks. In the rest of this section, I focus on two types of aggregation that I make use of personally, two means that I have of "remembering" my feeds.

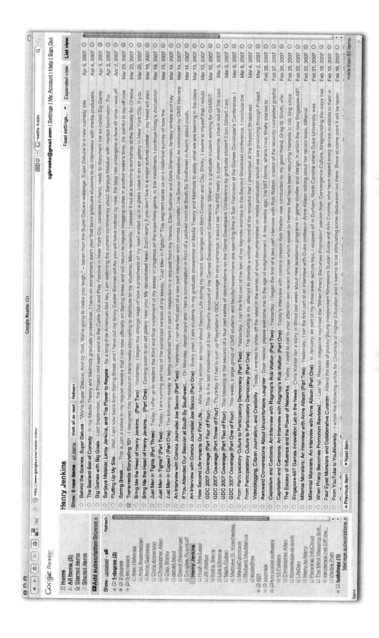

Figure 6.1. Screenshot of Google Reader

159

The first aggregator or feed reader is a more traditional one. Although there are many competing platforms out there, I happen to use Google Reader to keep track of weblogs. Google Reader (GR) is a web-based aggregator that allows me to check my feeds from any networked computer; because I work with three or four different machines, a web-based aggregator meets my particular needs quite well. The page is divided into two parts: Along a left column is a list of RSS or Atom feeds that the user wishes to keep track of; in the right column, when a feed is selected, the most recent content from that feed appears.

GR, and other aggregators like it, provides what is essentially a centralized portal, allowing me to keep track of more than 100 weblogs and frequently updated websites. Like many other technologies, my aggregator distributes my memory, freeing me of the need to remember each site individually. In this, it is something like a blogroll or a browser-based set of bookmarks. Where it differs from these other forms of distributive memory, however, is in the level of detail that the creators of GR are able to achieve. Unlike a bookmark or a weblink, GR tracks not only each feed, but when I last accessed it. Only content that has been added since my last reading is considered new, and GR indicates new content by boldfacing the feed (and including in parentheses the number of new entries since my last session). It allows me to "star" particular entries in a feed for future examination, storing them in a separate folder of saved entries. If I want to return to a feed and check an entry that I have meant to star but haven't, it supplies the option of displaying all of the entries published at the site. The site also provides me with some rudimentary "trends" about the feeds to which I subscribe, including information about how many entries I am reading, which feeds I most frequently save entries from, and the like (Fig. 6.2).

There are plenty of other features that GR provides, as does each of the other aggregators available, but I have focused here briefly on the ways that my own aggregation functions as a distribution of my memory. All things considered, GR's contribution to my personal media ecology is a fairly traditional one with respect to memory. The interface strongly resembles that of an e-mail program; although its service is more developed than other kinds of bookmarking services, GR is focused on storage— both of the particular feeds that I assign to it as well as my own reading of those feeds. At a glance, I can determine whether new content is present or absent in each of more than 100 feeds and I can preserve particular entries (in a few different ways) for measured consideration at a later date, and this is to say nothing of the convenience of having this service remember the many feeds that I prefer to check regularly. For those users who make regular use

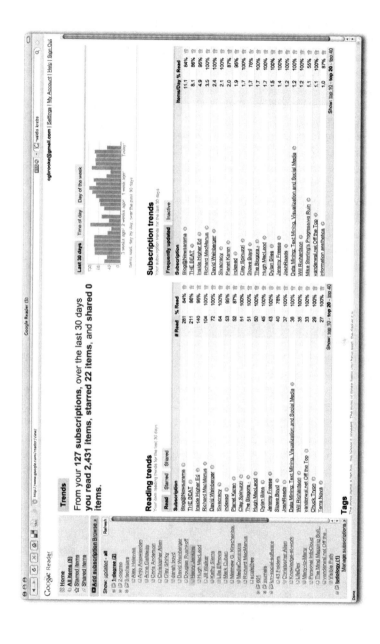

Figure 6.2. Google Reader Trends snapshot

of RSS or Atom feeds, aggregators have become, in a short time, an indispensable extension of their memory as we traditionally understand it.

The second memory practice I wish to consider here is a little bit different, however, because it corresponds to what I describe in the last section as persistence of cognition. In chapter 4, I discussed the pattern-making possibilities of tagclouds—almost nonsensical paragraphs of keywords where the color and size of terms reflect those terms' frequency in a particular text or set of texts. The social bookmarking service del.icio.us allows users to create tagclouds of the keywords they have used in bookmarking various sites, and Amazon.com now offers a "Concordance" for individual books in their inventory, a cloud of the 100 most frequently used words in a particular text. But there also are services on the Web that allow users to create tagclouds with RSS/Atom feeds (TagCloud.com and ZoomClouds.com) (Fig. 6.3). Tagclouds such as these differ from those found on Amazon (and, to a lesser degree, del.icio.us) in that the text that the clouds draw on changes regularly. As particular topics wax and wane in the feeds aggregated into a tagcloud, then the cloud would change along with it.

The parallels to the kind of feed-forward reading that DeWitt discusses, and the archetypal "surfing" activity of the Web, should be obvious. I store the feeds from blogs by my friends and colleagues in GR because I prefer to read them closely and reflectively. But when it comes to blogs and sites from the technology industry, for example, I am more interested in following particular trends than I am in reading each weblog entry closely. Assigning 20 or 30 feeds to a tagcloud allows me to distribute the kind of scanning, feed-forward reading that I would otherwise have to do myself. The cloud "remembers" the most important topics over the course of a week or a month. For example, as I was putting the finishing touches on this chapter, several of the sites that I aggregate this way made mention of Yochai Benkler's (2007) then new book *The Wealth of Networks : How Social Production Transforms Markets and Freedom*, and the number of mentions the book received were sufficient to show up in my own tagcloud (or feedcloud, which is how I think of it).

Unlike aggregators, which are typically software platforms containing a variety of options, tagclouds are the output of code that almost entirely remains behind the scenes. Other than typing in the feed addresses and setting up a page where the cloud will appear, this form of aggregation requires little involvement on my part unless I choose to follow a particular keyword for further investigation. Although tagclouds represent a fairly rough approximation of the kind of scanning we do when we surf from page to page on the Web, I would argue that this is indeed a form of mem-

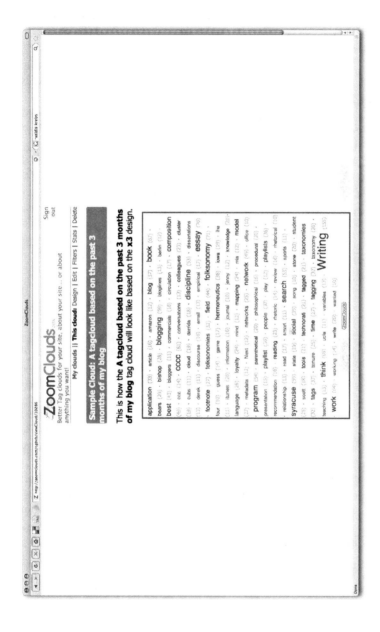

Figure 6.3. Screen shot of Zoom Clouds

163

ory, albeit one we are unused to discussing. Much like our brains fill in visual gaps, enabling us to perceive motion, tagclouds approximate the process by which we perceive connections among a set of texts to arrive at the conclusion that "everyone is talking about" a particular topic. My feedcloud remembers for me those topics that persist across a number of the feeds that I aggregate, allowing me to discern (and follow up on) particular patterns or intensities that emerge in the conversations that I wish to follow.

My final example is less personal in nature. In late 2006, Chirag Mehta created a site that applied the strategy of tagclouds to presidential speeches from 1776 to the present day (See Fig. 6.4). As he explains at the site,[4] he collated and converted more than 365 documents, running them through a tagcloud generator, removing common words, to arrive at clouds for each of the speeches, which include State of the Union Addresses, Inaugural Addresses, and speeches from any number of major events in the history of our country. As in the prior feedcloud example, Mehta's site allows researchers to chart terminology as it waxes and wanes in importance throughout the history of the presidency. The long horizontal line directly above the cloud is a "slider," which can be used to navigate from one cloud to the next with ease. As the legend to the site explains, both font color and size are used to indicate a term's importance at a given time. Interestingly enough, to be able to watch a term grow and shrink, the site makes use of persistence of vision to signify the kind of cognition that this chapter discusses. Because many of the terms change from one speech to the next, it is only the largest that persist across broad stretches of documents—a tendency that is easier to track if you unfocus your eyes as you watch the clouds change. Although the positions of the words may shift on the screen, loosely tracking the shape of a particular word (e.g., such as *constitution* in the years surrounding the Civil War) allows a viewer to watch it grow and fade over a period of time.

What is perhaps most fascinating about this site, however, is a feature that takes it beyond the scope of simply auto-indexing presidential speeches. As part of the script that generates the site, Mehta has programmed in a form of "stickiness," a kind of memory. That means that particularly important terms, even if they are not mentioned in every single speech during a time period, will stick around and fade more slowly. For example, the word *Cuba* figures prominently in President Kennedy's speech to the country during the Cuban Missile Crisis, as well it should. But the word appears in several of the documents after that, regardless of whether the word occurs in those speeches. Mehta describes these as "aging tag clouds," allowing users who adapt his code to set a variable for the persistence of prominent terms, which mimics the way that crucial issues and ter-

Figure 6.4. Screenshot of presidential speeches tag cloud

165

minology will persist in political discourse and fade only over time. Mehta's tagclouds mirror the way that we practice memory; we do not simply forget an issue or a keyword, particularly one as important as Cuba was in the early 1960s, as soon as another issue is raised by our leaders.

What begins then as an example of a thorough spatialization of discourse—the conversion of more than 300 presidential speeches to tagclouds—is on Mehta's site retemporalized by allowing for terminological persistence. To put it in the terms of this chapter, Mehta's site allows us to locate the presence or absence of a particular term at a specific time, and, in that sense, it functions as storage. But by programming stickiness into the clouds, Mehta also permits us to see the larger patterns that emerge over the course of time, establishing a rough form of cultural memory. Although that form may not offer us the reflective synthesis of a more careful reading of these speeches, Mehta's site generates a different kind of memory and knowledge—one that is no less valuable. For the casual researcher, this site might supply any number of hypotheses about political discourse in this country, testable claims that might then be followed up on through the more careful reading that is our stock in trade in academia.

Does this kind of aggregation and representation (in the form of tag clouds) signify a new form of memory? I would grant that these sites bear only some resemblance to what we traditionally think of when we consider memory. But this is partly a result of a habit of thought that has been with us since Plato. We take in information, sometimes without being aware of it, and only notice it when that information connects with other data to form a pattern worth investigating. One of the places where new media challenges our traditional notion of memory as storage lies precisely in its ability to emulate these sorts of background processes, whether it is through new tools for developing what Christina Haas (1996) calls text sense or through the kind of aggregation made possible by tagclouds. Our own minds are not simply sites of storage; they perceive connections and patterns that may only become present to us in the later stages of their construction. That this construction relies on the canon of memory should not be a point of contention, however, nor should the fact that new media stand to make significant contributions to our ecology of memory in the form of persistence.

NOTES

1. Whether Plato, as someone who wrote down his dialogues, genuinely takes this position is less relevant here than the effect that this position has had on our approach to memory.
2. The 2000 *College English* debate conducted among Xin Liu Gale, Susan Jarratt, and Cheryl Glenn remains one of the best illustrations of this conversation in rhetoric and composition. The three raise historiographical as well as ethical questions of what constitutes historical evidence when the object of study is a figure marginalized by traditional history.
3. See http://goatee.net/2003/rss-history.html for one such history.
4. http://chir.ag/phernalia/preztags/

7

PERFORMANCE

On those stepping into rivers staying the same other and other
waters flow.
—Heraclitus

You can never play a record the same way for the same crowd.
—Paul Miller (2004)

Much like the canon of memory, the canon of delivery has suffered from
neglect in contemporary rhetoric and composition. Although it is tempting
to lay the blame for this treatment at the feet of the printed page, John
Trimbur finds (as explained in chap. 2 of this book) that our discipline's
focus on the classroom and on the student-teacher transaction has as much
to do with our dismissal of delivery as the technologies we use. Kathleen
Welch (1990) also calls attention to the "truncation" of the canons perpe-
trated by writing textbooks, reducing the canons from five to three with the
"eradication" of memory and delivery. If Welch and Trimbur could write 5
years ago of the neglect of delivery, however, such a claim would be more
difficult to make in the present day. Kathleen Blake Yancey's 2006 collection *Delivering College Composition: The Fifth Canon* and Andrea Lunsford's

keynote address to the 2005 Computers and Writing Conference, "Writing, Technologies, and the Fifth Canon" (later published in *Computers and Composition*), are each instances of high-profile scholars attending to this "neglected" canon. In "Why Napster Matters to Writing: Filesharing as a New Ethic of Digital Delivery," published in the same issue as Lunsford's keynote address, Dànielle DeVoss and James Porter close their essay not by arguing for the recovery of the fifth canon, but for a "theory of digital delivery" that can help us come to terms with the ethical dynamics of the Internet. In short, we are rapidly approaching a time where we can dispense with prefacing discussions of delivery by bemoaning its neglect.

One of the factors that interferes with our ability to reconceive delivery in light of new media, however, is our tendency to view the canon through the lens of our commonsense definition of the term. Delivery, in everyday parlance, is a transitive process; it is rare to speak of delivering without an object that is being delivered. Our pizzas and newspapers are delivered to us, and we even speak of delivering conference presentations. In each of these cases, however, the practice of delivery has little appreciable impact on what is being delivered. We occasionally speak of someone "really delivering" when they have performed a task particularly well, but this intransitive use of the verb is not common. As Richard Lanham (2006) observes, however, delivery was far more constitutive for the ancient Greeks:

> Delivery did not deliver its messages as simply as United Parcel or FedEx, which bring the stuff to your door, ring the bell, and leave. It involved communicating the message in such a way that it would be accepted and attended to rather than refused, ignored, or thrown in the wastepaper basket unread. (pp. 23–24)

It is this sense of delivery, delivery as *performance*, that this chapter attempts to articulate in the context of new media.

The chapter begins by examining two of the more recent models for understanding delivery: Trimbur's (2000) discussion of circulation and Welch's (1990) equation of delivery with medium. Although there is merit to each of these positions, neither goes far enough in accounting for the constitutive force of delivery. If, as I argue in chapter 1, we should be working to avoid treating the practices of new media as discrete "objects," then correspondingly, we will have less use for theories of delivery that rely on the presence of such objects. The second section of the chapter returns to the argument sketched out here—that we need to think in terms of an intransitive, constitutive *performance*, rather than transitive or transactional delivery, when it comes to new media. The argument in this section draws an analogy between Richard Lanham's "Weak Defense" of rhetoric and our treatment of delivery to suggest that Lanham's insights should be extended to the fifth canon as well as the others.

Finally, I turn to an application of this discussion by examining some of the controversies surrounding Wikipedia, a site that has caused a great deal of concern on the parts of academics and librarians around the country. Much of this concern, I argue, comes from our misunderstanding of the significant differences between Wikipedia and more traditional encyclopedias. Wikipedia is often treated as if it were a traditional encyclopedia, albeit one that is imperfectly rendered online. As a consequence, its critics typically fail to recognize those elements that set it apart from its print-bound counterparts. Wikipedia entries are too often taken as static products—as objects that are simply correct or not, when in fact many of the "pages" are ongoing performances of values and interpretations, performances that in the long run may be more "accurate" than the corresponding entries in a traditional encyclopedia.

Before I turn to the next section, however, one important qualification is necessary. As crucial as it is to recognize the performative dimension of the canon of delivery, it would be foolish to argue that the canon must be *either* performative *or* transitive. The same Web whereon we can find Wikipedia also contains links to PDF files—graphic replications of printed pages that are frequently uneditable. Put simply, there are plenty of examples of each kind of delivery. This chapter argues, however, that without an understanding of delivery as *performance*, we are left with an incomplete grasp of new media. It may no longer be a question of neglecting delivery, but we still have work to do to recognize its constitutive powers.

DELIVERY AS CIRCULATION, MEDIUM

. . . the very task of deciding what media form a given rendering shall take no longer follows from the inherent differences between media (which have now become mere surface differences).

—Mark Hansen (2004)

DeVoss and Porter's (2006) chapter provides an example of how easy it can be to conflate these two senses of delivery. Referencing the tactics of the media conglomerates, DeVoss and Porter explain,

> They portray the individual participant as a "hacker" or "pirate"—the insurgent whose acts of production are really acts of theft. "Good users" are those who passively consume, respect intellectual property, and pay per use. "Bad users" are those who produce parody web sites, or who hyperlink without permission, or who distribute and download content without paying for it. Mostly, corporate producers are worried about the audience as co-producers of content and as active distributors of digital material. (pp. 190–191)

That final sentence regarding the "worries" of corporate producers blends together the two types of delivery we are considering in this chapter, although there is an argument to be made that filesharing has begun to blur the two as well. The most aggressive response from organizations such as the RIAA, however, have been reserved for those who distribute material that is the putative property of corporations in the music industry. There are obvious parallels to the vehemence with which the Star Wars franchise and the Disney corporation police their intellectual property. For these conglomerates, the Internet is simply another avenue for the kind of vertical distribution typical of earlier media, such as radio and cable music channels. Operating with a narrow definition of delivery, as these corporations do, Napster and other filesharing platforms undermine the centralized control by permitting widescale *lateral* or peer-to-peer (P2P) distribution.

It should be noted, however, that the challenge posed by P2P distribution is a more modest threat to the corporate oligopoly than either they or filesharing's advocates suggest.[1] It is difficult to imagine that corporate producers are particularly worried about audience production of content, for example, when we consider the heavily embedded technological, cultural, economic, and medial advantages that the various culture industries possess. If we reflect on how heavily these corporations are invested in distributive control, both directly and through the management of consumer attention, it is difficult to see their aggression in prosecuting so-called "bad users" as anything other than an overreaction. DeVoss and Porter (2006) urge us to extend our analysis in this way, beyond the point of delivery, asserting that "A renewal of interest in delivery requires that we take up the question of 'economies of writing'" (p. 194), a call that echoes John Trimbur's (2000) concerns in his article on circulation.

As I explained in chapter 2, one of the contrasts that Trimbur (2000) offers to explain the idea of circulation is the pairing of the *Wall Street Journal* and the *National Enquirer*, which "no longer figure simply as equivalent moments in the circulation of commodities, guided by the law of supply and demand" (p. 209). In other words, it is not simply that grocery shoppers demand one periodical and not the other, with the free market responding to this demand. Trimbur argues that each of these commodities participates in the broader system where the ability to read the *Enquirer* from a distance is tied directly to the types of stories appearing there and to the design that is typical of tabloids. Traditional economics tends to separate the elements of production and consumption, allowing them to be yoked together under the laws of supply and demand. "From a Marxist perspective, however," he explains,

> the point is not simply to describe the competition of the capitalist market, with its disciplinary force and underlying assumption that the fittest will survive and prosper—that, in effect, exchange value verifies use value. To do as much simply justifies the status quo as inevitable. (p. 211)

He goes on to critique the naive position that if academics would only write in less difficult prose, they could achieve a status as "public intellectuals." Such a position, he explains, involves a "one-sided view of production" without confronting the role that distribution plays in the insulation of academic discourse and expertise. We should not submit, he argues, to "the fallacy that by changing the manner of writing, one can somehow solve the problem of circulation" (p. 212).

One place that we might interrogate Trimbur (2000) is with his emphasis, following Marx, on the commodity form, the embodied contradiction between use value and exchange value. Indeed, one of the most persistent arguments against a practice like filesharing is its circumvention of the market. If an artist's work is posted to P2P networks, thousands of users might download it without any "value" returning to the artist or the studio. It is in this sense that filesharing blurs the lines between distribution and coproduction; an individual user might be responsible for producing hundreds or thousands of copies of an mp3 file with no more investment than storing the file in a net-accessible folder. It is possible to interpret the actions of groups like the RIAA, then, as a self-interested attempt at preserving the commodity form that Trimbur discusses, a reinforcement of the act of exchange. We can observe this attempt directly in the rerelease of Napster, a pay-per-use system that has never achieved the level of usage that it enjoyed prior to its shutdown at the hands of the recording industry.

To return more specifically to the question of delivery, one of the issues that new media raise is precisely this ratio between use value and exchange value. The danger of relying on Marx's formulation is that exchange as he conceives it is primarily an exchange of what Lanham (2006) calls "stuff," the exchange of currency for some physical object that has been produced and distributed and will eventually be consumed. Lanham contrasts "stuff" with "fluff," arguing that our economy is rapidly moving towards ephemera like style and attention. It would be a mistake to accuse Trimbur of ignoring this element of our economic systems, but, at the same time, he does ground his analysis in the "stuff-ness" of the commodity form. It is difficult to avoid inferring from this emphasis that he is speaking of the delivery, the circulation, of objects. Even in cases where the objects are less tangible, as in the case of academic knowledge, Trimbur references bibliometric analyses—attempts to materialize the exchange of ideas. We would be equally mistaken to imagine that the kind of circulation that Trimbur discusses fails to play an important role in our economic and social lives. Yet with phenomena such as filesharing, the open source movement in software development, and copyleft measures such as Creative Commons licenses, a model of delivery restricted to the physical distribution of commodities is insufficient for an understanding of new media.

At the close of his essay, Trimbur (2000) offers some examples of the kinds of classroom exercises implied by his exploration of circulation. One such, in his words, "may look at first glance to be a traditional genre exercise," but, in fact, it involves much more. While his students translate articles from medical journals into the kind of reports that might appear in the *New York Times*, Trimbur focuses on "how the act of translation necessarily participates in and shapes the circulation of biomedical discourse in ways that go beyond simple information transfer" (p. 213). In fact, it is assignments like these that keep Trimbur from fully drifting into the position of taking circulation to mean the simple transmission of physical objects. He is careful to note that translation from one medium to another works against a purely transitive notion of delivery. In this sense, the notion of *delivery as medium* may serve to keep circulation from becoming synonymous with the transitive form of delivery.

The reverse also may be true. Trimbur (2000) does not devote time in his article to the argument that delivery and medium are intimately connected; for that perspective, Kathleen Welch's (1999) *Electric Rhetoric* is a better place to turn. Welch argues that we should be thinking of delivery as medium and that this canon "is weakened if it refers only to the gesture, physical movement, and expression that so many commentators have dismissed it as limited to" (p. 153). Welch insists that delivery does not vanish with the shift from orality to literacy, but rather changes. Furthermore, as more recent developments in media have emerged, so too have new opportunities for the exploration of delivery. Welch may be the most outspoken critic of rhetoric and composition's willingness to ignore those opportunities, as *Electric Rhetoric* continues the critique begun much earlier in her writing.

Welch (1999) is critical of the kind of "form/content divide" imposed on our classrooms by the limitations of writing textbooks, and yet a simple equation of delivery with medium runs the risk of reducing to the position that she opposes. In chapter 1, I discuss the difficulties of working with the *medium* as a unit of analysis, and those cautions are worth considering in the context of delivery. One of the weaknesses of medium theory is the threshold of visibility that it requires: At the point that a particular set of practices is stable and visible enough to become a medium, it also possesses a certain level of inertial force. Academic blogging, for example, has grown substantially over the past 3 years, enough so that it is taking on the shape of a particular genre within the medium of blogging. Without intending it, those of us who blog consciously as academics have been constraining the medium for newcomers. It is not uncommon to see newer bloggers struggle with the tension between what they perceive as an "established category" and their own interests in the practice. Few academic bloggers would admit to believing that everyone else should blog as they do,[2] and yet the presence of a critical mass of this type of writing creates this pressure. Although it may be more precise to speak of academic blogging as a specific genre within a medium, my point here is that both genres and media, as units of analysis, both reflect and produce a level of stability that may work against a conception of delivery as performance.

Welch (1999) offers an example of the kind of classroom exercise implied by her discussion, just as Trimbur (2000) does. She suggests, as one possibility, "interpreting an apparently ordinary electronic text, such as a Coca-Cola advertisement, and probing its ideological positioning as it emerges from the rhetorical canon of delivery" (p. 160). Additionally, she suggests a variety of questions that would make up such probing, questions related to camera and actor positioning, editing, lighting, production quality, and so on. There is an ironic subtext to the majority of these questions—namely, that they could be asked of nearly any televisual or cinematic text. In other words, the questions she offers are highly formalistic. In part, this is a function of the medium within which she operates, an academic book that advocates certain generalizable strategies. These are not questions meant to address *only* the putative advertisement, but rather a whole host of related texts, and, in this sense, they are perfectly reasonable. But it is here where Trimbur's notion of circulation provides a corrective to an emphasis on medium. Attention to circulation involves asking about more than medial features; students would inquire into the way that the advertisement circulated on particular TV channels, at specific times, during certain shows, and so forth. Welch's final question, regarding intertextuality, takes on much greater importance with an emphasis on circulation.

Both medium and circulation prove valuable additions to the critical vocabulary that we use in our consideration of delivery, but neither seems entirely adequate to the task of discussing delivery as practice and performance. Circulation captures the importance of movement in the way that information spreads, but it is too easy to fall back into traditional characterizations of physical transfer. The equation of delivery with medium acknowledges the shaping role that information and communication technologies play, but it can too quickly become a static set of features that decontextualizes delivery. Neither Trimbur nor Welch necessarily falls prey to these risks, but the picture that they present of delivery is one on which we can productively build. The strategy that I advocate here sees both circulation and medium gathered under the idea of performance. As part of that strategy, it is worth turning our attention to the work of Roland Barthes and Richard Lanham and their contributions to the practice of delivery.

TO DELIVER: AN INTRANSITIVE CANON?

The title of this section alludes to Roland Barthes's essay ("To Write: An Intransitive Verb?") that has suffered from poor circulation, exiled to a collection of essays (*The Rustle of Language*) that has not received nearly the attention as have *Image Music Text* (Barthes, 1978) or the selection of essays edited by Susan Sontag (1983), *A Barthes Reader*.[3] As a result, we in rhetoric and composition are largely unaware of "To Write," although it begins by contrasting then-contemporary literary criticism with the "genuine theory of language" that, for Barthes, was represented by classical rhetoric. Much of the essay concerns itself with structural linguistics and the role that it might play in literary criticism. Specifically, Barthes identifies linguistic features that might provide him with a "weapon against the general 'bad faith' of discourse which would make literary form simply the expression of an interiority constituted previous to and outside of language" (p. 141). Those familiar with his better circulated work may recognize the parallel here between "the expression of an interiority" and the capital-A Author whose death Barthes is famous for declaring. Prefiguring his later claims about the transitions from Author to writer and from Work to text, Barthes asks "at what point the verb to write began to be used in an apparently intransitive manner" (p. 141).

The significance of this shift signals for Barthes a turn to the middle voice when it comes to writing: It is no longer sufficient for him to say that an author writes. We must also acknowledge the degree to which the Author is written, as Foucault (1977) does in his essay on the author function. Although this may strike contemporary readers as a *fait accompli*, the intransitive manner of *to write* means that the author is as much a product of her text as the text is the result of her labor.

> The meaning or the goal of this effort is to substitute the instance of discourse for the instance of reality (or of the referent), which has been, and still is, a mythical "alibi" dominating the idea of literature. The field of the writer is nothing but writing itself, not as the pure "form" conceived by an aesthetic of art for art's sake, but, much more radically, as the only area [espace] for the one who writes. (p. 144)

The instance of discourse, as later essays would explain, not only includes the reader, but assigns to the reader a great deal more responsibility than criticism of the time presumed. To put it another way, the model against which Barthes is writing is one where an Author delivers "reality" to a passively consuming reader through the medium of language. Much of his subsequent work helps to demonstrate that "reality," as portrayed by even the most "realist" of French authors, is indeed performed in the instance of discourse, and that performance relies heavily on the readers' faculties (see especially Barthes, 1974, 1978).

Close to the end of his talk, Barthes explains that the features he has discussed "oblige us to conceive language and discourse no longer in terms of an instrumental and reified nomenclature but in the very exercise of language [parole]" (p. 144). Although Barthes would later reject structuralism as too reified and instrumental, the goals that he sets here for the structuralist project are not difficult to see even in his final works. In *Camera Lucida* (1982), for example, he makes space for the *punctum*, an individual's response to visual art that takes place in what he calls here the "instance of discourse." Our point here, however, is to follow Barthes in conceiving of new media in the exercise, the practices, of new media. Particularly in the case of delivery, we must consciously resist the impulse to reduce that canon to a transitive, instrumental process of transmission.

This fundamental opposition to the instrumentality of language is one of the places that we might draw connections between Barthes' work and that of Richard Lanham, whose *Electronic Word* (1993) remains one of the foundational texts for establishing a relationship between the humanities and technology. That relationship is elaborated in his most recent book *The Economics of Attention* (2006), but this book follows *The Electronic Word* more than it signals a change in direction and so, as in chapter 5, it is to Lanham's earlier work that I wish to turn. In that earlier chapter, we considered the at/through distinction from *The Electronic Word*, but the "bistable decorum" Lanham suggests is for him an answer to a broader question, one whose parameters include much of Western civilization as well as one that represents for Lanham "the root problem I was trying to address in my scholarly life" (p. 154). He labels this "the 'Q' question" in honor of Quintilian, who, according to James Murphy (1986), raises it himself no fewer than 23 times in his work. The question is a simple one: Is the perfect orator a good person as well as a good speaker? At the root of this question is the Platonic critique of rhetoric—if rhetoric can be put to both good and bad uses, then its potential for abuse (in the form of dishonest manipulation) outweighs its possible benefits, and one would better spend one's time pursuing only good, and in Plato's case, this pursuit would take the form of philosophy.

Because the "Q" question starts from a Platonic presumption of amorality, both of the answers that Lanham lays out are described as defenses of rhetoric. Lanham (1993) begins his chapter on the "Q" question, then, by laying out the terms of what he calls the Weak Defense:

> So, like Quintilian, we first deny the problem resolutely, and then construct something that I shall call "the Weak Defense." The Weak Defense argues that there are two kinds of rhetoric, good and bad. The good kind is used in good causes, the bad kind in bad causes. Our kind is the good kind; the bad kind is used by our opponents. This was Plato's solution, and Isocrates', and it has been enthusiastically embraced by humanists ever since. (p. 155)

Lanham ties the Weak Defense not only to Plato and Isocrates, but also to Peter Ramus' division of the rhetorical canons into "properly" philosophical ones and the "decorative" canons of style and delivery, which would remain the province of an impoverished rhetoric. The result is one that is familiar to us contemporarily as that strategy which denounces an opponent's claims as "mere rhetoric" and valorizes one's own as the truth. With the Weak Defense, rhetoric is purely decorative and parasitic on the ideas or positions it is called on to represent.

The Strong Defense, in contrast, does not presume the existence of *a priori* positions that are then expressed through a rhetoric that corresponds in value to the ideas it represents. According to Lanham (1993):

> The Strong Defense assumes that truth is determined by social dramas, some more formal than others but all man-made. Rhetoric in such a world is not ornamental but determinative, essentially creative. Truth once created in this way becomes referential, as in legal precedent. The court decides "what really happened" and we then measure against that. The Strong Defense implies a figure/ground shift between philosophy and rhetoric—in fact, as we shall see, a continued series of shifts. (p. 156)

The "series of shifts" to which Lanham refers here is the bistable oscillation of looking at and through a text that we took up in chapter 5; more important for our purposes here is the shift from rhetoric as a decorative art to one that is architectonic (Lanham cites McKeon's work approvingly in this chapter). According to the Strong Defense of rhetoric, the proof of its value does not rest with some *a priori* content, but rather in the performance. As Lanham writes of Ramus' choice to formally institute his own Weak Defense, "we can hardly make too much of this decision" (p. 158). In other words, what may seem to be an obvious reversal of the hierarchical relationship between philosophy and rhetoric in fact has wide-reaching implications that cannot be understated.

Those implications place the canon that we call *delivery* at the center of the relationship between identity and discourse, a relationship that Lanham (1993) argues is mutually constitutive. Yet as Trimbur (2000) argues, our treatment of delivery has tended to reduce "discourse" to student papers and "identity" to the "middle-class family drama" of the composition classroom. It is difficult not to see precisely the sort of Weak Defense that Lanham argues against when we consider how delivery has been handled in our discipline. But this "afterthought" is grounded in more than Ramus' severing of specific canons; it also is a function of a particular technology. For delivery to be a matter of "physical presentation," there must be some sort of object to be presented—an attitude toward discourse typical of print culture.

Lanham's (1993) Weak and Strong Defenses, in other words, encompass more than our attitudes toward language; they also can be extended into a consideration of technology. In fact, I would argue that there are similar Defenses to be made on behalf of media. Lanham makes much of Deirdre McCloskey's remark that there is "virtue in virtuosity," and we might suggest a corresponding virtue in virtuality. The Weak Defense of technology treats it analogically as separable into good or bad technology or, to put it in more familiar terms, into technologies that liberate or oppress. In this view, values such as these are located within technologies, rather than being rooted in particular practices. The Strong Defense, in contrast, would see technologies valued only in specific uses; information technologies, in particular, would not simply represent messages conceived prior to their "physical presentation," but rather would be understood as a crucial element in the constitution of those messages. In short, returning to the issues of chapter 1, a Strong Defense of technology sees it as an interface, rather than an object.

Lest we assume that we are somehow beyond Weak Defenses of technology, a recent example might prove instructive. In a 2003 essay entitled "Why the Web Will Win the Culture Wars for the Left: Deconstructing Hyperlinks," Peter Lurie argues that the structure of the web will produce a particular cultural outcome:

> The architecture of the web, and the way users navigate it, closely resembles theories about the authority and coherence of texts that liberal deconstructionist critics have offered for thirty years. . . . Anyone who has spent a lot of time online, particularly the very young, will find themselves thinking about content—articles, texts, pictures—in ways that would be familiar to any deconstructionist critic. And a community of citizens who think like Jacques Derrida will not be a particularly conservative one.

Lurie continues, arguing that "These basic technical tools are similar to deconstructionist analytical tools," but this ignores that, in Derrida's case particularly, those "deconstructionist analytical tools" are simply the analytical tools provided by the philosophical tradition. Derrida breaks from that tradition in the ways he employs those tools; this does not mean that the tools are responsible for deconstruction. Ultimately, Lurie poses a homology that is not an unusual one—more recently, weblogs have been heralded as a new, more democratic form of media—but it buys unthinkingly into a Weak Defense of technology. Lurie assumes that there is a particular value that predates the technology, and that technology practice will simply inculcate users with that value. Lurie's argument here carries no more weight than would the inverse, a claim that the cultural values instantiated by books (stability, coherence, authorship) have resulted in a "particularly conservative" culture.[4] Each views technology as a conduit for particular values, a "delivery system" that plays little, if any, role in what is being transmitted.

Although he is a little more nuanced about it than many of the writers at the time, Lanham (1993) employs a Weak Defense with respect to technology from time to time, assuming the democratizing force of the electronic word. In this sense, Lanham is not too far away from Lurie, who likewise assumes particular cultural outcomes as a result of the technology. Technology, for both Lanham and Lurie, runs the risk of being reduced to mere instrument, just as rhetoric does in the Weak Defense. The technologies simply represent or instantiate values that preexist any specific practice. It is not necessarily that these claims are invalid, but rather that the Weak Defense ultimately preempts any attempt to achieve them. If it is enough to simply use certain media to achieve a particular value (be it democracy, liberalism, critical thinking, etc.), then that absolves users of any responsibility for working toward that outcome. We see this frequently in educational contexts, where emphasis on the raw use of technology often supercedes concerns about *how* technology is used.

In the case of new media, the distinction between instrument and interface (as forms of the Weak and Strong Defenses) is even more crucial. It is debatable whether new media exist outside of performance, whether we can even speak of such media as objects in the same way that we refer to books or videotapes. A discussion list is simply a list of e-mail addresses, for example; it is only in the performance, the consensual invocation of a discussion space, that the list exists as a medium for conversation. Most of the software with which writers create weblogs are simply database interfaces that must be used in a particular fashion to create that particular medium. In both of these cases, and others besides, there is no "physical presentation" of a preexisting discursive object; although the products of these media can be reappropriated into other forms, their status as new media comes through delivery, through performance.

Both Lanham's (1993) discussion of a Strong Defense of rhetoric and Barthes' (1972) attention to the "instance of discourse" emphasize performance over transmission when we consider their work in light of the canon of delivery. It is easy to forget, in a culture still heavily influenced by print technology, that delivery was at one time a key constitutive element in discourse, and I take both Barthes and Lanham to be harkening back to that model of discursive production. There are certainly contexts where a more traditional, transitive version of delivery is appropriate, but this chapter focuses on performance as a competing version, partly as a corrective for those cases where the transitive model of delivery is misapplied. In the final section of this chapter, I turn to a couple of different examples, one brief and one extended, where an understanding of delivery as both practice and performance should be applied.

DELIVERY AS PERFORMANCE

> The question of whether the Web is a medium or a world mat-
> ters if you think it's a medium and nothing more. A medium is
> something through which a message travels from A to B. The
> communication succeeds if the message arrives at B unaltered.
> Obviously, the Net is a medium in that sense, complete with
> noise and error-correction, etc. But if that's where you stop—
> and who does?—you don't ever see the Web and can't explain
> why it matters to us.
> —David Weinberger (2005)

One place we might begin when considering the different models of delivery at play in new media is with the Web. As students have turned to electronic resources in ever-increasing numbers, there has been a parallel turn
on the parts of instructors, librarians, and anyone concerned with education. Whereas younger generations have turned to the Internet with enthusiasm, our more conservative social institutions (like the RIAA as discussed
earlier) have done so with something more resembling panic. Educators,
even those of us who advocate for information technologies, are no exception. One of the ways that we have tried to get a handle on the proliferation of electronic sources and resources is through an emphasis on "credibility," or *ethos* in the parlance of classical Greek rhetoric. A Google search
on pages with both *web* and *credibility* will net more than 47 million
results, from tutorials on assessing Web pages' credibility to advice for
enhancing one's own credibility online to Stanford's Web Credibility Project
(Fig. 7.1), which, among other things, will provide users with a "two-week
teaching outline and resource materials" for "teaching Web credibility."

Nearly every discussion of online research has in common a single
injunction. Much like the universality of the writing handbook command to
"Use definite, specific, concrete language," discussions of electronic
research beseech students to take great care in critically evaluating sources
located on the Web. Justification for this care is usually couched in terms of
the Web's lack of quality control. Unlike print materials, according to this
argument, which have been subjected to editorial review, the low publication threshold of the Web makes it necessarily suspect. Chris Anson and
Robert Schwegler's (2004) *Longman Handbook* provides an explanation that
is typical:

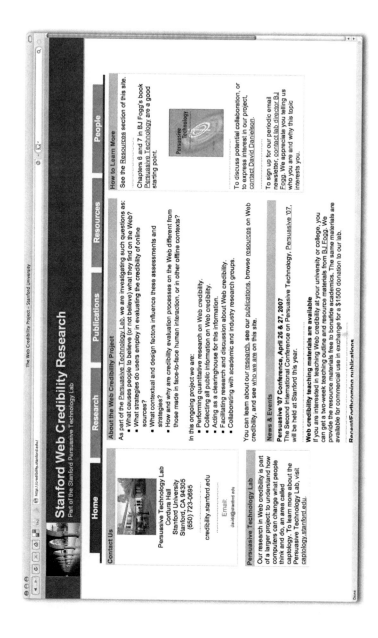

Figure 7.1. Screenshot of Stanford's WCP

183

> Although you must judge all your sources critically, Internet resources
> require more careful evaluation than library materials, which have
> been evaluated prior to publication. Because anyone can place materi-
> als online, the Internet provides the largest repository of information—
> and much questionable information. (p. 250)

This notion, that "Internet resources require more careful evaluation," has
sparked a veritable cottage industry of tutorials promising to make us more
careful and critical consumers of Web information—an industry that
extends now to the writing handbooks produced in our field. For example,
The Curious Researcher (2006) offers the domain test, suggesting that, "in
general you're wise to rely more heavily on material sponsored by groups
without a commercial stake [.gov or .edu instead of .com] in your topic."
Research Strategies for a Digital Age (2006) presents tips for "verifying the
web site author," for as she explains, "anonymity destroys credibility." The
Little Brown Compact Handbook (2004) explains that a design that "reflect[s]
the apparent purpose of the site" serves to "indicate that the sponsor takes
its purpose seriously and has thought out its presentation." *Bookmarks: A
Guide to Research and Writing* (2005) provides an eight-category, cross-media
taxonomy for assisting students, exceeded only in detail by *The Curious
Researcher*'s 16-step flowchart for a "rigorous review of a Web document."

None of this advice is incorrect *per se*, although it is relatively easy to
find exceptions for most of it. The underlying assumption behind most of
these evaluation checklists, however, is something that we should find
more problematic. Put simply, much of the advice for evaluating Web-
based information posits credibility or *ethos* as a quality that is decontextualized from the technology, an attitude toward delivery that sees it simply as transmission. Drawing on Roland Barthes' distinction between Work
and Text, Barbara Warnick (2004) describes this "one-size-fits-all"
approach as inappropriate:

> we need to move away from the tendency to think of credibility assess-
> ment on the Web in modernist terms. A modernist approach consid-
> ers the source or author of a site as an essential gauge of its trustwor-
> thiness and expertise. But clear indication of authorship, sponsorship,
> and credentialing is not ubiquitous on the Web.

Credibility, as it is presented in our textbooks, is something that Websites
have only by virtue of some traceable connection to the "real world," what
Barthes calls above "the instance of reality (or a referent)." Online sources
are presumed faulty unless they are able to verify that connection, to

demonstrate the quality control that we assume is lacking online. As Warnick explains, however, that presumption rules out a great deal of what happens online.

As an alternative to the one-size-fits all" approach to credibility (and to delivery), Warnick (2004) follows Nicholas Burbules in a discussion of "distributed credibility," the introduction of a range of other conditions under which a site might be deemed credible, including "skillful design, image quality, usability, information structure, comprehensiveness, absence of self interest, usefulness," and many others. As Warnick explains, "it is the quality of the performance that counts," and this is where the canon of delivery might be enter into the discussion. Also, it is in this sense that Trimbur's circulation can be a helpful addition to our vocabulary. For the remainder of this chapter, it might prove useful to turn to a couple of concrete examples of the kind of distributed, performed credibility that we are after here.

In August 2004, an unusual congruence of subject matter took place across a broad range of academic weblogs, centered around the question of whether one should blog, as an academic, under one's given name (or "real" name) or using an alias or pseudonym. The discussion that ensued could probably be described as what Kumar et al. (2005) have described as a "burst" in blogspace—an extended, concentrated series of blog entries occurring across a range of sites, interlinked and responding to each other in a fairly short period of time. Although the issue has resurfaced on several occasions since that original discussion, often in connection to articles appearing in either *The Chronicle of Higher Education* or *Inside Higher Ed*, subsequent discussions have not either the breadth or passion of the original "pseudonym" debate. Unfortunately, the conversation must be reconstructed indirectly because some of the sites central to the discussion have been taken down in the 4 + years since.

The question of whether to blog with a pseudonym is one that most academic bloggers ponder at one or more points during their writing. In a profession where the competition for positions is fierce and where decisions sometimes ride on the smallest of factors, writing publicly carries as many risks as it does rewards. In the past few years, there have been high-profile cases of experienced academic bloggers either being refused tenure or losing out on positions, which has led, naturally, to speculation about whether their blogs played a role in those decisions. The pseudonym debate began in the comments to a blog entry where the author wondered out loud whether blogging under one's own name posed a risk to tenure and promotion decisions. As often happens in such spaces, comments quickly polarized the discussion, and commenters took to their own blogs to compose lengthy arguments and refutations. One of the chief issues was one that fits well within the bounds of this chapter—namely, how are other academics to trust anything that is written by someone under an alias when they have no way of measuring their remarks against reality? Particularly when it came to issues of academic culture and life, they argued, there was no reason to take anything that pseudonymous bloggers wrote as "real" or serious.

One of the arguments that emerged on the other side, however, and one that helped to crystallize my own thinking on the matter concerned the nature of credibility. To treat only eponymous blogs as credible was to fall prey to the attitudes under question in this chapter—to assume that weblogs were only credible insofar as they provided a conduit or channel for the credibility that their authors had accumulated offline. Yet dozens and maybe hundreds of readers had come to rely on these bloggers for advice, community, and insight. In cases like the now-defunct Invisible Adjunct (Fig. 7.2), pseudonymous weblogs have provided (and still provide) a space for exposing and critiquing the gender, race, class, and/or labor politics of the academy, with a forthrightness that would be inadvisable (if not impossible) for someone blogging eponymously. Most important, some of these pseudonymous bloggers argued, the personae that they had crafted had earned the kind of distributed credibility that Burbules and Warnick discuss. By maintaining their pseudonyms consistently in the comments on countless other blogs and by maintaining their own weblogs, they had invested in their personae no less energy than we all do in our "real" names. Unless we have met someone face to face, there is little, in fact, to distinguish a pseudonym from a "real" name in blogspace.

The warrant underlying pseudonymous bloggers' claim to credibility is that such credibility can be distributed throughout a social network, a warrant that has a basis in our everyday experiences. When we are looking for book or movie recommendations, for example, we do not necessarily turn to the critics who are "most qualified" to make that decision in an objective sense. We turn to our friends, people in our immediate social network whose taste we perceive as similar to our own. In fact, as the recommendations provided by services like Amazon and iTunes demonstrate, we do not even need to know the person to find his or her recommendations credible. It is possible to argue, however, that it is one thing to rely on a stranger's taste when selecting a book to read and quite another when it comes to the kind of information that sites like Wikipedia provide. Our second example, therefore, provides a closer look at this massive multi-author online reference work, which has, in recent years, proved to be a con-

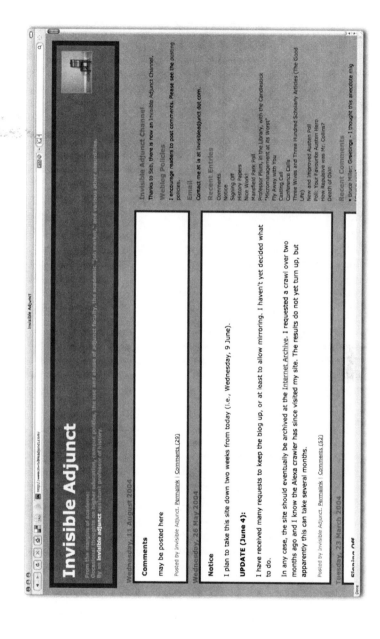

Figure 7.2. Invisible adjunct blog

187

tentious site among educators of every stripe, not just those who maintain weblogs.

Wikipedia (Fig. 7.3) was founded in January 2001 to be an interactive encyclopedia,[5] a reference work built on a platform of wiki software, which allows anyone to edit content. Some 5 years later, according to Stacy Schiff in *The New Yorker*, Wikipedia celebrated the publication of its millionth article (on March 1, 2006) and achieved the lofty position of the "seventeenth most popular site on the Internet," generating far more traffic than its "more traditional" competitors. Thanks partly to the PageRank algorithm at Google, which rewards densely interlinked sites like Wikipedia, and partly to the vision of its founders, Wikipedia has become an issue for many educators. Most frequently, it is compared with the Encyclopedia Britannica, with the obvious exception of its authorship. Wikipedia articles are authored by anyone who wishes to contribute; although the site has been reorganized to attempt to restrict abuse and vandalism, it is open in the sense that potential contributors are only blocked for demonstrably bad behavior. Although much of the content is supplied by a select few—Schiff reports that only 3,300 of the English language site's more than 200,000 registered users have contributed 70% of the work—Wikipedia is far more open than comparable reference works.

It is this openness—what its detractors would describe as the absence of any quality control—that makes Wikipedia a prime site for considering the canon of delivery. In December 2005, *Nature* published a study comparing 42 entries from Wikipedia with their corresponding articles in *Britannica* and concluded that the accuracy rate was similar in each (on average, Wikipedia entries contained four errors for every three in *Britannica*). If the content provided by each of these reference works is substantially similar, then the primary differences between them lie elsewhere. Obviously, there is a difference in authorship. The traditional approach to encyclopedias involves assembling a large staff of qualified experts to write entries; their expertise (and hence credibility) precedes anything that they might write. The *Encyclopedia Britannica* collects their expertise together, but otherwise simply transmits that expertise in the form of a static reference work. The coordination required to organize and produce a reference work like an encyclopedia is sizable; to keep the work (and eventual price) manageable, print reference works must make choices about what material to include and exclude.

Many of the features of Wikipedia turn this model for reference work on its head. No particular expertise is required to contribute to Wikipedia, although inaccuracies and misinformation are not likely to last long. It may be more accurate to say that a person's credentials have little impact if the

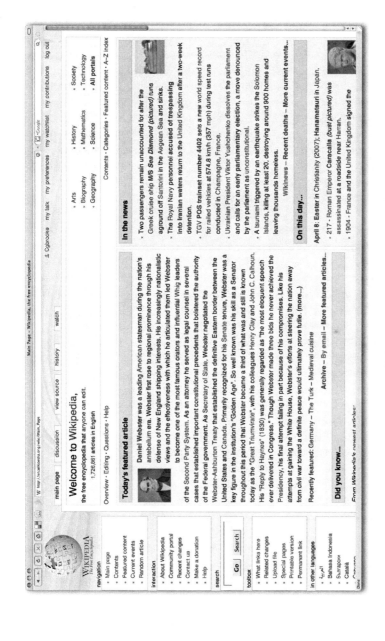

Figure 7.3. Wikipedia front page

quality of the work is considered sufficient. Although marginal topics are sometimes folded into other pages or deleted eventually, there are no topical restrictions. In 2005, Jon Udell published a screencast detailing the evolution of a Wikipedia page, on the "heavy metal umlaut," that began as a joke and eventually matured into an actual entry. Nor does a topic need to "ripen" or be finished; there are often Wikipedia entries posted the day that something happens. The staff that maintains the project is small, and although superusers have been drafted to settle disputes and oversee site edits, the level of organization at Wikipedia reflects a growing need more than it does an organizational plan. Of course, Wikipedia is freely available, has entries in more than 200 languages, and aspires to the kind of global reach and relevance that no encyclopedia, print or otherwise, has ever enjoyed.

For all of its advantages, Wikipedia also has its share of detractors, many of whom can be found on the "Criticism of Wikipedia" entry on the site. Their criticism gathers around the issue of credibility. If authors are multiple and anonymous, the argument goes, how can there be any accountability? How can we know whether to trust a Wikipedia entry? One answer to these questions is to carry over the idea of a socially distributed credibility. Wikipedia authors now occupy different tiers of editorial responsibility, with more trusted writers working further up the ladder than random contributors. In other words, one measure of an entry's accuracy is the reputation earned by its author(s) in their participation on the site.

A second answer, to my mind a less satisfying one, has been to simply ban students from using Wikipedia. Unfortunately, there are many instructors across the disciplines taking just such a step. In fact, the Wikipedia "crisis" has grown to such proportions that one of the most popular memes to circulate among academic technologists in June 2006 was Alan Liu's memo on the "Appropriate Use of Wikipedia." In it, Liu explains to potential students that encyclopedias are not primary source materials and that Wikipedia is, at best, an uneven source with respect to quality, one that is not properly an encyclopedia at all. "Students should feel free to consult Wikipedia," he writes, "as one of the most powerful instruments for opening knowledge that the Internet has yet produced. But it is not a one-stop-shop for reliable knowledge." Liu's memo does not evince the kind of hostility with which many commentators view Wikipedia, but his acceptance is begrudgingly pragmatic at best.

What many commentators on Wikipedia accuracy fail to acknowledge is that there are other forms of distributed credibility at work on the site. Each entry on Wikipedia is, in fact, the tip of a much larger iceberg of activity. Each entry has a version history, records of every change made to the page, as well as a discussion page where authors debate the page's content and direction. If a user visits Wikipedia and simply samples an entry, she or he may be missing out on a great deal of the information that the site can provide. Ben Vershbow (2006) describes the alternative as reading Wikipedia "in the fullest way: by exploring the discussion pages and revision histories that contextualize each article, and to get involved ourselves as writers and editors." He even goes so far as to suggest that accuracy is in some ways beside the point, which makes sense when we consider it from the point of performance and delivery. Some entries become the subject of "edit wars," rapid changes, and reverts centered around key phrases or claims, and pages like these can be all but useless to the visitor looking for clear, definitive answers to a question. One way to look at these pages, however, as Vershbow explains, is to consider them in their full contexts. If we expect Wikipedia to deliver (in the traditional sense) a definitive answer, then the site will often fail. But if we approach the site, and particularly its contested pages, as sites where the questions are not yet answered, where there are *no* definitive answers, then Wikipedia becomes a site where the debates over these issues is performed, in a much more "accurate" fashion than attempts at encyclopedic objectivity could be. Version histories and content debates should be of particular interest to scholars and teachers in rhetoric and composition because debates over content often take place at the level of language. It is not unusual to see arguments over particular phrasings and terminology and whether they are the best expression of neutral point of view.

The credibility of Wikipedia (and sometimes lack thereof) is something that occurs, to borrow Barthes' phrase once more, at the instance of discourse. Rather, we might describe it as both circulating and distributed among many instances of discourse. Credibility is not delivered prepackaged at Wikipedia; it is performed, sometimes *ad nauseam*. As a discursive system, Wikipedia collects both the process and product of reference work, and the result sometimes can be messy. But it also can represent the kind of opportunity that traditional encyclopedias can never dream of providing—an *ethos* that is interactive, democratic, public, and, at times, contentious.

I should conclude this chapter by acknowledging the wealth of material on performance that goes unexamined in this chapter. There is a long history in the study of technology of work that focuses particularly on the performance of identity that is too extensive to go into here. The transdiscipline of performance studies has taken up questions of technology readily and contributed a great deal of valuable work. In some ways, the question of online or virtual identities is one that parallels the questions I raise and answer in this chapter. If, on the Internet, "no one knows you're a dog," as the *New Yorker* cartoon would have it, the question of trust and credibility can extend quite easily to questions of identity. Sociocultural questions of access are posed routinely in blogspace and answered in a full range of behaviors. The dangers of adhering to traditional notions of delivery on a MySpace or FaceBook page, providing predators with all-too-real information about ourselves, are well documented in the media and, as I write this book, the object of current legislation.

Although we understand at some level the idea of performing a role or particular identity, however, the notion that discourse is performed is largely foreign, except in certain contexts (e.g., dramatic or cinematic scripts). On the one hand, it is a small change in attitude that this chapter suggests—seeing discourse as circulating rather than some*thing* that we circulate—but on the other hand, it is a change that has far-reaching implications for the practice of new media. As I explained in the introduction to this chapter, delivery is not an either/or proposition; we need not choose to view it as *either* transitive *or* intransitive. With new media, however, the importance of considering delivery in its intransitive incarnations becomes important. As Mark Hansen (2004) explains in *New Philosophy for New Media*, "digitization underwrites a shift in the status of the medium—transforming media from forms of actual inscription of 'reality' into variable interfaces for rendering the raw data of reality" (p. 21). Paul Miller (2004) puts it more colloquially in one of the epigraphs to this chapter, noting that "you can never play a record the same way for the same crowd." Both writers speak to that property of new media that draws us away from the "instance of reality," the one true rendering of reality in discourse, and closer to the "instance of discourse," where it is a particular performance, one that constitutes reality, that is taking place. As should be becoming increasingly clear to us, even the unmarked scenario that Trimbur discusses, the classroom submission of printed pages, is a performance of certain values—values that are being challenged by contemporary information technologies. Rethinking our approach to delivery is one of the ways we might begin to account for those values.

NOTES

1. Youtube may ultimately prove an exception to this statement.
2. One notable exception to this is the "nymous" debates that swept through the academic blogosphere in 2004, which I discuss later in this chapter.

3. The essay also was delivered as a talk at the 1966 Johns Hopkins symposium on "The Languages of Criticism" and collected in *The Structuralist Controversy*. My own preference is for this version because it also transcribes the discussions that followed the presentations. Page numbers refer to this volume.
4. Neil Postman was fond of pointing out in lectures to predominantly left-leaning humanities audiences that the majority of "inner circle" members of the Nazi party were humanities majors. Weak Defenses can be found in both advocacy and criticism of rhetoric, discourse, technology, and so on.
5. The site actually began in 2000 as Nupedia, but was relaunched as a wiki in 2001.

DISCOURSE EX MACHINA,

A CODA

Now let us imagine an extreme case: that a book speaks of
nothing but events that lie altogether beyond the possibility of
any frequent or even rare experience—that it is the first language for a new series of experiences.

Friedrich Nietzsche (1992)

I am not so presumptuous as to imagine that this book provides the sort of
"first language" that Nietzsche (1992) describes in *Ecce Homo*, and yet he
gets at part of what I have hoped to accomplish in my own writing. Over
the past 15 years or so, we have moved from the niche status of e-mail and
Usenet to a Web that, although not genuinely yet WorldWide, would have
been difficult to imagine or appreciate back then. Although I do not mean
to insult the various attempts, our ability to generate a productive vocabulary for describing these new media has lagged behind the development of
the technologies. Already certain terms sound quaint and others clunky,
while even the category of *new media* can be vague to the point of mean-
inglessness. This book is not an attempt at "defining, once and for all,"
these technologies; there is no quicker route to obsolescence than by
depending on the stability of the technology industry. New tools, platforms,

interfaces, genres, practices, and/or products may rise and fall, seemingly overnight.

What I have attempted, then, in this light is to articulate some of the practices that I see cutting across varieties of new media. By grounding them in revisions of the classical canons of rhetoric, I have tried to hint at both the fundamental continuities in our production of discourse and the ways that such production changes over time. Like such scholars as Eagleton, Barthes, McLuhan, and so on, I have always found the canons to be a particularly robust framework for understanding discourse. As I explain in chapter 2, however, I do not see the canons as naming specific practices, but rather as ecologies of related practices that shift and change as our technologies do. One advantage of understanding them ecologically is that we can resist concerns of technological determinism, which, oddly enough, are more relevant to, for instance, arguments that memory and delivery were erased by the development of the printing press. We may invent new practices within a particular canon/ecology, but this does not erase or supplant those that already exist. To put it simply, the canons speak to the need for invention, arrangement, style, memory, and delivery, but our available information technologies (from voice and gesture to YouTube and MySpace) both constrain and enable the way that those needs are actualized in discourse.

I also hope that the canons serve a heuristic function in this project— that is, that they might help us to make valuable distinctions among the myriad interfaces available to us. Obviously, I can speak to my own experience and the fact that writing these chapters changed the way I perceived the various platforms and interfaces that I examine here. But ultimately the test of any heuristic is its portability—the extent to which others can take it up and use it. Too often the critical vocabulary we have developed to write about new media has been definitional, answering questions like: What is/are new media? What is hypertext? What is multimedia? What is interactive? In some ways, this book is an expression of my own frustration with that line of questioning, which can only ever arrive at the conclusion that something is or is not X. They can be important questions under certain circumstances, but more often, in my experience, the more valuable questions to be asked have to do with function, value, and practice. At different scales of an interface, the "need to know" can vary widely. For most users, it is more important to know that Movable Type works, for example, and that it makes publishing a weblog easier than it is to know that MT is a database system or even to know how it works. My hope, then, is that the canons, as I describe them here, will be of use at many different scales in focusing our attention on the practices made possible (and on those made more difficult or impossible) by the interfaces we encounter.

Perhaps the single most important goal that I hold for this book is the one that I lay out in the introduction; this book seeks to stage a mutually transformative encounter between rhetoric and technology. It is an encounter that took place in my own graduate study long ago and one that has had far-reaching implications for the ways that I see both rhetoric and technology. For me, they have served as barely distinct perspectives on the same phenomenon. I find it increasingly irresponsible to study rhetoric and writing without accounting in some way for the various impacts of information and communication technologies. Likewise, I do not think that it is possible to understand these technologies without an appreciation of their rhetorical effects, both qua technology and as players in our discursive ecologies. In our discipline, it is still commonplace to think of technology as one specialization among many, an attitude that I have critiqued elsewhere and find less and less viable as time goes on. If this book can help to persuade some in my discipline that technology is a more central concern than they previously thought, then I will consider it a success. If it sparks (or rekindles) interest in rhetoric on the parts of those who study technology across the disciplines, I will be similarly pleased. My interest is in raising the concerns outlined in this book, not in answering them with any sort of finality.

In that interest, rather than closing this afterword with grand proclamations of the sort that plague many of our critical texts on discursive technologies, I want to conclude with a FAQ of sorts. With any large project, there are inevitably questions or issues that lurk in the background—choices that writers make that may go undefended (or even unexamined) due to the particular directions their texts take. Some of these questions are addressed to one degree or another in the book, whereas others are simply concerns that have developed for me as I have written. At any rate, I hope that they provide some resolution without closing off what I have intended to be a fairly open project.

WHAT'S WITH THE LETTER P?

Partly, this project partakes of my passion for problematizing propriety paired with the preponderance of productive perspectives and practices proffered by P words. Yes, I am kidding. The choice of terms that begin with P began as a coincidence and was later elevated into heuristic. In my mind, the terms we use to designate the canons are largely arbitrary—certain of my revisions will undoubtedly appear as casuistic stretches, whereas other may seem obvious or redundant. The point is not to happen on the "correct" term for invention or style in the context of new media. Rather, it is to acknowledge that the practices associated with these canons change in that context and will continue to do so. Insofar as it has been useful to have certain terms to designate the traditional interpretations of the canons, on the one hand, and my revised versions, on the other hand, I have deployed these terms. Just as I am not arguing that contemporary rhetorical practices somehow supplant those of previous eras, I do not suggest that anyone begin using these terms in lieu of our traditional translations for the canons. If they provide some assistance in recasting the canons for our current era, I am satisfied.

IS THE INTERFACE/OBJECT DISTINCTION THAT CRUCIAL?

I believe so, although it does not receive the attention it perhaps deserves here. Like Steven Johnson (1997), I think that the future of criticism, and rhetoric for that matter, requires us to come to terms with interfaces and to recast our understanding of texts in such a way that sees them as particularly stable interfaces (although not completely so). As I explain in chapter 3, I think it possible to read Roland Barthes (1974) *S/Z* as a demonstration of the interfaciality of even the most relentlessly referential of print texts. We also might see Jacques Derrida's work as an extended argument for the ways in which individual texts are simply interfaces with the whole of language, as much as they strive to conceal that fact. In other words, there is a philosophical commitment to the interface on my part that underlies this book, only surfacing on occasion. There is a great deal of fine work being done on interface design in the practical sense, which lies outside of the scope of this project. In other words, we know more now about the nuts and bolts—the grammar—of interface design than ever before. My sense is that the practices I describe in this book might productively be combined with such work because I do not address the "how" of interface design.

WHAT ABOUT ALL THE SOCIAL FACTORS THAT AFFECT TECHNOLOGY?

Just as I consciously elect in this book to focus at the scale of practice (as opposed to code or culture), I also chose to operate at a certain level of generality when it came to describing these practices. I think it almost self-evident to say that different communities are going to take up (or ignore or resist) technology in different ways, and that this difference would extend to the scale of practice seems equally obvious. The question of how widespread (or minor) these various practices might be would be more relevant if I were advocating certain of them at the expense of others. This book can only hint at the sum total of possibilities; thus, in many cases, I drew on examples of practices familiar to myself. However, another rich vein of potential research might come from combining this framework with diffusion studies or by examining specific communities.

This answer may be unsatisfying to some and this framework more limiting than I have found it, but I believe there is an important need for scholarship that is not simply descriptive. Such work also has its place, but it assumes a degree of stability and locality that can doom us to reaction rather than action. As important as it is to experiment with new media, it is equally important to take an inventive attitude toward the ways we think *about* technology and the vocabularies we use to describe it. I do not question that factors such as gender, race, and class have profound effects on technology, but I would dispute the notion that technology studies should be reduced to an exploration of those factors to the exclusion of all else. In rhetoric and composition, we have access to some of the most robust theories of discourse ever devised, and yet most of the persistent theoretical frameworks for examining discursive technologies come from writers in other disciplines, often whether they fit our own work. If I have underrepresented the importance of social factors in this book, it has been in the interest of developing a framework that might productively be refined in a range of such contexts.

WHAT ELSE IS MISSING?

For better or worse, there is no explicit focus in this project on pedagogy, although I believe that there are some obvious classroom implications for many of the examples I offer. One of the equally obvious implications of the increasing trend toward online education is that we have begun to think of our classrooms, whether f2f or online, as interfaces as well, and in that sense, the writing classroom may ultimately take its place among the media I describe in this project. But there are no direct pedagogical consequences to this project other than its attitudes toward rhetoric and technology.

Missing also is a fair amount of advocacy on the part of technology in general. I do not think that it is necessary to be a "power user" to understand my arguments here, nor do I see this project as an attempt at conversion to technophilia. My own interest in technology is undoubtedly apparent, but advocating particular practices would be to run counter to the framework for this project. We each build our own personal media ecologies, according to our needs, our abilities, and what is available to us. This project supplies a vocabulary for describing these ecologies, one that also might be of use in transforming and/or improving our practices.

WHAT EXACTLY IS IT THAT THIS BOOK *DOES* DO AGAIN?

It is natural, I suspect, to be hyperconscious of those "areas for further study" and the factors bracketed off for a project's manageability. As I explain in the Introduction, this project is both grandly ambitious and paradoxically modest. This project recasts two of our more venerable frames from classical rhetoric, the canons and the trivium, setting them almost as axes along which to plot a rhetorical approach to technology. A revised trivium, I argue, can help us to map out differently scaled ecologies (code, practice, and culture), and the canons provide a rich articulation of ecologies of practice. This framework is particularly useful in the case of interfaces, those imperfectly bounded encounters where users, technologies, and contexts intersect. Instead of describing a process that culminates in the production of a textual object, the trivium and canons help us envision a discursive space that is ongoing—one that is shaped both by the intentions of individual users and contextual constraints.

As part of this overall framework, this project also visits each of the individual canons in turn, considering how various new media have served to challenge and/or augment the various practices gathered under each heading. The framework described in the first two chapters is not a map in the sense of stably locating each of the canons; rather, it is an attempt to focus our attention as we examine media, isolating those practices (and sets of practices) that the canons indicate. In short, I suggest that the canons can help us understand new media, which add to our understanding of the canons as they have evolved with contemporary technologies. Neither rhetoric nor technology is left unchanged in their encounter.

Although it is grandiose to propose a revision to the classical tradition, the revision is backward compatible. In other words, I believe that this project lays out a framework that is no less useful for the study of ancient media than it is for their contemporary descendants, and that requires a certain degree of modesty. This book does not propose a radical break from classical rhetoric. In some ways, I believe that this project restores to the canons some of the vitality and richness that they held for the ancients, although I am less qualified than others to make that determination. This book, then, works to maintain some continuity with the history of rhetoric even as it looks to new forms, genres, and technologies with the hope of enriching our understanding of both past and future. I hope that it proves to be a strong contribution to our discipline's efforts at developing a rhetoric of new media.

BIBLIOGRAPHY

Aarseth, Espen. *Cybertext: Perspectives on Ergodic Literature*. Baltimore: Johns Hopkins University Press, 1997.

Adamic, Lada A. and Natalie Glance. "The Political Blogosphere and the 2004 U.S. Election: Divided They Blog." LinkKDD-2005, Chicago, IL, Aug 21, 2005.

Alexander, Christopher. *A Pattern Language*. New York: Oxford UP, 1977.

Anjewierdan, Anjo and Lilia Efimova. "Understanding Weblog Communities Through Digital Traces: A Framework, a Tool and an Example." *International Workshop on Community Informatics* (COMINF 2006). Montpellier, 2006 (November). http://staff.science.uva.nl/ ~ anjo/cominf2006.pdf

Anson, Chris M. and Robert A. Schwegler. *Longman Handbook for Writers and Readers*. 3rd ed. New York: Longman, 2004.

Aristotle. *On Rhetoric: A Theory of Civic Discourse*. Trans. George Kennedy. New York: Oxford UP, 1991.

Banks, Adam. *Race, Rhetoric, and Technology: Searching for Higher Ground*. Hillsdale, NJ: Erlbaum, 2006.

Barber, John and Dene Grigar, eds. *New Worlds, New Words: Exploring Pathways for Writing About and in Electronic Environments*. Cresskill, NJ: Hampton Press, 2001.

Barta-Smith, Nancy and Danette DiMarco. "Same Difference: Evolving Conclusions About Textuality and New Media." *Eloquent Images*. Eds. Mary Hocks and Michelle Kendrick. Cambridge, MA: MIT Press, 2003. 159–178.

Barthes, Roland. *Camera Lucida*. Trans. Richard Howard. New York: Hill and Wang, 1982.

_____. *Critical Essays*. Evanston, IL: Northwestern UP, 1972.

_____. *Image Music Text*. Trans. Stephen Heath. New York: Hill and Wang, 1978.

_____. *S/Z*. Trans. Richard Miller. New York: Hill and Wang, 1974.

_____. "To Write: An Intransitive Verb?" *The Structuralist Controversy: The Languages of Criticism and the Sciences of Man*. Eds. Richard Macksey and Eugenio Donato. Baltimore: Johns Hopkins University Press, 1972. 134–144.

Barzun, Jacques. *From Dawn to Decadence*. New York: Harper Collins, 2000.

Bateson, Gregory. *Steps to An Ecology of Mind*. Chicago: U of Chicago P, 2000.

Bawarshi, Anis. *Genre and the Invention of the Writer: Reconsidering the Place of Invention in Composition*. Logan: Utah State UP, 2003.

Bazerman, Charles. "The Life of Genre, the Life in the Classroom." *Genre and Writing: Issues, Arguments, Alternatives*. Eds. W. Bishop and H. Ostrom. Portsmouth: Boynton/Cook, 1997. 19-25.

Bender, John and David E. Wellbery, eds. *The Ends of Rhetoric: History, Theory, Practice*. Stanford, CA.: Stanford UP, 1990.

Benjamin, Walter. "Unpacking My Library." *Illuminations*. Ed. Hannah Arendt. New York: Schocken, 1978.

Benkler, Yochai. *The Wealth of Networks: How Social Production Transforms Markets and Freedom*. New Haven: Yale UP, 2007.

Bernstein, Mark. "Cycle." Patterns of Hypertext. 1 Oct 1998. 13 Aug 2006. < http://www.eastgate.com/patterns/Patterns3.html > .

_____ "The Virtue of Irregularity." Hypertext Gardens: Delightful Vistas. 1 Oct 1998. 13 Aug 2006. < http://www.eastgate.com/garden/ Virtue_of_Irregularity.html > .

Birkerts, Sven. *The Gutenberg Elegies: The Fate of Reading in an Electronic Age*. New York: Fawcett Books, 1995.

Bolter, Jay David. "Hypertext and the Rhetorical Canons." *Rhetorical Memory and Delivery*. Ed. John Frederick Reynolds. Hillsdale, NJ: Erlbaum, 1993.

_____. *Writing Space: The Computer, Hypertext, and the History of Writing*. Hillsdale, NJ: Erlbaum, 1991.

_____, and Diane Gromala. *Windows and Mirrors: Interaction Design, Digital Art, and the Myth of Transparency*. Cambridge: MIT Press, 2005.

_____, and Richard Grusin. *Remediation: Understanding New Media*. Cambridge: MIT Press, 1999.

Booth, Wayne C. *The Rhetoric of Fiction*. 2nd ed. Chicago: U of Chicago P, 1983.

Bowden, Darsie. "The Limits of Containment: Text-as-Container in Composition Studies." *CCC* 44.3 (1993): 364-379.

Brooke, Collin Gifford. "Forgetting to be (Post)Human: Media and Memory in a Kairotic Age." *JAC* 20.4 (Fall 2000): 775-795.

_____. "Perspective: Notes Toward the Remediation of Style." *Enculturation: Special Multi-journal Issue on Electronic Publication* 4.1 (Spring 2002): < http://enculturation.gmu.edu/4_1/style >

Brooks, Kevin, Cindy Nichols and Sybil Priebe. "Remediation, Genre, and Motivation: Key Concepts for Teaching with Weblogs." *Into the Blogosphere*. (2004). 13 Aug 2006. < http://blog.lib.umn.edu/blogosphere/remediation_genre.html > .

Burgin, Victor. *In/Different Spaces: Place and Memory in Visual Culture*. Berkeley: U of California P, 1996.

Burke, Kenneth. *A Grammar of Motives*. Berkeley: U of California P, 1969a.

_____. *A Rhetoric of Motives*. Berkeley: U of California P, 1969b.

Bush, Vannevar. "As We May Think." *Atlantic Monthly* 176.1 (July 1945). 17 Feb 2003. 14 Aug 2006. < http://www.theatlantic.com/unbound/flashbks/computer/bushf.htm > .

Clark, Irene L. *Concepts in Composition*. Mahwah, NJ: Erlbaum, 2003.

Cooper, Marilyn. "The Ecology of Writing." *College English* 48.4 (1986): 364–375.

Coover, Robert. "The End of Books." *New York Times Book Review*. 21 Jun 1992: 1 + .

Corbett, Edward P. J., and Robert Connors. *Classical Rhetoric for the Modern Student*. 4th ed. New York: Oxford UP, 1999.

Corder, Jim. "Varieties of Ethical Argument, With Some Account of the Significance of Ethos in the Teaching of Composition." 1978. *Landmark Essays on Rhetorical Invention in Writing*. Eds. Richard E. Young and Yameng Liu. Mahwah, NJ: Erlbaum, 1995.

Cresswell, Peter. "A More Convivial Perspective System for Artists." *The Virtual Embodied: Presence, Practice, Technology*. Ed. John Wood. London: Routledge, 1998.

Crowley, Sharon. *The Methodical Memory*. Carbondale: Southern Illinois UP, 1990.

_____. "Modern Rhetoric and Memory." Reynolds, 31–44.

_____, and Debra Hawhee. *Ancient Rhetorics for Contemporary Students*. 2nd ed. Boston: Allyn & Bacon, 1999.

Davis, D. Diane. *Breaking Up [at] Totality: A Rhetoric of Laughter*. Carbondale: Southern Illinois UP, 2000.

deCerteau, Michel. *The Practice of Everyday Life*. Berkeley: U California P, 1988.

Deleuze, Gilles, and Felix Guattari. *A Thousand Plateaus: Capitalism and Schizophrenia*. Trans. Brian Massumi. Minneapolis: U of Minnesota P, 1987.

Derrida, Jacques. *Archive Fever: A Freudian Impression*. Trans. Eric Prenowitz. Chicago: U of Chicago P, 1996.

_____. *Dissemination*. Trans. Barbara Johnson. Chicago: U of Chicago P, 1981.

_____. *Of Grammatology*. Trans. Gayatri Chakravorty Spivak. Baltimore: Johns Hopkins UP, 1976.

_____. "White Mythology: Metaphor in the Text of Philosophy." *Margins of Philosophy*. Chicago: U of Chicago P, 1982.

DeVoss, Dànielle Nicole and James E. Porter. "Why Napster Matters to Writing: Filesharing as a New Ethic of Digital Delivery." *Computers and Composition* 23.2 (2006): 178–210.

DeWitt, Scott Lloyd. *Writing Inventions: Identities, Technologies, Pedagogies*. Albany: State University of New York Press, 2001.

_____, and Kip Strasma, eds. *Contexts, Intertexts, and Hypertexts*. Cresskill, NJ: Hampton Press, 1999.

Douglas, Jane. *The End of Books—or Books without End? Reading Interactive Narratives*. Ann Arbor: U of Michigan P, 2000.

Eagleton, Terry. *Literary Theory: An Introduction*. Minneapolis: U of Minnesota P, 1996.

Edbayer, Jennifer. "Unframing Models of Public Distribution: From Rhetorical Situation to Rhetorical Ecologies" *Rhetoric Society Quarterly* 35.4 (2005).

Ede, Lisa S. *Situating Composition*. Carbondale: Southern Illinois UP, 2004.

Efimova, Lilia. "Visual Settlements on Weblog Visitations." *Mathemagenic*. January 16, 2005. < http://blog.mathemagenic.com/2005/01/26.html >

Ehses, Hanno H. J. "Representing MacBeth: A Case Study in Visual Rhetoric." *Design Discourse: History, Theory, Criticism*. Ed. Victor Margolin. Chicago: U of Chicago P, 1989. 187–197.

Elbow, Peter. "The Music of Form: Rethinking Organization in Writing." *CCC* 57.4 (2006): 620–666.

Eskilinen, Markuu. "Cybertext Theory and Literary Studies, A User's Manual." *electronic book review* 12 (Fall 2001). < http://www.altx, com/ebr/ebr12/eskel.htm >

Ezzy, Ebrahim. "Search 2.0 vs Traditional Search." *Read/Write Web*. Ed. Richard McManus. 20 July 2006. 13 Aug 2006. < http://www.readwriteweb.com/archives/search_20_vs_tr.php > .

Fahnestock, Jeanne. "Arrangement." *Encyclopedia of Rhetoric and Composition: Communication from Ancient Times to the Information Age*. Ed. Theresa Enos. New York: Garland Publishing, 1996.

Fleckenstein, Kristie S. "Words Made Flesh: Fusing Imagery and Language in a Polymorphic Literacy." *College English* 66 (2004): 612–631.

Foucault, Michel. "What Is an Author?" *Language, Countermemory, Practice: Selected Essays and Interviews*. Ed. Donald F. Bouchard. Trans. Donald F. Bouchard and Sherry Simon. Ithaca: Cornell UP, 1977. 113–138.

Fuller, Matthew. *Media Ecologies*. Cambridge, MA: MIT Press, 2005.

Giddens, Anthony. *The Giddens Reader*. Ed. Philip Cassell. Stanford: Stanford University Press, 1983.

Gilfus, Jonna. "Students and Authors in Introductory Composition Textbooks." *Authorship in Composition Studies*. Eds. Tracy Hamler Carrick and Rebecca Moore Howard. New York: Wadsworth, 2006.

Grusin, Richard. "What Is an Electronic Author? Theory and the Technological Fallacy." *Virtual Realities and Their Discontents*. Ed. Robert Markley. Baltimore: Johns Hopkins UP, 1996. 39–54.

Haas, Christina. *Writing Technology: Studies on the Materiality of Literacy*. Mahwah, NJ: Erlbaum, 1996.

Handa, Carolyn, ed. *Visual Rhetoric in a Digital World: A Critical Sourcebook*. Boston: Bedford/St. Martin's, 2004.

Hansen, Mark. *New Philosophy for a New Media*. Cambridge, MA: MIT Press, 2004.

Havelock, Eric. *The Muse Learns to Write: Reflections on Orality and Literacy from Antiquity to the Present*. New Haven, CT: Yale UP, 1986.

Hayles, N. Katherine. *How We Became Posthuman: Virtual Bodies in Cybernetics, Literature, and Informatics*. Chicago: U of Chicago, 1999.

_____. *My Mother Was a Computer: Digital Subjects and Literacy Texts*. Chicago: U of Chicago P, 2005.

_____. "Narrating Bits." *Vectors*. 1.1 (Winter 2005). 16 Aug 2006. < http://vectors.iml.annenberg.edu/narrating_bits/ > .

_____. *Writing Machines*. Cambridge: MIT Press, 2002.

Higgason, Richard E. "A Scholar's Nightmare." *Journal of Digital Information*. 3.3 (2003). 13 Aug 2006. < http://jodi.ecs.soton.ac.uk/Articles/v03/i03/Higgason/ nightmare.html > .

Hocks, Mary E. "Understanding Visual Rhetoric in Digital Writing Environments." *CCC* 54.4 (2003): 629–656.

Ihde, Don. *Postphenomenology: Essays in the Postmodern Context*. Evanston: Northwestern UP, 1993.

Jarratt, Susan. "New Dispositions for Historical Studies in Rhetoric." Olson 65–78.

Johnson, Steven. *Interface Culture: How New Technology Transforms the Way We Create and Communicate*. New York: HarperCollins, 1997.

Johnson-Eilola, Johndan. *Datacloud: Toward a New Theory of Online Work*. Cresskill, NJ: Hampton Press, 2005.

_____. *Nostalgic Angels: Rearticulating Hypertext Writing*. Norwood, NJ: Ablex, 1997.

_____. "Reading and Writing in Hypertext: Vertigo and Euphoria." *Literacy and Computers: The Complications of Teaching and Learning with Technology*. Eds. Cynthia L. Selfe and Susan Hilligoss. New York: MLA, 1994. 195-219.

Joyce, Michael. *Afternoon, a Story*. Boston: Eastgate Systems, 1990.

_____. *Of Two Minds: Hypertext Pedagogy and Poetics*. Ann Arbor: U of Michigan P, 1995.

Kaufer, David S., and Brian Butler. *Designing Interactive Worlds with Words*. Mahwah, NJ: Erlbaum, 2000.

Kendrick, Michelle. "Interactive Technology and the Remediation of the Subject of Writing." *Configurations* 9.2 (2001): 231-251.

Kent, Thomas. "The Consequences of Theory for the Practice of Writing." *Publishing in Rhetoric and Composition*. Eds. Gary A. Olson and Todd W. Taylor. Albany: SUNY P, 1997. 147-162.

Kerne, A. "Interface Ecology: An Open Conceptual Space of Collage and Emergence." *ArtLab23* 1 (Spring 2002). School of Visual Arts, NYC.

Kinneavy, James. "Kairos: A Neglected Concept in Classical Rhetoric." *Rhetoric and Praxis: The Contribution of Classical Rhetoric to Practical Reasoning*: Ed. Jean Dietz Moss. Washington, DC: The Catholic U of America P., 1986. 79-105.

Kinsey, Anthony. *How to Make Animated Movies*. New York: Viking, 1974.

Kirschenbaum, Matthew. "'So the Colors Cover the Wires': Interface, Aesthetics, and Usability." *A Companion to Digital Humanities*. Eds. Susan Schreibman, Ray Siemens, and John Unsworth. Oxford: Blackwell Publishing, 2004. 523-542.

Kittler, Friedrich A. *Gramophone, Film, Typewriter*. Stanford: Stanford UP, 1999.

Kolb, David. "Socrates in the Labyrinth." *Hyper/Text/Theory*. Ed. George P. Landow. Baltimore: Johns Hopkins UP, 1994. 323-344.

Krebs, Valdis. "Divided We Stand." *Orgnet.com*. 2004. 13 Aug 2006. < http:// www.orgnet.com/divided3.html > .

Kress, Gunther. "Design and Transformation: New Theories of Meaning." *Multiliteracies: Literacy Learning and the Design of Social Futures*. Eds. Bill Cope and Mary Kalantzis. London: Routledge, 2000. 153-161.

_____, and Theo van Leeuwen. *Reading Images: The Grammar of Visual Design*. London: Routledge, 2006.

Kumar, Ravi, Jasmine Novak, Prabhakar Raghavan, and Andrew Tomkins. "On the Bursty Evolution of Blogspace." *World Wide Web* 8.2 (2005): 159–178.

LaCapra, Dominick. *History and Memory After Auschwitz*. Ithaca NY: Cornell UP, 1998.

Landow, George. *Hypertext 2.0: The Convergence of Contemporary Critical Theory and Technology*. Baltimore: Johns Hopkins UP, 1997.

Lanham, Richard. *The Economics of Attention: Style and Substance in the Age of Information*. Chicago: U of Chicago P, 2006.

_____. *The Electronic Word: Democracy, Technology, and the Arts*. Chicago: U of Chicago P, 1993.

Latour, Bruno. *Michel Serres with Bruno Latour: Conversations on Science, Culture, and Time*. Trans. Roxanne Lapidus. Ann Arbor: U of Michigan, 1995.

LeFevre, Karen Burke. *Invention as a Social Act*. Carbondale: Southern Illinois UP, 1987.

Leitch, Vincent B. *Theory Matters*. New York: Routledge, 2003.

Lemke, Jay "Metamedia Literacy: Transforming Meanings and Media." *Handbook of Literacy and Technology*. Eds. David Reinking et al. Mahwah, NJ: Erlbaum, 1998. 3–13.

Lévy, Pierre. *Becoming Virtual: Reality in the Digital Age*. New York: Plenum Press, 1998.

Lurie, Peter. "Why the Web Will Win the Culture Wars for the Left: Deconstructing Hyperlinks." *CTheory.net*. 2003. 14 Aug 2006. < http://www.ctheory.net/ articles.aspx?id = 380 > .

Lyotard, Jean-Francois. *Peregrinations: Law, Form, Event*. New York: Columbia UP, 1988.

Manovich, Lev. Foreword. *The New Media Reader*. Eds. Noah Wardrip-Fruin and Nick Montfort. Cambridge, MA: MIT Press, 2003.

McLuhan, H. Marshall. *Understanding Media: The Extensions of Man*. Cambridge: MIT Press, 1994.

_____. *The Language of New Media*. Cambridge, MA: MIT Press, 2002.

Mijksenaar, Paul. *Visual Function: An Introduction to Information Design*. Princeton: Princeton Architectural Press, 1997.

Miller, Paul D. *Rhythm Science*. Cambridge, MA: MIT Press, 2004.

Miller, Susan. "Writing Studies as a Mode of Inquiry." *Rhetoric and Composition as Intellectual Work*. Ed. Gary A. Olson. Carbondale: Southern Illinois UP, 2002. 41–54.

Mitchell, W. J. T. *Picture Theory: Essays on Verbal and Visual Representation*. Chicago: U of Chicago P, 1995.

_____. *What Do Pictures Want?: The Lives and Loves of Images*. Chicago: U of Chicago P, 2005.

Moretti, Franco. *Graphs, Maps, Trees: Abstract Models for a Literacy History*. London: Verso, 2005.

Mowitt, John. *Text: The Genealogy of an Antidisciplinary Object.* Durham: Duke UP, 1992.

Moxey, Keith. "Perspective, Panofsky, and the Philosophy of History." *New Literary History* 26.4 (1995): 775–786.

Murphy, James J. "Introduction." *Arguments in Rhetoric Against Quintilian: Translation and Text of Peter Ramus's* Rhetoricae Distinctiones *in Quintilianum* (1549). Trans. Carole Newlands. DeKalb: Northern Illinois UP, 1986.

Nardi, Bonnie, and Vicki O'Day. *Information Ecologies: Using Technology With Heart.* Cambridge, MA: MIT Press, 1999.

Nietzsche, Friedrich. *Ecce Homo: How One Becomes What One Is.* 1979. Trans. R. J. Hollingdale. New York: Penguin, 1992.

_____. *Twilight of the Idols.* Trans. Duncan Large. New York: Oxford UP, 1998.

O'Reilly, Tim, and Rael Dornfest. "An Invitation to Attend the 2006 O'Reilly Emerging Technology Conference." O'Reilly Emerging Technologies Conference. 14 Aug 2006. < http://conferences.oreillynet.com/pub/w/43/invite.html > .

Panofsky, Erwin. *Perspective as Symbolic Form.* New York: Zone Books, 1991.

Pearce, Celia. *The Interactive Book.* Indianapolis: Macmillan Technical Publishing, 1997.

Plato. *Phaedrus.* Ed. Benjamin Jowett. 16 Aug 2006. < http://classics.mit.edu/Plato/phaedrus.html > .

Poster, Mark. *The Mode of Information: Poststructuralism and Social Context.* Chicago: U of Chicago P, 1990.

_____. *What's the Matter With the Internet?* Minneapolis: University of Minnesota Press, 2001.

Postman, Neil. "The Reformed English Curriculum." *High School 1980: The Shape of the Future in American Secondary Education.* Ed. Alvin C. Eurich. New York: Pitman, 1970. 160–168.

Quintilian. *The Insitutio Oratoria of Quintilian.* Trans. H. E. Butler. Cambridge, MA: Harvard UP, 1953.

Rettberg, Scott. "Editor's Introduction: *Reconfiguring Place and Space in New Media Writing." The Iowa Review Web* 8.2 (July 2006). 16 Aug 2006. < http://www.uiowa.edu/~ iareview/mainpages/new/july06/intro.html > .

Reynolds, John Frederick, ed. *Rhetorical Memory and Delivery.* Hillsdale, NJ: Erlbaum, 1993.

Reynolds, Nedra. "Composition's Imagined Geographies: The Politics of Space in the Frontier, City, and Cyberspace." *CCC* 50.1 (1998): 12–35.

Richardson, Will. "Posting vs. Blogging." *Weblogg-ed: The Read/Write Web in the Classroom.* May 7, 2004. < http://www.weblogg-ed/com/2004/05/07 >

Ricoeur, Paul. *The Rule of Metaphor.* Toronto: U of Toronto P, 1977.

Romanyshyn, Robert D. *Technology as Symptom and Dream.* New York: Routledge, 1989.

Ronell, Avital. *Finitude's Score: Essays for the End of the Millennium.* Lincoln: U of Nebraska, 1992.

Saper, Craig. *Artificial Mythologies.* Minneapolis: U of Minnesota P, 1997.

Saul, MaryLynn. "The Limitations of Hypertext in the Composition Classroom."
    Contexts, Intertexts, and Hypertexts. Eds. Scott DeWitt and Kip Strasma.
    Cresskill, NJ: Hampton Press, 1999.

Selfe, Cynthia L., and Richard J. Selfe, Jr. "The Politics of the Interface: Power and
    Its Exercise in Electronic Contact Zones." *CCC* 45.4 (1994): 480–503.

Serres, Michel. *Conversations on Science, Culture, and Time*. Trans. Roxanne Lapidus.
    Ann Arbor: U of Michigan P, 1995.

_____. *Statues: Le second livre des foundations*. Paris: Éditions François Bourin,
    1987.

Shenk, David. *Data Smog: Surviving the Information Glut*. San Francisco, CA.: Harper
    Edge, 1997.

Skjulstad, Synne, and Andrew Morrison. "Movement in the Interface." *Computers
    and Composition* 22 (2005): 413–433.

Smith, Catherine. "Reconceiving Hypertext." *Evolving Perspectives on Computers
    and Composition Studies*. Eds. Gail E Hawisher and Cynthia L. Selfe. Urbana:
    NCTE, 1991. 224-252.

Snyder, Ilana. *Hypertext: The Electronic Labyrinth*. Melbourne: Melbourne UP, 1996.

Sontag, Susan, ed. *A Barthes Reader*. New York: Hill and Wang, 1983.

Spinuzzi, Clay. *Tracing Genres Through Organizations: A Sociocultural Approach to
    Information Design*. Cambridge, MA.: MIT Press, 2003.

Stafford, Barbara M. *Good Looking: Essays on the Virtue of Images*. Cambridge, MA:
    MIT Press, 1998.

Steinberg, Leo. *Other Criteria: Confrontations With Twentieth-Century Art*. New York:
    Oxford UP, 1972.

Stevens, Anne H. and Jay Williams. "The Footnote, in Theory." *Critical Inquiry* 32.2
    (Jan 2006): 208-25.

Stroupe, Craig. "Visualizing English: Recognizing the Hybrid Literacy of Visual and
    Verbal Authorship on the Web." *College English* 62.5 (May 2000): 607–632.

Syverson, Margaret A. *The Wealth of Reality: An Ecology of Composition*. Carbondale:
    Southern Illinois UP, 1999.

Trimbur, John. "Composition and the Circulation of Writing." *CCC* 52.2 (2000):
    188–219.

Tufte, Edward R. *The Visual Display of Quantitative Information*. Cheshire, CT:
    Graphics Press, 1983.

Ulmer, Gregory L. *Applied Grammatology*. Baltimore: Johns Hopkins UP, 1985.

_____. *Electronic Monuments*. Minneapolis: U of Minnesota P, 2005.

_____. *Heuretics: The Logic of Invention*. Baltimore: John Hopkins UP, 1994.

_____. *Teletheory: Grammatology in the Age of Video*. New York: Routledge, 1989.

Valesio, Paolo. *Novantiqua: Rhetorics as a Contemporary Theory*. Bloomington:
    Indiana UP, 1980.

Vershbow, Ben. "Wikipedia Not Safe for Work." *if:book*. July 25, 2006.
    < http://www.futureofthebook.org/blog/archives/2006/07/wikipedia_not_safe_
    for_work.html >

Warnick, Barbara. "Online Ethos: Source Credibility in an 'Authorless' Environment." *American Behavioral Scientist.* 48.2 (2004): 256–265.

Weathers, Winston. *An Alternate Style: Options in Composition.* New York: Hayden Book, 1980.

Weinberger, David. *Small Pieces Loosely Joined (a unified theory of the Web).* Cambridge, MA: Perseus Publishing, 2002.

_____. "Web as World." *JOHO the Blog.* January 13, 2005. < http:// www.hyperorg.com/blogger/mtarchive/003569.html >

Welch, Kathleen. *The Contemporary Reception of Classical Rhetoric: Appropriations of Ancient Discourse.* Hillsdale, NJ: Erlbaum, 1990.

_____. *Electric Rhetoric: Classical Rhetoric, Oralism, and a New Literacy.* Cambridge: MIT Press, 1999.

White, Eric Charles. *Kaironomia: On the Will-to-Invent.* Ithaca: Cornell UP, 1987.

Wysocki, Anne Frances, and Johndan Johnson-Eilola: "Blinded by the Letter: Why Are We Using Literacy as a Metaphor for Everything Else?" Eds. Gail E. Hawisher and Cynthia L. Selfe. *Passions, Pedagogies, and 21st Century Technologies.* Urbana, IL.: NCTE, 1999. 349–368.

Wysocki, Anne F., et al., eds. *Writing New Media: Theory and Applications for Expanding the Teaching of Composition.* Logan: Utah State UP, 2004.

Yancey, Kathleen Blake. *Delivering College Composition: The Fifth Canon.* Portsmouth, NH: Boynton/Cook, 2006.

Young, James. *The Texture of Memory: Holocaust Memorials and Meaning.* New Haven, CT: Yale UP, 1993.

AUTHOR INDEX

SUBJECT INDEX

CPSIA information can be obtained at www.ICGtesting.com
Printed in the USA
BVOW040102301211

279399BV00001B/37/P